EXTERNAL

Backpacking through Life On (and Off) the Appalachian Trail

DUSTIN E. WAITE

Without Limits Publishing Company
DENVER, COLORADO

All events, locations, timelines, and conversations in this book are recalled from the author's memory and have been investigated diligently to ensure their accuracy. Permission to use names and likenesses has been obtained as often as possible to ensure authenticity. Some names and identifying details of individuals and places have been changed, altered, or withheld by request or an inability to contact for permission, but the underlying stories are based on events that did occur.

The author and publisher have made every effort to ensure that the information in this book is correct and do not assume liability to any party for any loss, damage, or disruption caused by errors or omissions, whether such errors or omissions result from negligence, accident, or any other cause.

Copyright © 2019 by Without Limits Publishing Company
Published in the United States.

All rights reserved. No part of this book may be duplicated, reproduced, published, or distributed in whole or in part except with the prior written permission of the publisher. For more information, contact Without Limits Publishing Company at info@withoutlimitspublishing.com.

Designed and typeset by Timm Bryson, em em design, LLC
Illustrations by Daniela Liberona

Library of Congress Control Number: 2018913599
ISBN: 978-1-7329239-0-4 (paperback)
ISBN: 978-1-7329239-1-1 (ebook)
10 9 8 7 6 5 4 3 2 1

For Ryken, Monty, Larkyn, and Dora

*In the future, you may be the only proof that I existed.
I hope you have some good stories to tell.*

"Long-distance hiking has really established my faith in mankind. There [are] good people everywhere. After hiking the Appalachian Trail, ask yourself this: What did you learn about yourself and other people on the white blazes that you can use for the rest of the journey?"

—Bob Peoples, Owner of Kincora Hiking Hostel, Appalachian Trail Advocate, Maintainer, Legend

CONTENTS

Prologue: Iowa 1997 — 1

PART I

Chapter 1: California 2008 — 7
Chapter 2: Appalachian Trail 2014 — 17
Chapter 3: Colorado 2009 — 31
Chapter 4: Appalachian Trail 2014 — 39
Chapter 5: Colorado 2009 — 47
Chapter 6: Appalachian Trail 2014 — 51
Chapter 7: Colorado 2011 — 63
Chapter 8: Appalachian Trail 2014 — 74
Chapter 9: Colorado 2011 — 85
Chapter 10: Appalachian Trail 2014 — 91
Chapter 11: Hawaii 2012 — 103
Chapter 12: Appalachian Trail 2014 — 110
Chapter 13: Hawaii 2012 — 124
Chapter 14: Los Padres National Forest 2014 — 130
Chapter 15: Hawaii 2013 — 140
Chapter 16: Appalachian Trail 2014 — 144
Chapter 17: Iowa 2014 — 157
Chapter 18: Appalachian Trail 2014 — 161

Chapter 19: Iowa 2014	175
Chapter 20: Appalachian Trail 2014	181
Chapter 21: Georgia 2014	197
Chapter 22: Appalachian Trail 2014	200

PART II

Chapter 23: Iowa 2015	215
Chapter 24: Appalachian Trail 2016	222
Chapter 25: Iowa 2015	237
Chapter 26: Appalachian Trail 2016	243
Chapter 27: Iowa 2015	253
Chapter 28: Appalachian Trail 2016	263
Chapter 29: Iowa 2016	274
Chapter 30: Appalachian Trail 2016	285
Chapter 31: California 2016	290
Chapter 32: Appalachian Trail 2016	297
Chapter 33: California 2016	304
Chapter 34: Appalachian Trail 2016	308
Epilogue: Colorado 2018	317

Acknowledgments, 321

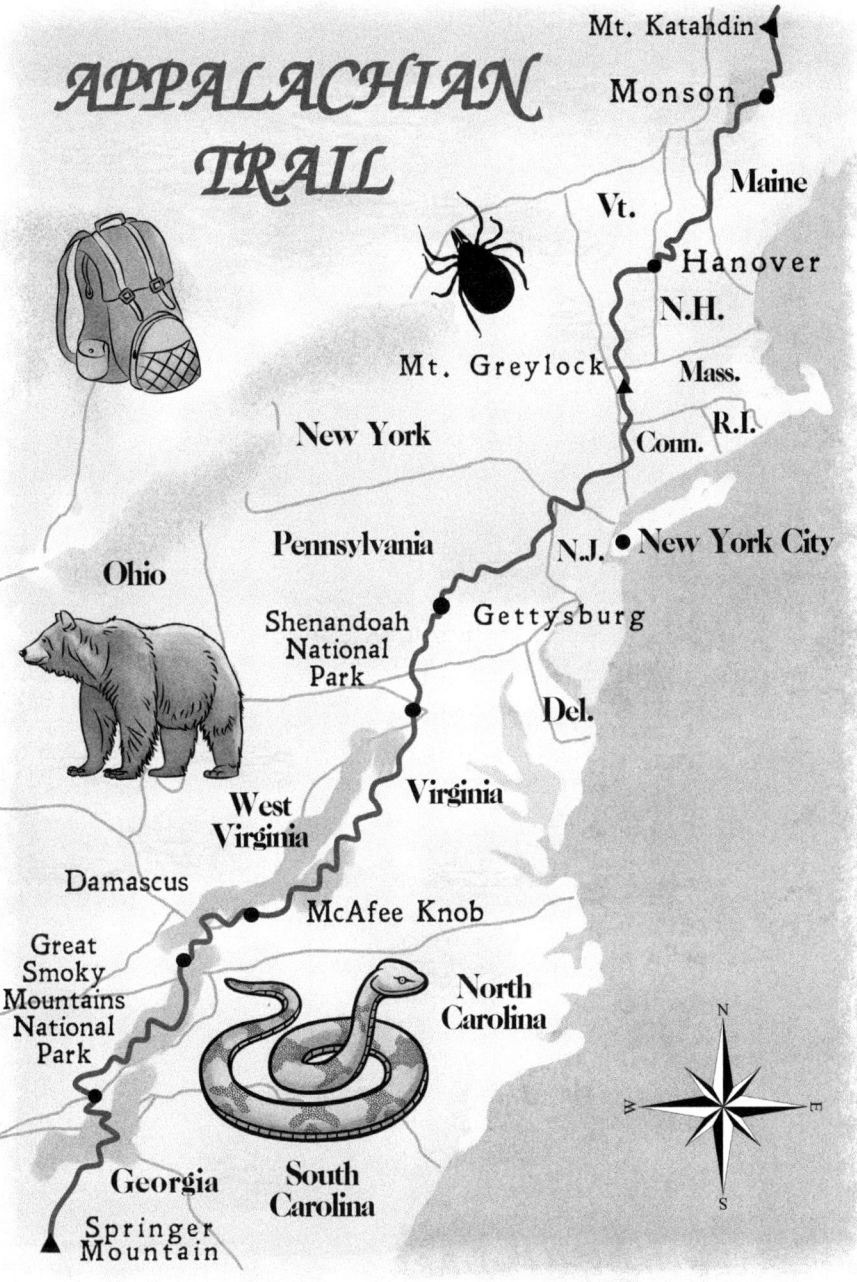

PROLOGUE

Iowa 1997

Pffffft.

Come on! I thought nervously as the thick plastic weights from my dad's cheap workout set forced the air out of my lungs. I moved my tongue across the rough, sticky inside of the piece of duct tape that was tightly secured over my mouth.

Why isn't it working?!

I was a skinny, freckled, Catholic, thirteen-year-old white kid. I was athletic and earned good grades, and I was a decent (by adolescent-guy standards) human being. I was also totally naive and, in retrospect, very depressed.

I had just finished spying on my next-door neighbor's party to which I hadn't been invited (despite the neighbor being a kid I had been friends with for most of my childhood). I was certain the party was some combination of every Molly Ringwald movie ever made, and I felt totally rejected and isolated.

"Just jump the fence!" some friends encouraged.

No way, I thought as I imagined the social suicide that would surely result and envisioned myself being beaten up by a girl at school the next day. I'd hopped that aluminum fence hundreds of times to play Wiffle ball or chase after Max, our half-Pomeranian/half-Chihuahua family dog that looked like a fox, but none of that mattered now. We were in middle school and things were different.

Emotionally vanquished, I slowly returned to my basement bedroom. I sank down onto my bed and knew I was alone in the house. Like the dutiful Catholic boy I was at the time, I began praying, but this time I gave God an ultimatum: help me get more friends or kill me. Living this lonely life was no longer worth it, and if God couldn't help me change that, I figured that he might as well make room for another person who could do a better job at being happy than me.

Thanks to watching shows like *The Real World*, I thought that dressing or talking in a certain way was supposed to get me more friends, maybe even a girlfriend. But it wasn't working for me and I was tired of waiting.

The problem with my ultimatum to God was that I wasn't so sure he could pull it off. This first time of doubting my faith was intense, and I was afraid that God would decide that finding me friends would prove too difficult of a task and that he would choose to take my life instead. When that fear sunk in, I decided it wasn't worth waiting for God's decision, so I tried to commit suicide.

My brilliant plan was to stack enough weight on my stomach to force all the air out of my lungs; I figured if I stopped breathing long enough, my body would finally just give up. As it turns out, the body is designed to do the exact opposite. No matter how hard I tried to not take a breath, my lungs would involuntarily win the battle.

But I was determined. I stacked heavier items on my stomach, like several big volumes from our antiquated encyclopedia set. I put more duct tape over my mouth. Still, no matter what I did, the oxygen inside my basement bedroom found its way into my deprived lungs. Although my methods were poorly conceived, the intention of wanting my life to end was very real.

Spoiler alert: it didn't work.

❖ ❖ ❖

Like most people, the vast majority of my experiences haven't been life changing or even memorable. But, collectively with the more influential experiences (like trying to end my life), they've guided my journey and for that I'm grateful.

It was on September 12, 2016, that all of my life choices, even those small, seemingly insignificant ones, led me to Baxter State Park in northern Maine—to the top of Mount Katahdin at the northern terminus of the 2,189-mile Appalachian Trail—where the only distraction was a swift current of wind brushing across my face as I stood next to the famous wooden summit sign.

There's nothing special about my story, except that it's everyone's story. Mine is a tale that involves learning from my mistakes and finding the strength to move forward. I'm not perfect—far from it, in fact. I've made many mistakes and though I'm sorry, I know I'll make more. "It's all part of the experience."

My hope in sharing this story is to offer a reminder to put aside the distractions, to keep searching your soul to discover what is truly important, and to keep putting one foot in front of the other—because you never know what trail magic lies ahead.

Part I

CHAPTER 1

California 2008

The journey that led me to the top of Mount Katahdin was catalyzed one night in the fall of 2008, in the small town of Bell Gardens, California. I had just finished eating dinner and quenching my thirst with four or five beers at a small bar in Monterey Park, just east of Los Angeles. It was a "grill-your-own-steak establishment," which meant that on any night of the week, for less than fifteen dollars, you'd be handed a plate with a baked potato and a raw piece of meat to cook on an open grill. The place didn't have a lot of seating, but it was a regular spot for me and my colleagues when work took us away from our swanky Santa Barbara offices.

Although it was a Saturday, I had just finished working at a project site because the school district didn't particularly want children, teachers, and parents watching a geologist collecting hazardous gas samples from below the outdoor cafeteria area. It had been an especially rough day—I had trouble pulling a good sample from one of our gas probes and the troubleshooting didn't go very well—so I was already excited about sinking into the fancy sheets and pillows of my newly renovated hotel. In spite of the stunning views of the Pomona Freeway, a parking lot, and a landfill, the hotel appeared to be relatively nice, and the complimentary breakfast was satisfactory.

Besides the bar, my other viable restaurant choice for the evening was an Applebee's, but that would require getting back on the freeway—something no one ever wants to do in Southern California after arriving home. The bar, on the other hand, was straight down a side road from my hotel. I also loved the bar's quirkiness: the dim lighting made it feel like a secret gentlemen's club from *Goodfellas*, but in the blink of an eye, the DJ would switch on the amplifiers and the fog and karaoke machines, and the place would transform from Joe Pesci's hangout to a trailer-park disco.

It was on that evening, with no regard for the fact that I had to be back at the job site at seven the next morning, that I began drinking and sulking about my loneliness and the fact that I *thought* I was in love. The woman's name was Karla and she had been a bridesmaid at my brother's wedding. We had shared a fun weekend and, ultimately, a night in a hotel room. (In other words, we got drunk and had sex.) Afterward, for some reason, I convinced myself that we should be together. The problem was that she lived in Iowa City and I was currently drinking by myself in Southern California while listening to a surprisingly well-performed karaoke version of Toby Keith's "I Love This Bar." Also, when I said I had four or five beers, what I meant was that I had six and they were each 22 ounces of Fat Tire Amber Ale. So, with 132 ounces of liquid depressant in my system, combined with a hatred for my job and a recently built-up sense of loneliness, I had just the right ingredients to make at least one ill-planned, potentially life-altering decision that evening.

Thanks to 2008's modern conveniences like text messaging and Facebook, I was able to keep in touch with Karla, and sometimes those conversations included phrases such as "I really miss you" and "I would be happier if you were around." Looking back on it, what I was really trying to say was, *You're the last woman I've seen naked and I'm lonely, so. . . .* There was no love involved. I didn't know her. She didn't know me. We had shared one night of drunken fun that included fooling around in a church basement coat closet and again in my room at the Clarion Hotel. Hell, she wasn't even *my* bridesmaid. When her groomsman had to leave early, I swooped in.

Somewhere between my fourth and fifth beer, after I had already finished eating my steak, my mind began concocting all sorts of plans as to how I could fix these feelings of loneliness. I left the bar drunk and depressed, and instead of driving the short distance back to the hotel, I decided that going for a longer drive would help clear my head. However, as I drove my newish Ford Focus rental car down a road on which I had never been, and on which mine was surprisingly the only vehicle, my head never really cleared up. Instead, a torrent of emotions continued to occupy it, and I couldn't shake them. I couldn't shake the idea that I needed to make a change in my life, and that I needed to start making good on promises to myself: promises to travel, promises to become a better person for a future relationship, promises to never remain stagnant if life wasn't going the way I planned.

There's no poetic way to describe what happened next. Between the alcohol, the depression, and the fact that I was driving a vehicle that wasn't mine, I somehow decided to pull into a parking lot and start doing donuts in my rental car. I guess I thought it would help take my mind off things—it seemed like a promising idea at the time.

❦ ❦ ❦

After about fifteen minutes passed, for the most part I was having fun and my mind was no longer thinking about Karla. There were a few concrete lampposts in the parking lot that made great improvised cones around which I could whip the back end of my rental and then punch the gas as I headed toward the next post to repeat the process. Because of the inertia disruption, miscellaneous items in my car were tossed around each time I pulled and released the emergency brake; data sheets and daily journals from the job site were scattered around the passenger floor mats, and bags of leftover Jack in the Box exploded onto the console. I was having a wonderful time.

This immature activity actually *was* helping to clear my mind of all the nonsense, but that clarity wouldn't last long. Just as I was about to finish my rebel escapade and leave the parking lot, I saw something that drunk drivers never anticipate—the police.

Almost out of nowhere, two cars with cherries rolling whipped into the lot quicker than I could begin to grasp the consequences of my recent actions and blocked me in between them. I was asked to produce my license and registration, but when I turned to my right, I discovered that my wallet was among the items that had been tossed to the floor during one of my laps around the lampposts and was now buried somewhere in a pile of debris in front of the passenger seat. They pulled me out of the car and forced me to put my hands on the hood of the first police cruiser. While one officer searched for my wallet, the other stood right beside me and started the questioning. He was the good cop. His voice was calm, and he asked me questions that would have seemed almost friendly if the situation had been different.

As the other footsteps approached, I heard, "What in the hell do you think you were doing?!?!" He was the bad cop, and he had found my wallet and license. The second officer repeated the same line of questioning as the first, except at no point did he seem friendly.

It may have been the alcohol talking, or maybe I was just so fed up with my current life scenario that I really didn't care if I went to jail, but my attitude became cocky after the initial round of questioning and I began stating all my answers proudly. I remember giving a brief laugh and saying, "I'm sure the news would like to hear this," after I informed them I was working on a project for local schools. When they asked me how much I had to drink, my word-for-word answer was "Probably four or five, so let's call it five."

At that point, both officers were shaking their heads, either in disgust or just utter confusion about the scene that was unfolding. It was about eleven on a Saturday night in east Los

Angeles, and here was a college-educated, freckled white kid from Iowa—complete with an Iowa driver's license—who had admitted to drinking enough beer to make anyone blow over the legal limit while doing donuts in an open parking lot. I had wanted to make a change in my life and there I was, hands pressed against the hood of a police cruiser, making changes, although this was not quite the change that I had intended.

The source of the officers' confusion was still unknown to me since all I could see was the black reinforced bumper attached to the front of the police cruiser. The second officer finally expressed his anger in words that I'll never forget: "Son, you're gonna have to give me some more information than this. You seem like a good kid, but you gotta tell me, what on earth possessed you to start doing donuts in a parking lot *across the street from a police station?*"

As he said those words my eyes opened wide, my heart skipped a beat, and a lump about the size of a grapefruit developed in my throat. At that moment, all formality of the situation went out the window as I took my hands off the cruiser and stood straight up. I should have been a bit more cautious as both officers quickly moved their hands toward their hips, clearly ready to draw their firearms when I stood. (Thankfully, they didn't.) With my back now against the hood of the police cruiser, I looked across the street and, sure enough, written on the top of the building directly across the street from the well-lit parking lot was the word "POLICE." It was only then that I noticed the many bright windows with black silhouettes of people staring in my direction.

The second officer continued, "We've all spent the last fifteen minutes watching this idiot across the street wondering what the hell is he doing?!?!"

Me. I was the idiot.

I can't make this up. In my drunken stupor, I honestly had not noticed the police station across the street.

My initial response was to say, "Well that's just dumb luck right there." Without missing a beat, the second officer quickly responded, "It sure was dumb!"

Until that point in the interrogation, I had been impressed as to how it was these officers pulled up *right* as I was leaving the parking lot. Now, it was very clear they were merely done enjoying the show and thought it best to come talk to the drunk idiot who decided to do donuts across the street from a police station. These officers had not come out of nowhere; they had come down the steps, maybe used an elevator, probably discussed which one would talk to me first, got into their vehicles, drove four seconds across the street, and in the shortest police chase ever, caught their perp. I bet the oil in their cruisers wasn't even at a normal operating temperature by the time they reached me in the parking lot.

"So what's the deal, Dustin? What are you doing?" said the first officer.

I paused, looked once more at the police station across the street, glanced at both officers again, and began to think about all the possible things I could say at that very moment—a moment that had finally become all too real. A moment of sobriety in an otherwise drunken spectacle. A moment that could change the course of my life in a very drastic and negative way, and yet all I could I think of in that moment was how lonely and unhappy I was.

A DUI is a terrible thing. It's expensive, it usually means jail time, it sometimes means losing your job, and it's a terrible blemish on your record. Ask anyone with a DUI and they'll confirm this. But, at that moment, none of that really mattered to me. Depression has a way of making your mind think in mysterious ways, but how was I supposed to explain that to these officers? How was I supposed to explain the entirety of all the emotions that had been running through my head that night, let alone for the previous few weeks, months, and years? So, I took a deep breath, and as the weight of all the pain in my heart culminated in that moment and tears formed in my eyes, I looked right at the first officer and said, "I can tell you the whole story or I can say I just needed to have a few drinks and do some donuts."

There are many moments of pause that happen in peoples' lives that mark the reshaping of their current path. Like the pause when a couple is waiting to learn if they're going to have a baby or the pause when a patient is waiting to hear the results of a cancer screening. That pause while waiting for the officers' response was one of those moments for me. I knew, even as I stood there, drunk and sad, that what the officers decided to do next was going to reshape my life's path.

After looking at his partner and then back at me, the first officer handed me my wallet and said with a firm voice, "Dustin, get back in your car, drive directly to your hotel, and go to bed."

That was the end of it.

To this day I can't tell you why they let me go. Perhaps the entire situation was just too much to comprehend and they didn't want to deal with it. Maybe they just didn't want to do the paperwork. Perhaps they thought I was trying to get caught by doing something so blatantly stupid. Or maybe, just maybe, that first police officer knew that I was looking for something else that evening, that I wasn't trying to get caught or even have a joy ride, that I was just looking for someone to talk to that wasn't myself.

Nah, they probably just didn't want to do the paperwork.

His partner was visibly angered when he told me to drive home, and rightly so seeing as I had already admitted to being intoxicated. In no way do I condone drinking and driving, but the mistakes I have made in my life have shaped my current path, and the response from that first police officer, a man I will likely never meet again, unequivocally shaped the rest of my life.

❖ ❖ ❖

In the following months, I finished up projects at work as well as I could. I began selling my possessions on Craigslist—the first of many purges of material items from my life—and as December 2008 rolled around, I began letting close friends know of my plans. Ironically, in the process of finally pulling the trigger on making changes in my life to make myself happy, I kept noticing all the good things that were already *in* the life that I was planning to leave. I was surrounded by amazing people and friends, but my mind hadn't been able to see that before. My job wasn't all *that* terrible, there had merely been a few not-so-great events that compounded my existing feelings of depression and loneliness.

Our brains are filled with a chemical called serotonin and when this chemical is out of balance, so are we. Some people can manage this with everyday habits, but others struggle immensely. For my entire life, I had been trying to manage this imbalance on my own. But the pressure can build like in a magma chamber, the churning and decay creating a giant pressurized vat of molten lava, until one day it explodes and manifests itself in our outwardly expressed emotions or behavior. Depending on the person, that manifestation can take many different forms—from buying a new sweater to walking into an elementary school with an AK-47.

Thankfully, my explosion of emotions manifested itself in a road trip, and on January 9, 2009, I quit my job and set off on a candy-cane loop around the country to see family and friends in San Bernardino, Scottsdale, Albuquerque, Dallas, Tampa, Charleston, Trenton, Boston, Chicago, and Cedar Rapids.

There is nothing quite like being moments away from having your license revoked and then, four months later, driving eight thousand miles to see people who care about you. If I was writing a manual on how to help people with depression, I would put this activity at the top of the list. After six weeks on the road, in the early spring of 2009, I finally settled in Denver and for the first time in a while, I was happy again.

CHAPTER 2

Appalachian Trail 2014
7 Days; 70 Miles

I was dropped off in northern Georgia at the trailhead for Springer Mountain, the southernmost terminus of the Appalachian Trail (AT), by a driver who looked eerily like Philip Seymour Hoffman, the recently deceased actor. Another pair of hikers from Michigan, Larry and Terri, took the same shuttle and provided me a reprieve from our driver's continuous self-congratulatory talk regarding his "unmatched system" of long-distance hiking. Although we reached the trailhead in the afternoon, because it was late February, I only had about four or five hours of hiking before nightfall. I scurried to the top of Springer Mountain where I made a few quick friends: Kacie and Margery, who had just returned from a mission trip to Uganda, and Stan and his son Erik from New England. After dreaming about this adventure for the previous decade, knowing I was attempting to hike two thousand miles over the next few months had my adrenaline pumping.

I left the top of Springer and began my first eager steps north on the AT. I left in such a hurry that I forgot to sign the trail register at the top of the mountain. This marked the first of many times while hiking the AT that I got to use one of my favorite quips. Whenever someone asked, "Where are you headed?" I would smile, stare them right in face, and say, "North." Depending on the scenario I would sometimes say it with a deep, mountain-man voice and abruptly walk away into the woods; however, more times than not, I would stick around, have a conversation, and make a new friend.

The AT is marked with what are called "white blazes" (small rectangles of white paint on trees, rocks, road signs, or any other permanent structure), which inform hikers that they are still on the trail. The distance between white blazes can range from a few hundred feet to even an eighth of a mile, depending on the terrain. Although it may sound a bit destructive to the environment to paint so many trees and rocks, it's less harmful than other forms of signage that can rot and fall apart, and it also helps promote hiker safety. Because these trail markers are so prevalent along the trail, many hikers don't carry a GPS device or even a map. The AT, in my opinion, is a very pampered trail in some sections. It's well maintained compared to other backcountry trails, largely due to the extensive volunteer networks in each state that the AT passes through. But, as I learned on night one of my Appalachian adventure, even with these markers showing the way, it's still possible to get turned around.

Ironically, I was carrying a map *and* a GPS device when I realized that I had lost my bearings. The problem was that I didn't know I was lost until I was well off the trail, and it was getting dark. I was so excited when I left the top of Springer

2: Appalachian Trail 2014

On top of Springer Mountain, the southern terminus of the Appalachian Trail

Mountain that I practically ran down the trail. I kept seeing white blazes and the trail was well traveled, so it was obvious where the path was. I can't remember exactly what thoughts I had that day. I'm sure it was a jumble of awe and excitement at what I was doing, or perhaps there was even a song in my head that helped with my hiking cadence, but at some point after my first few miles I had an eerie thought that a lot of AT hikers experience on the trail: *How long has it been since I've seen a white blaze?* All of a sudden, my soft and cushy confidence became hard and nervous uncertainty as it dawned on me that the trail was appearing less and less traveled with more overgrowth of plants and weeds. The only solace I found was when I passed a makeshift "cowboy camp," which is the term for unofficial campsites that often exhibit signs of human activity like tent depressions or a ring of rocks for a fire pit. While my spirits lifted slightly, it was clear that this particular cowboy camp had not been used in quite some time.

I pulled out my map, at which point I realized that my map was horrible; there were no contour lines whatsoever and the waypoints were unclear. The whole map looked as if it might be a restaurant place mat on which young children could color before receiving a small portion of mac 'n' cheese. Also, maps are only helpful if you also have a compass (I didn't) and at least some idea of where you are in relation to other landmarks on the map (a process called "triangulation"). I had determined that I was in a ravine that seemed to be a less-traveled access road for all-terrain vehicles, but since I had no landmarks with which to triangulate my exact position, this was just a guess. My adrenaline was still very high, so I didn't spend too much time pondering my options and quickly decided it was probably best to just keep moving. Everything I had read about the AT said there were lots of side trails that reconnected with the main trail, so I went with the decision that I would ultimately find myself back on the main trail soon. Thankfully, this access road took me back up the ravine and an hour or so later I emerged onto a gravel road. At that point, I still wasn't completely sure I was off the AT and I hoped that maybe the white blazes were just placed far apart in this section. I saw another cowboy camp set up beside the gravel road, giving me hope that I wasn't completely lost.

The sun was beginning to set and the wind was picking up. Admittedly, I was a bit scared at this moment. Although I had a tent, a zero-degree sleeping bag, and enough food to last me a week, I was still in the middle of a wooded area where I didn't know a soul. Also, my pride was on the line because I didn't want to admit I got lost on my first night of a two-thousand-mile backpacking trip. I knew my hiking pace after years of previous trips, so I reckoned I had probably hiked about ten miles—a calculation that didn't assuage my fears because the campsite I was trying to find was only eight miles from where I started. For what would be the first of many times, I took my pack off in frustration, sat down next to a tree, and weighed my options. The cowboy camp near the road was less than desirable for my first night, so once again I made the decision to keep walking.

About a half mile down the main road was an access road that led to the top of a small mountain, and I figured that if I was going to be lost, I might as well be lost on the top of a mountain with a good view. I soon discovered I was not the first person to have this idea because when I reached the top there was a small, previously used campfire ring left by another hiker. Although I had not accomplished my goal of reaching my intended campsite that day, the small fire ring at the top of this mountain was the best thing I could have hoped for in that moment. I quickly set up my tent, blew up my Therm-a-Rest camping pad, and as the sun set over the Appalachian ridgeline, I enjoyed my first of many backcountry meals on (or near) the AT. It was cold, I was tired, and I fell asleep watching my breath form a tiny cloud near my face as the inside of my tent slowly warmed up with my body heat. I would later learn this first night was spent on Hawk Mountain.

When I woke up in the morning, not only was I still frustrated about getting lost the previous day, but, like pouring salt on a fresh wound, I discovered my brand new (and expensive) headlamp didn't work!

❖ ❖ ❖

A common topic of conversation among outdoor enthusiasts is gear. Everyone is curious about what gear other people are carrying and discussions abound regarding the newest lightweight sleeping pad, or the advantages of an isobutane stove versus a denatured-alcohol stove, or how many pairs of underwear are necessary (for many hikers the answer is *one*). The phenomenon of gear talk has been highlighted in many books written about the trail. Some of the books express disdain for anyone who engages in too much gear talk and I would be remiss if I didn't say there were multiple times I felt the same way. That being said, I'm going to talk about my gear now.

One of my major purchases prior to flying into Atlanta to begin my journey was a rechargeable Black Diamond headlamp. It could be charged with a micro-USB charger or the lithium batteries could be replaced with regular AAAs, so it was the best of both worlds. It also boasted a high lumen output and waterproof construction. Among outdoor gear companies, Black Diamond is consistently named one of the best brands in the industry. I figured that if so many other people trusted this company, I could, too, so I bought a seventy-dollar headlamp from them and it broke on night one.

Apparently, the waterproof construction wasn't so waterproof. To avoid having my water freeze in the colder evening temperatures (a very real possibility that I have experienced), I kept my water reservoir in my sleeping bag during that first night, right next to my headlamp. Over the course of the night, even though the mouthpiece lock on the water reservoir was engaged, water still escaped. I woke up the next morning to see tiny droplets of water *inside* the headlamp casing and a red light was blinking on the device. My seventy-dollar headlamp never worked again. If my ego wasn't already destroyed from my navigational mistakes the day before, this was just another nudge toward the edge of my cliff of sanity. As I packed my bag and prepared for my second day (hopefully) on the AT, I shoved my broken headlamp into the bottom of my pack, where I discovered that I had packed a backup headlamp—a simpler $2.99 model I had purchased at Walmart a few years prior. I forgot I had thrown it in my pack at the last second before flying into Atlanta. For the next week, until I reached an outfitter to replace the (still under warranty) Black Diamond model, through rain and rugged terrain, this inexpensive, basic headlamp was my beacon as I cooked dinner and set up camp each night.

❊ ❊ ❊

Although I was grateful to have a working light source, I still had to figure out how to get back on the AT before I left the campsite at the top of Hawk Mountain. After another unsuccessful attempt to use my map, I decided to turn on my phone and try a GPS mapping app I had downloaded. You may be facepalming right now thinking that I am an idiot for not opening this app the night before; however, it was my understanding that it would only work with data connectivity and there was absolutely no cell phone service in that area. My mind was blown when I saw a little blue dot pop up on the topo map within the app. (Apparently, the GPS feature operates with a different antenna than the one used for cell and data service. Who knew? Not me. Clearly.) This was a great reminder to always test my gear before leaving for a trip.

After fearing an exhausting day ahead of walking on a gravel road trying to find the trail, seeing that blue dot was incredibly exciting, especially once I realized I wasn't too far off the trail. The app included a very distinct red line representing the location of the AT, and it informed me that my current location was only about a quarter mile away from the trail. It turned out that the gravel road would *not* have crossed the trail and that walking in that direction any farther would have been disastrous.

Although I do not condone "blazing" new trails in the woods if they are not needed, I was sincerely lost and off-trail in an area I did not know, so in this scenario I justified sidestepping my way down the side of the mountain until my little blue dot was firmly on the red line. Although I usually escape to the woods to get away from all the screens and technology that surround us, I reminded myself in that moment that even Lewis and Clark used the best instruments and tools available to them at the time, and I was happy to have some help in finding my way.

After another eight miles I made it to Gooch Shelter, a three-sided wooden structure that is one of hundreds of shelters scattered throughout the thousands of miles of trail that—depending on how your day is going—can look like a damn castle in the middle of the woods. Although some people prefer not to stay in the shelters, they offer a nice alternative to setting up your tent. Despite the abundance of daylight that was still available, I felt I deserved a little rest and decided to relax for the rest of the day until nightfall.

The next day brought a delightful surprise when I had my first experience of "trail magic." This is the term given to random acts of kindness that sometimes happen along the trail. My first taste of trail magic came in the form of a jolly character named Fresh Ground. He adopted this trail name when he attempted to hike the AT in 2008. Since then, he had taken it upon himself to pick random road crossings along the trail and offer up hot dogs, Kool-Aid, fresh fruit, snacks, and a friendly smile—all for free (though donations were welcome). He named his roadside stand the Leap Frog Café (in reference to his leaping around to various road crossings to offer his services). I devoured five hot dogs, a bag of Doritos, and some bananas and oranges. He asked me to sign his guest log (mine was the first entry for 2014), and it was then that I decided on my trail name. After a few hours of chatting and expressing my gratitude, I made it another three miles down to my stop for the night at small stream called Lance Creek.

❦ ❦ ❦

Every person on the trail is encouraged to adopt a trail name. My trail name was Batman (and still is, as trail names absolutely stay with you in your post-trail life). There were a few reasons for this choice: I had two Batman shirts with me that I had received as Christmas gifts from family members just before leaving for the AT; I have a bat tattoo on my left arm (a realistic bat, not the bat symbol from the comic); and Batman is my favorite superhero, largely because he doesn't have any super powers. He's merely a man who uses available resources to accomplish goals for the greater good, and I thought that on a two-thousand-mile hike, I better be as resourceful as possible. I have been scolded a few times for picking my own trail name because some hikers think a trail name needs to be given, but I suppose that depends on what hiking blogs you read. However, I figured if I was going to be called a new name for all of eternity by a new group of friends, why not choose Batman? I passed one hiker who was given the trail name Skunk due to her excessive flatulence, so I am happy my name is something that I don't mind using off the trail as well as on (although I'm sure Skunk *is* quite proud of her name). If the way I chose my hiking name offends some people, I've decided that's not a battle with which I'm going to concern myself. *Hike your own hike.*

❖ ❖ ❖

The fourth night and all of its festivities were determined by pure luck and good timing. After hiking over Blood Mountain, one of the first grueling climbs of the AT, I stumbled toward Neel Gap and into Mountain Crossings, which is an outfitter where the trail literally goes through a part of the building. Not only was this an efficient place to resupply and sleep in a bed at their on-site hostel, but that night they were also throwing a party to celebrate the start of hiking season. There was music and free food, and veteran AT hikers were sharing stories and just having a good time. I met Mama Goose, a friendly woman who hiked the trail in 2013 and who bought me a few snacks and isobutane fuel at the shop. I also had the great honor of meeting Baltimore Jack, a trail legend who had hiked the AT nine times at that point. I was beginning to learn about the amazing culture of people who only want to see new hikers succeed.

It was very humbling for me because I'm not used to accepting help from people, but after almost thirty miles of hiking it was nice to know that others were looking out for me. There was also a church group from Louisiana serving hamburgers and other goodies, so I ate like a king *and* made some new friends. Two people, Caleb and Whitney, chatted with me throughout the evening and, even though my own feelings toward God and world religions had waned at that time, they gave me some wonderful words of encouragement that nourished me both physically and spiritually.

A group of us departed from Neel Gap and hiked for twelve miles to Low Gap Shelter. It was the nicest day so far, which made for some good photos. The group of people I left the hostel with would become my trail family for the next few weeks. Most of them were in their late teens or early to mid-twenties, so that made me the old guy at the age of twenty-nine. The youngest in the group, Beast, was from Massachusetts and fresh out of high school. The other hikers in that first small group that left Mountain Crossings were Forget-Me-Not, Knapsack (and his dog, Bailey), Z Man, and Rambo. A couple of other guys, Money Maker and Night Whisperer, would come and go from our group as well.

We woke up to rain dripping off the shelter the next morning. After packing up some wet gear and hiking ten miles to Unicoi Gap, we discovered that the same church group from the outfitter had driven ahead and set up a canopy and grill at the road crossing in the gap and was again serving free burgers and snacks. I destroyed three burgers, three bananas, and a couple of snack bars before hiking another six miles to the top of Tray Mountain, a 4,430-foot climb with spectacular views of the sunset on the horizon.

❊ ❊ ❊

Regardless of what is expounded in hiking blogs and extreme workout magazines, the AT is far from a race. There are no trophies at the top of Mount Katahdin in Maine; however, sometimes being the first to a campsite where a lot of hikers plan to stay has its benefits. Although I can't remember the exact

Posing with Beast shortly after leaving Mountain Crossings

number of hikers that evening, there were enough to necessitate a few of them setting up their tents because the shelter was packed full. As I mentioned, some hikers prefer not to stay in the shelters, but it's nice to avoid setting up and tearing down your tent if your energy is drained after a long day of hiking, especially if it's raining. On this evening, I was one of the fortunate ones in the shelter. When the eclectic group of hikers awoke the next morning, we were greeted with an incredible view. The rain from the previous day had frozen and everything was covered in ice. It was quite amazing. Long icicles hung from every tree branch you could see and it looked like something straight out of a children's fantasy novel.

This was one of those experiences that you can't really recreate with words. Most people have seen icicles, and lots of people have been camping, but what I saw that morning cannot be fully described, and even the photos I took don't do it justice. Ice was dangling from every tree branch like a delicate array of crystals, with light glistening and refracting off every piece: it truly was a winter wonderland. On mornings like this, I would linger a bit longer at the campsite and make a second cup of freshly ground coffee before starting my day. After a half hour or so, I packed my bag and continued north. Even though it was still cold, the icicles began to melt away. As the sun began to rise and I got a few miles into the day, they were all gone.

One state and 70 miles down. Thirteen states and 2,119 miles to go.

CHAPTER 3

Colorado 2009

I settled in Denver in the spring of 2009 to pursue a career in education, or at least a position working with children. I realized after some time as a geologist that I needed to try something different, although I did (and still do) enjoy a good discussion about climate change or the possible reasons why the earth's magnetic field has switched polarity multiple times.

❦ ❦ ❦

After leaving my job in California, I embarked on my six-week road trip around the United States. During my two years in the Golden State, I found myself saying "we should get together soon" to a lot of people in my life who lived elsewhere around the country. I used the road trip to make good on all those promises: I travelled from Jensina in Scottsdale to Julia in Albuquerque, from Aunt Jackie in Dallas to my brother Devon in Clearwater, from Justin in Charleston to Joe in Boston, and finally ended with Marie in Chicago before going back home to Cedar Rapids. It felt good for my soul to see these friends and family, and to finally catch up.

I also had a few interesting and unexpected encounters, like when I was in the panhandle of Florida near the small town of Holt. It was getting dark and since I had recently splurged for a hotel in New Orleans, I was hoping to set up my tent for the evening. After driving down a dirt path toward a local park hoping to find a campsite, I came across some gentlemen who were standing outside a small trailer drinking some beers. As I approached to inquire about possible campsites, two of the men took my arrival as their cue to leave, and I began to chat with the remaining man, Avery, who owned the trailer. Perhaps it was the 6 percent ABV Natty Ice beers we were consuming, but whatever the reason, after a few drinks Avery got emotional and said I reminded him of his son who he hadn't seen for a few years. While he was drying the tears from his eyes, he invited me to crash on a couch in his trailer for the evening, which I accepted. However, soon after accepting his invitation to stay, I began to suspect why the two other men had left as soon as I arrived and, possibly, why Avery's son hadn't seen him in a few years.

Avery was a member of the KKK. I know this because he told me. Over the course of the evening, I learned other curious facts about Avery's life. The inside walls of his entire trailer were lined with mirrors so that he could always see the front door from any room. The outside of his trailer was modified to look as if it was a submarine surfacing out of the nearby Gulf of Mexico to "trick" any overhead aircraft that might be trying to spy on him. A few times during the evening, Avery informed me that, "If I wanted to kill you, I would have done it by now, but I like you." Lucky me, I guess.

We watched a movie, had DiGiorno pizza, and drank a few more beers as we both talked about our respective views on life. He offered me a few books to read. One of these books, Stephen Covey's *First Things First*, a self-help book about managing your time effectively, would later influence one of my tattoo choices. However, I imagine Avery and I interpreted the guidance of that book in very different ways. As midnight rolled around and my eyes got heavy, Avery informed me he needed to wake up at 6:30 a.m. for a weekly phone call he had with members of his "secret group of friends" who were on the East Coast (apparently forgetting his earlier blatant admission that he was a member of the KKK).

Soon after Avery fell asleep, it dawned on me that I should have been a bit more cautious with my screening process for whose couches on which I'm willing to crash. I also realized that there was a slight chance this inebriated gentleman, who informed me about his arsenal of weapons in the back room, once sober, could forget he invited me to stay with him the previous evening and it might be in my best interests to leave before any of that confusion could take place. It would be a lie to say I woke up at 5:00 a.m. as I never really fell asleep. There's just something about a man with a lot of guns who semi-threatened to kill me that kept most of my nerve endings firing that evening. Even though we didn't share too many interests, I didn't want to seem rude to Avery, so before I left, I implemented a lesson I learned from my mother: I wrote a note. After leaving the note (thanking him for the pizza and books) on the kitchen counter, I snuck out as quietly as possible to my

2006 Chevy HHR, sped away as fast as I could, and didn't stop until I reached Tallahassee.

Although there were a few other unanticipated events that happened during the six-week road trip (like finding out that my dad was engaged and that my trip schedule would have me back in Iowa for his courthouse wedding), I felt spending an evening with a member of the KKK in the panhandle of Florida best encompassed my purpose for the road trip: to meet people, new and old, and to reflect on my own goals in life. To be sure, Avery and I do not share the same life goals, but he did offer me shelter, food, and drink. Although these small acts of kindness do not make up for his membership in a terrible hate group, it does give me a sliver of hope that someone like him might have the capacity for change if given the right opportunity. There were things I didn't like about my own life prior to the road trip, and my hope was to find the capacity to make the changes that I wanted to make, no matter how challenging.

❦ ❦ ❦

Living in Colorado seemed like a more financially feasible option than living in California, where I once paid twelve bucks for a small Jack and Coke in Santa Barbara (no ocean view is worth that), and Colorado was also home to a few relatives I hadn't seen in a while. However, another draw to the region was the large collection of my college friends who were loitering in the Mile High City at that time. One would think that since I had decided to make a career change from geology to education, one of my reasons for choosing a new city would have been career prospects. Nope. I had absolutely zero education job prospects and not the slightest idea as to what the first step in attaining my teacher license would be when I arrived in Denver. To be clear, I didn't necessarily think I needed to be a traditional classroom teacher, I just wanted to work with kids, so, naturally, my first thought was to teach. I was open to any position that would give me the opportunity to work with children and, ideally, teach them in some capacity, to see if that would be a career I wanted to pursue further. However, there was one tiny problem I faced when I got to Denver, and that was the state of our nation's economy.

Although I had willfully quit a well-paying job and was able to find relatively sustainable part-time employment while I worked toward my Colorado teaching license, for a short while, I was the most famous unemployed guy in Denver, and possibly the entire United States. Like that business executive in New York who made headlines because his daughter gave him the idea of wearing a sandwich board and handing out resumes to people on the street, my unemployment status also found its way into the national media. My riches-to-rags story of being a geologist who was raking leaves for a living made headlines twice in the *Denver Post*. It started when I submitted my resume to a local staffing agency that focused on finding long-term employment but offered temporary positions from time to time. I told them I would take any job available.

The owner of the company needed her lawn raked and some other landscaping needs addressed, so she hired me and another gentleman who is still in my phone contacts simply as "Al."

The job only took about two days to complete (although Al constantly pleaded with me to slow down to prolong the work for another day). Shortly after this job I received a phone call from the agency. They had told a reporter from the *Denver Post* about my work history and the *Post* wanted to know if I'd be willing to do an interview for an article about the employment situation in Denver. At first I felt a little uncomfortable because I had voluntarily quit a well-paying job to pursue another career path, and I knew there likely were other, more deserving stories of the painstaking efforts of those facing unemployment—stories about families struggling to make ends meet or of home foreclosures and personal loss. But since I was bored and not doing anything that day, I agreed to do the interview.

To exonerate myself just a little bit from sounding like a fame-hungry social media star, from the start of the interview, before any questions were asked and any photos were staged of me looking stoic and concerned as I was drinking coffee or walking down some steps, I told them exactly what my real story was: that I had quit my job, road-tripped around the country hanging out with friends, and was just doing what I needed to make ends meet while pursuing another career path. I made it clear this was completely voluntary and that I really didn't think there was a story to be told. They assured me that it was more a piece about job searching in general.

They ultimately played the sympathy card ("Scams Prey on the Jobless" the headline blared) but by the time they published the story, the level of responsibility I felt for making sure the truth was told had dwindled and it all had become somewhat of a joke within my circle of friends. But it didn't stop there. Media outlets have contacts and informants with other news agencies, so story sharing is quite common, at least according to my interviewers. The next phone call I received from the staffing agency was not only to thank me for doing the article (they had received some good press) but to tell me they also had my next gig. They wanted me to do an interview for a nationally syndicated news program. You may have heard of it: it's a little show called *Good Morning America*. I could barely contain my surprise while they were telling me how the ABC consultant for the *Denver Post* read my story and wanted to spotlight me in *Good Morning America's* televised report on the struggles of the job crisis in America. At that point, the humor of it all was at its peak and I immediately agreed to do the interview.

I was to go back to the staffing agency owner's yard where I would be filmed raking leaves—even though I had just raked them about a week prior to the filming and few leaves had fallen since then. If you look closely at the footage, you'll notice there were almost no leaves on the ground and I was merely raking up dead grass and the occasional felled needle from a nearby conifer. They also filmed me taking bags of "leaves" and placing them in the yard waste bin. To be sure, there were very few leaves in those bags, they were mostly filled with other random trash that was found at the house that day.

The day of the interview, I made sure to wear one of my favorite college t-shirts, one we made to commemorate a trip I took with five other friends to a cabin in Canada. The shirt read "Canadian Excursion 2004" with an outline of my buddy's

Canadian neighbor holding a beer, and the word "Eh!" in a word bubble above him. Once again, I told the true story of the events leading to my voluntary unemployment to ABC's representative, but at least she had the boldness to just say, "Oh, we don't care." The best part of the experience was receiving phone calls from various friends across the country—some of whom I had just hung out with on my road trip while drinking and eating out and spending money freely—who were shocked in disbelief at the sad story of a jobless geologist that scrolled across their television screens that morning.

The clip also featured two separate interview segments of me telling more job-searching stories, all of which were true. Unfortunately for the staffing agency, the interviews that ABC did with their employees (who had encouraged me to do the interviews in the first place) were mostly edited out of the version that aired, so I had quite a bit of screen time. The staffing agency had greatly helped me find much-needed temporary work, so I was hoping they would at least get some more press from all of this. But no, it was just me wearing my "Canadian Excursion 2004" t-shirt on national television.

The best description of the whole situation came from my friend Andy, who captioned a link to the news clip on his Facebook page, "Free Loading Couch Surfer Dupes *Good Morning America*." For the next few nights, my friends and I shared a few drinks and some laughs at the Irish Snug bar on Colfax, using the pick-up line, "Hey, do you want to meet the most famous unemployed guy in America?"

It didn't work.

CHAPTER 4

Appalachian Trail 2014
15 Days; 166 Miles

In one of my favorite holiday movies, *National Lampoon's Christmas Vacation*, the family is searching for the perfect Christmas tree. Upon hearing that his daughter Audrey is frozen from the waist down, Clark Griswold calmly explains that "it's all part of the experience." This movie quote seemed very applicable to what I experienced while hiking my first mile through the mountains of North Carolina, which included a brutal uphill climb that kicked my butt. After waking up the following morning to a four-inch layer of snow surrounding my tent, I calmly thought to myself, *It's all part of the experience.*

I packed up my gear and made breakfast quickly, but I made the common mistake of bulking up on layers of clothes to counteract the chilly morning without remembering to shed a few of those layers before beginning to hike. It's incredible how quickly the body can work up a good sweat, especially carrying a heavy pack and hiking up mountains. So even though it was still snowing with freezing temperatures when I departed camp that morning, after about twenty minutes I was sweating. Naturally, it only made sense to stop in the middle of the woods and take my pants off; I assumed this would be a safe place to be half naked. But even in the middle of the woods, you are never truly alone. With my pants dangling around my ankles, another hiker walked past and we exchanged a simple nod—an acknowledgement between two men who understood the situation.

After putting my regular hiking pants back on and walking a few more miles, I came across a moral dilemma. While I hike, I try to pick up trash (bottles, wrappers, etc.) to do my part in keeping the trails clean. However, on this day, what I came across was not a small candy bar wrapper, but a large, soaking wet, heavy winter parka that someone had left on a tree on the side of the trail. I wish I could say that this was a rare occurrence along the AT, but sadly it's all too common to find items, large and small, left behind in the woods. Most of the larger, nonfood items I found were likely left by someone who didn't want to carry extra weight, which, in my opinion, is not cool. Unless it's a life or death scenario, choosing to not carry out your gear is just selfish and wrong.

❦ ❦ ❦

Trail trash is often a simple accident. A hiker will pull a snack bar from a pant pocket, open and eat it while walking, and then shove the wrapper back into the pocket without breaking stride. All too often I came across either parts of or entire wrappers from snack bars sitting in the middle of the trail because they didn't make it back into the owner's pocket. There is a theory that most of the trash found in the woods is from a previous era of hikers who were unaware of the importance of "pack it in, pack it out" backpacking principles. But I would often come across a hiker taking a break at a stream crossing and see him or her eating the exact same snack as the wrapper I'd found. I'd also find trash many miles away from road crossings, which debunks another theory that the trash comes from all of the day hikers using the trail, and not the long-distance backpackers. Unfortunately, the truth is that even the most avid backpackers and outdoor enthusiasts—the people who decide to hike a 2,189-mile trail—are still leaving trash in the woods, even though a lot of times it's completely by accident.

There is a gray area between the (presumably unintended) practice of leaving garbage in the woods and the practice of intentionally sprinkling trail magic for other hikers to find. Not all trail magic comes in the form of people who set up chairs and a canopy and hang out at a road crossing all day to wait for hikers (like Fresh Ground and the church group). Sometimes people will just leave a box of food next to a road. Although finding a free Snickers bar after a long day of hiking is amazing, I personally feel it really isn't a good practice to leave food unattended in or near the woods. The food could draw unwanted wild animals to the area and the packaging of such trail magic is often left behind. I understand the intentions are truly noble, but there's a high probability of it ending up as trash in the woods.

When discussing this topic with other hikers—usually after finding some trash—I felt like I was always preaching to the choir because everyone seemed to only know the responsible people who provided trail magic: those who returned to clean it up at the end of the day. Yet over the course of my AT adventure, I constantly saw remnants of trail magic that were obviously more than a day (and possibly even weeks or months) old. Sometimes it was the trash leftover from a box of trail magic that was never picked up, or soda cans scattered around an area where someone had left a cooler. Although I benefitted many times from delicious trail magic that someone left for people hiking the AT, if it's not done properly, trail magic can quickly become trail trash. These observations are not meant to be a negative blast toward the trail angel community (those amazing individuals who leave trail magic), but to emphasize that if there's one group of people who can work to keep the woods trash free, it's the hiking community.

❖ ❖ ❖

So there I was, staring at a giant, soaking wet, heavy winter parka. After spending almost three years as an environmental consultant cleaning up contaminated sites, and two years as an environmental educator teaching elementary students to pick up trash, I was at a crossroads. My pack was already wet and heavy from packing up in the snow that morning and, after checking my map, I knew it was seventeen miles to the next viable road crossing where I would *possibly* be able to properly dispose of the jacket. After staring at it for five minutes and almost walking away twice, I finally picked up the parka, threw it on my pack, and starting walking. Immediately, I felt the added weight—at least five pounds—but just like that, I had committed myself to carrying someone else's mistake.

Although the parka was heavy, it wasn't unbearable. I kept my mind busy with other hiking activities such as observing the snow melt as the sun rose toward the middle of the day, and subsequently watching it disappear completely as the sun began to set that evening. After a night in a shelter, and with the jacket tied tightly to my external-frame pack, I made it the seventeen miles to the road crossing. There, I met a retired fella named Ralph who was offering some trail magic in the form of coffee, orange juice, fresh fruit, and homemade cookies. Ralph offered two additional things: first, he told me his wife's church was having an auction and that he'd take the coat, wash it, and ensure it would go to a new home; and, second, he told me a delightful story.

When Ralph was younger, his parents were driving through an area near Great Smoky Mountains National Park when they came upon a lot of cars parked along the road. People were standing outside of their vehicles and staring down into a nearby valley, which was littered with dead cowboys and Indians. Off in the distance, fighting continued between the two groups. Shocked, Ralph and his family didn't know what to think of the scene in front of them. This would shock anyone in the old west, but it was the 1950s! Then, out in the distance, they heard a loud voice yell "CUT!" At that moment, all the dead cowboys and Indians stood up and walked away. Ralph and his family had just witnessed firsthand a scene being filmed for Walt Disney's *Davy Crockett*.

As I have said many times since completing the AT, the best experiences are sometimes the people you meet. *It's all part of the experience.*

❖   ❖   ❖

After a few more nights in various shelters, my family of hikers and I made it to the Nantahala Outdoor Center (NOC), affectionately referred to by many hikers as "Hiker Mecca." It's a large complex with dormitory-style rooms for rent, an outfitter, a restaurant, and, more importantly after five days of hiking, cold beer on tap. The NOC also has outdoor activities like rafting and zip-lining, but a cold beer and a hot pizza were good enough for me.

As much as the first couple of days through North Carolina kicked my butt, they offered some of the best, unobstructed landscape views that I had seen on the AT. Georgia was beautiful, but the viewpoints were limited. North Carolina had many mountain tops without trees that offered incredible panoramic vistas (at least while I was in the area), and after leaving the NOC we continued to enjoy these views as we reached one of the more famous sections of the entire AT: Great Smoky Mountains National Park. Here, the group decided to take what is known on the trail as a "zero-day" (no hiking) and after fifteen consecutive days of walking through the woods, my body was grateful! We stopped at Fontana Dam Shelter, located just outside the park, which would be our starting point for the roughly eighty miles of trail that traverse the Smokies.

Shirtless, underwear, mittens, and coffee. What else do you need?

After resupplying in a nearby town, we spent the rest of our zero-day meeting new hikers and playing cards (amazingly, there were three other people in my crew who played spades). I was getting used to people being impressed that I carried a coffee grinder and whole bean coffee with me. (I was carrying four different kinds of single-origin beans at one point, shipped to me from my favorite coffee shop in Denver.) However, after a couple weeks, it was another unique piece of gear I had that caught people's attention, and I was subsequently known on the trail as "the guy with the cutting board." In the world of lightweight backpacking—a world where people cut off the ends of their toothbrushes to save weight—having a cutting board seems like carrying a load of bricks, but I wouldn't have traded it for the world (besides, it wasn't *that* heavy). The level of satisfaction that I gleaned from that luxury was beyond description. It's amazing how spending time in the woods makes you appreciate the little things, like a cutting board.

One state and 166 miles down. Thirteen states and 2,023 miles to go.

CHAPTER 5

Colorado 2009

Her name was Lauren. She was waiting in line at my new favorite coffee shop in Denver, Novo Coffee, where it often took a while to get a caffeine fix because they brewed black coffee one cup at a time. I was in line to buy coffee for myself and my buddy Evan when Lauren and I began chatting, which quickly shifted into mutual flirting. After some generic banter about coffee shops, the conversation took an organic turn toward the topic of jobs: what she did for work, why I wanted to get into teaching, and things of that nature. This offered an opportunity for me to retell the story of my interview on *Good Morning America*, which drew a quick laugh from Lauren (it can literally take this long for a cup of coffee at this place, but it's totally worth it).

Before we could exchange numbers, she abruptly stopped talking and her eyes froze as another gentleman made his way through the crowd and said, "There you are," as he gave her a hug—the type of hug that indicated a different connection between them than just friends. I would later learn this was their first date. I've learned over the course of my life that I'm not the brightest at reading certain kinds of relationship cues from women, but I interpreted the look Lauren gave me as *I would love to keep talking but I have to deal with this.* Thankfully, my coffee was ready by that point, offering an easy exit strategy. I left with a simple "nice talking with you" to show the man that nothing was going on between Lauren and myself. After bringing Evan his coffee, I told him about Lauren and the somewhat awkward situation when the other guy arrived, but I wrote the experience off as just an enjoyable conversation with an attractive woman. I thought the odds were slim that we would meet again.

I thought wrong.

My friend Evan had developed a keen ability to find funny news stories online and always generously forwarded them to our friends. Another source of entertainment for him was the habitually ridiculous personal ads and quirky items for sale that he regularly discovered on Craigslist. Some of the writing in the old Craigslist personal ads were literary gold of the highest caliber.

Evan particularly enjoyed perusing Craigslist's subsection "Missed Connections." These were typically posted by individuals who danced with somebody at the bar but didn't get their number, or by guys who saw a cute girl driving down Broadway and decided afterward to "hit 'er up," as some of the posts said. Some of the ads were so utterly ridiculous that it's hard to imagine that real people might actually be using this site to find a *connection* with someone they missed! While browsing one night after our coffee at Novo, Evan saw a post titled "Dustin at

Novo." This made him (in his own words) "almost shit himself" and call me immediately.

My friends, however, also had a history of posting fake Craigslist ads, like the time Andy posted an ad in Wisconsin where our friend Gary lived at the time. The ad stated that Gary had tickets to a local concert and that whoever proved they were the biggest fan of the band would get two free tickets. In the ad, Andy instructed anyone interested to call Gary's cell phone number and immediately begin screaming their favorite song by the band over the phone. Just as Andy had hoped, Gary received nonstop phone calls and messages from fans screaming into the phone trying to convince him that they deserved the (nonexistent) tickets. Because of this history with my friends, Evan made sure to confirm the validity of the "Dustin at Novo" ad before calling me.

After exchanging a few messages via the Craigslist email server, Lauren and I met for coffee and, a few days later, for dinner. We hung out two other times: once at "Film on the Rocks" where a movie is shown on a screen at the famous open-air Red Rocks Amphitheater, and then again with some of her friends at "Jazz in the Park" in Denver's City Park. After that date, though, it was clear that she wasn't interested anymore. There had been a few kisses between us but no more than that. I liked her a lot, but it just wasn't mutual. She told me she liked someone else and she was going to pursue that relationship.

So what did the end of my time with Lauren mean? It meant she was being an adult and took responsibility for her role in the relationship. She decided it was not me who she wanted to be with exclusively, and she was upfront about her feelings, and for that I commend her. Some men would have just chalked this up as a loss and never thought about it again. However, Lauren played a crucial role in my story because of one simple gesture: While we were dating, she told me about an email list for the Colorado Alliance for Environmental Education (CAEE). She forwarded me a link to a job posting from that list for a part-time job with an organization called South Platte River Environmental Education (SPREE), which was the educational branch of a larger nonprofit called the Greenway Foundation. The job included developing curriculum and leading excursions for elementary students at urban parks and waterways. I applied and got the job, which turned into a full-time salaried position for the next two years and gave me the amazing opportunity to provide environmental education to thousands of students at outdoor parks.

Although Lauren didn't turn out to be my significant other, it felt as if a series of cosmic events aligned us to first meet at a Denver coffee shop and then reunite over a Craigslist Missed Connections ad, which subsequently led to an opportunity to fulfill my employment goals and expand my professional experience in a way that I could have never imagined. Besides, if Lauren had decided to stay with me, or if I hadn't gotten that job working with the Greenway Foundation, I might never have moved to other side of town and met Jessa at Annie's Café and Bar.

CHAPTER 6

Appalachian Trail 2014
22 Days; 274 Miles

After crossing over Fontana Dam, the tallest dam in the eastern United States, I began the uphill climb into the most visited national park in the country. Before reaching this part of the AT, we heard a lot of rumors about the Smokies and the difficulties these mountains pose to thru-hikers. Maybe it was the pleasant weather that day or maybe my legs were stronger, or maybe it was the four beers, two pizzas, and one hot dog I consumed the day before, but whatever the reason, after we crossed the dam, I dominated the initial eleven-mile climb into the park. It was definitely a workout, but it was nothing compared to what we had heard about this section, and many of my fellow hikers agreed with that sentiment. We finished the day with seventeen miles under our belts and smiles all around.

The following day, we left the shelter to begin what would be our longest hike yet, and to climb the tallest peak along the entire AT: Clingmans Dome. The weather was pleasant when the day began, but we immediately experienced the aftermath of the previous weeks' melting snow: massive puddles of mud were lingering in the middle of the trail like mini lakes just waiting to crest the top of my waterproof boots (and they did). Thankfully, the adrenaline from summiting the tallest peak on the whole trail was enough to stop some wet socks from bothering me, at least not at that point. Clingmans Dome was everything I hoped it would be. The observation tower offers stunning 360-degree views of the whole park, including the one directly down the ridgeline that is the North Carolina/Tennessee border. I was able to see how I had just crossed back and forth between the two states with my recent steps. This moment also presented one of the first major psychological tests that the AT gave me as a thru-hiker. Hiking hundreds of miles to reach the tower and achieve the views I just described was humbling, perhaps even more so because I immediately noticed the very well-maintained access road that allowed anyone with a driver's license the very same views.

This occurs frequently at many of the major peaks and climbs along the AT. Most are accessible to non-hikers, which may seem to take away from the sense of accomplishment gained by having just hiked hundreds or thousands of miles to get there. For example, the second-tallest peak along the trail, Mount Washington in New Hampshire, is accessible by road, cog rail, and worse yet—shorter hiking trails. So even those who say they hiked to the top didn't necessarily hike over a thousand miles, like thru-hikers do. My favorite of the alternate methods used to reach the top of mountains are the ski lifts that operate during the summer months on a handful of peaks. It's pretty sobering to finally reach the top of a serious climb, only to see the ski lift come to a stop and some grandma with a cane step off and give you a smile. (Yeah, that happened.)

If your only goal while hiking the AT is to summit a lot of the peaks along the trail, then take this advice: rent a car, drive the Blue Ridge Parkway through Virginia, explore Harpers Ferry, skip the entire state of Pennsylvania, head straight to the White Mountains of New Hampshire, and then stop for some lobster in Maine on your way to Mount Katahdin. That would only take a few weeks, save you a lot of money, and accomplish the goal of seeing most of the major peaks along the trail. To me, though, the point of hiking over two thousand miles through the woods isn't about checking things off a list or meeting schedules. Seeing these folks step out of their cars (or off ski lifts) and enjoy the same views that I felt I had *earned* while hiking meant learning to manage my expectations of what the journey meant to me.

Thankfully, the access road to the observation tower on top of Clingmans Dome was still closed for the winter, so although I knew people could drive to where I stood, I didn't have to face that reality in that particular moment. Because the weather can change drastically near Newfound Gap—the pass where Highway 441 crosses the mountains from Cherokee, North Carolina to Gatlinburg, Tennessee—the park rangers leave the tower's access road closed until the weather improves. So, after taking in the crisp air for about thirty minutes and an impromptu

A view from the observation tower at Clingmans Dome

snowball fight with other hikers, we finished our twenty-mile hike for the day.

❦ ❦ ❦

We woke up the next morning to the start of a rainstorm that didn't let up for two days. Given the freezing temperatures, wind gusts that were likely in the range of fifty to sixty miles an hour, and puddle-soaked boots from the day before, the day was doomed from the onset—and I forgot to manage my expectations properly.

I could sense my body was going to need a break soon, so when we arrived at camp the previous evening, I started polling my trail family as to how they'd feel about taking a break in Gatlinburg the next morning. At first, it was clear that most people in my group were not interested in taking a break. Regardless, I had already decided I was going to stay a night in town to dry off, get a nice meal, and come back refreshed and energized (at least, that was the idea). The next morning, with rain falling and snow and ice still on the ground, everyone's boots still wet, and a temperature that was less than enticing, some members of my trail family began to change their tune about finding a warm hotel shower. Incidentally, Forget-Me-Not's inflatable sleeping pad had sprung a leak during the night, so going into town to replace it became a priority for her.

I had arranged for a ride into town with another hiker's buddy who was already scheduled to pick him up. The hiker said he would wait for me at Newfound Gap and wasn't concerned when I told him I would be behind him by about a half hour. I was usually one of the last people to leave camp in the morning because of one simple fact: I made coffee and breakfast, which was unusual for most thru-hikers. Everyone has a dietary plan that works for their needs, but my experience with camping and hiking has shown me that morning coffee in the woods is one of the best things a human can experience. No cup of coffee is better than the one you make in the woods. Period. This little indulgence in my morning routine usually got me out of camp about thirty minutes later than the others.

After I finished my coffee and oatmeal that morning, I departed camp, and I reached the road after about five miles of hiking through very strong winds and rain, my hands frozen and nearly numb. Once my body became compromised it quickly affected my mental state in a negative way. This negativity was exacerbated when I arrived at Newfound Gap and my ride was nowhere to be found. I learned that Forget-Me-Not had met up with the hiker who had offered me a ride and *she* hopped in the car to go into town. Whether she knew she had taken my ride or if it just wasn't clear who in our group the ride was for, I'll never know, but at that moment my frustration was high and I knew I had to get out of the numbing cold, and fast.

I called a local motel that was listed in a guidebook as offering free shuttles from the pass. Sadly, the man on the other end of the phone said they didn't have a shuttle but that he could give me the number of a cab service. I called the number, and after about forty-five minutes of waiting in the wind and cold an old van arrived with a small child riding shotgun. This was our "cab." (The rest of my group had gathered and the decision to go into town had changed from a "no" the night before to a resounding "yes!" that day in the cold.) As we piled into the van, the driver told me the price and it was double what the motel owner said it would be. After a few minutes of debate, when he still wouldn't budge on the price, I reluctantly instructed him to "just go" and said we would figure out the money situation in town. It turned out that we had extra time to figure it out since the small child in the front seat needed the driver to pull over multiple times so he could throw up outside of the car. At this point, I was really questioning the legitimacy of this so-called "cab" and especially the motel owner who referred me to it.

When we arrived at the motel, one thing immediately grabbed my attention: a large white van parked directly in front of the motel office with the word "Shuttle" painted on the side. I walked in and had a war of words with the owner. He boldly explained that he simply didn't want to send his driver out that day and decided to give his buddy a chance to make some extra cash by picking us up in his van. To cap it all off, even the price of the motel room was more than he had originally said. I was furious.

Perhaps the motel owner assumed I was a typical poor hiker looking for the cheapest room and therefore would rent his room anyway since it was still the cheapest in town—which wouldn't be out of the norm to assume for most hikers—but not all of us thru-hikers were searching the gutters for spare change, free meals, or the cheapest motel rooms. I was by no means disregarding the financial cost of this journey, but at that point, even with my body cold and wet, and with a mental state on the brink of collapse if I didn't get a cheeseburger soon, this guy was not about to get a single dime from me. So I stormed off and headed to one of the more mainstream chain hotels that, although more expensive, would undoubtedly have better rooms and, most importantly, allow me to avoid dealing with the motel owner. I told the group I would front the extra cost, and even though forty dollars can go a long way for a backpacker, I was more than happy to pay it out of spite—not my finest hour, but far from my worst.

❖ ❖ ❖

It's quite the scene watching a group of hikers unload their gear into a double queen room at a Days Inn. Everything immediately became a hook as we scrambled to hang anything that might need drying. (The space above the window-mounted heater is prime real estate for hanging wet clothing and footwear.) If this sounds disgusting then that means you're a normal human being, but to us thru-hikers, it was just another day.

Although my frustration about the "stolen" shuttle, the cab with the sickly child, and the slumlord motel owner was beginning to subside, I still wanted a beer and a burger to return all the good feels to my mind and body. After finding what looked like a sports bar on Google Maps and suggesting it for dinner, I was outvoted for a place of which I had never heard. Since I still wanted to stay with my trail family, I was okay with the decision, especially when they informed me that this place might have some bottled beer available.

They took me to a big chain restaurant, essentially the amusement park equivalent of southern burger joints. Nothing about this place was going to help me forget the frustrations from the day. Don't get me wrong, the burgers were good, but the environment could easily have been a very effective condom commercial: loud, echoey walls, running children, and not a single beer in the cooler. Perhaps it was a generational thing, but for some reason the low-key sports bar and restaurant just didn't appeal to the rest of the group, yet this restaurant and all of its ruckus was like the holy grail of places to eat for some folks in my trail family. In the end, after the burger joint, a few of us did go to the other restaurant, but I felt as if they were only there out of pity for me. Regardless, it was the best pity beer of my life.

Back at the hotel, the final straw of what I have since determined to be the second most frustrating day of my entire AT journey was when Forget-Me-Not (who I still blamed at that point for stealing my ride) rejoined us and wanted to stay in the hotel room. I really didn't care, except that adding another female to the group changed the sleeping arrangements in the room and resulted in me not getting a bed for the evening.

At the time, I was frustrated. However, as with many things along this (or any) journey, in retrospect I see the events of that day in Gatlinburg very differently now. I don't actually think Forget-Me-Not stole my shuttle ride. I was just cold and hungry, and I let my failure to manage my expectations get the best of me. I do not hold any ill will toward her nor any of the others in the group—that would be silly and unjustified. Forget-Me-Not and everyone in our trail family were (and are) amazing people, but on that particular day, my experience with the AT was challenging due to many factors, including the delicate process of building relationships with the other hikers.

From discussions with other thru-hikers, I've learned that being frustrated with the interpersonal aspects of having a trail family is common. As much as the AT can be an enlightening solo experience, it is also a time of being in very close quarters with new friends, most of whom are pushing their bodies to their physical limits. Sometimes those experiences were great and sometimes they didn't go as planned. While hiking the AT, and as I continue to age, I've discovered that while any relationship will have high and low points, even the worst of the low points don't usually warrant destroying a good friendship.

❖ ❖ ❖

As we could have expected, one night in a hotel room was not enough time to entirely dry out six people's gear, and the fifteen miles we hiked the next day through torrential rain was the beginning of my feet really starting to hate me. We did have some clear weather on our last day in the Smokies and knowing that I had just hiked across the entire park in four and a half days was a good confidence booster. The highlight of the last few days was seeing an outcropping of rocks called Charlies Bunion. We saw it just as the clouds were burning off, and Beast accurately captured our awe by saying, "It looks like the mountains are going into an ocean."

The conclusion of the Smokies hike brought us to the hostel at Standing Bear Farm, a place highly recommended by many hikers, including Pappy Joe, whose trail name was bestowed upon him by his grandchildren. Pappy Joe was probably in his late sixties and he was hiking the AT for the *third time*. He and I had been leapfrogging each other for a few days and we officially met when I picked up his hat on the trail and he was hiking back to find it. When I asked why he was hiking the AT again he said, "Well, I read somewhere that less than seventy

A view from Charlies Bunion in the Great Smoky Mountains

people have ever hiked the entire trail three times, so I figured, why not?" Seemed to me as good of a reason as any.

Standing Bear Farm was everything you could want in a hostel: a laid-back setting with enough modern conveniences to make you feel like a king (or queen) for a day. We had to hand wash our clothes and even though they had a dryer, I chose to hang mine to dry. There was a fire pit, food for sale, and cold beer in the fridge. After four days of hiking in wet boots, I was experiencing what would be the start of many blisters and very sore feet. I met some new hikers there, like Jalopy and her dog, Coyote, who were hiking with dried fruits and nuts as their only food source. I didn't leave Standing Bear Farm until late the next day because I vowed to not walk another step until my boots were dry.

❦ ❦ ❦

After hiking thirty-five miles in the next two days, I finally made it to the town of Hot Springs, North Carolina, located just before the Tennessee border. The trail literally goes along the main street through town, which is only about four blocks long and complete with two taverns, a Dollar General, an outfitter, and an amazing coffee shop and art gallery called Artisun Gallery & Cafe. It was also home to some of the nicest people you could ever hope to meet. A few other hikers had learned from some locals that there would be a town potluck that evening (open to the public for a small donation), so that quickly answered the question of where I was having dinner. There I met Queen Diva, a woman who would come to town for a few months out of the year to work in the Hiker's Ridge Ministry Center, located in a small building in town. It appeared her only job was to make cookies (which I ate) and talk story with the hikers (which we did). At the potluck I also met Shannon. She was an artist visiting from Chicago and was staying just outside of town at an art residency center called Azule. She offered me the opportunity to stay at the center, so I decided to call Hot Springs home for a few days. Those few extra days in town undoubtedly cost more money than I was planning to spend, but I don't think I'll ever tell my future grandchildren, "I regret having had so much fun."

One state and 274 miles down. Thirteen states and 1,915 miles to go.

CHAPTER 7

Colorado 2011

After leaving California, where dating had proved to be difficult for me, Denver, on the other hand, was very kind. After Lauren, I never had a shortage of dating opportunities and I was enjoying life as a single male in a very vibrant city. Admittedly, I was not always looking for love, partly because I was ready to take a break from finding "the one." My heart and soul were tired from all the searching I had done up to that point in my life and I figured if I was changing career paths from a geologist to an educator, I might as well make a change in my dating intentions as well. I'm not going to sugarcoat it: I was a single man in my mid-twenties dating a lot of women and enjoying every minute of it.

I suppose you could also say I was bitter from all the times I sincerely made efforts to be a good friend or boyfriend and was subsequently shut down. This isn't a unique story—the nice guy who is always "just a friend." This concept, albeit somewhat childish, is a real struggle for some people. I don't mean for this to come off as a pity-party, but to ignore the ways that dating experiences shape a young man or woman's life would be to shortchange an important part of their whole story.

❋ ❋ ❋

Back in college, I was studying in the campus library with my friend Natalie. After being very vocal about her craving for Ben and Jerry's ice cream, it was clear that a pint of it would mean the world to her. Natalie was single at the time, and even though I was nowhere close to being on her dating radar, I nonetheless enjoyed spending time with her and becoming her friend.

I "finished studying" before she did, hopped in my pinkish-beige 1992 Ford Taurus, drove to the local grocery store, bought the ice cream she so desired, sped back to her dorm, parked illegally, convinced her roommate to let me in, placed the ice cream in her minifridge, and left a note on her laptop wishing her luck on the test the following day.

Upon finding the ice cream and the note, was I expecting her to run across campus to find me, hug me, kiss me, and promise to marry me forever? Maybe. But even a "thank you" via AOL Instant Messenger would have sufficed. Instead, Natalie didn't respond to the gesture for well over two weeks until, while passing me in the Commons of our college, she quickly said, "Oh thanks for the ice crea—" as she walked in the other direction.

Although our efforts don't always pan out the way we might expect them to, and sometimes we just have to get over it, the reality is that it can be difficult to manage those expectations, especially for young adults. Sure, it was just a pint of ice cream, but as is true for almost every emotionally challenging life event, there is a point where—after the mind, heart, and soul have endured repetitive pain—one's outward emotions and actions begin to change in response. I think that's why, after repeatedly experiencing heartache, I had altered the way I approached dating when I arrived in Denver.

❦ ❦ ❦

Things felt different after my first date with Jessa, though. She was a bartender at a local diner called Annie's Café and Bar, at the corner of Colfax Avenue and Saint Paul Street. I would go there for late night pie and coffee. Jessa was beautiful and fun to chat with. She was warm and caring, and she always seemed to make me want to come back for more pie (no pun intended). As one of her friends would later say, Jessa was "the smile on your face." She really was.

When she crossed "that" boundary, the one that separates all bartenders from their customers, I knew she was taking an epic risk by giving me her phone number. Despite all the rules I have learned about how long I should wait to call a woman, with Jessa, I didn't follow a single one. The moment she gave me her number, I immediately called it right then at the bar, she answered, and I asked her out. Thankfully she said yes because otherwise it would have made for a seriously awkward moment. We agreed on a simple night out at a few bars later that week. She had already proven to me that she was fun to be around, I just hoped she shared that sentiment about me.

By that point in my single-man escapades, I was starting to tire of the monotony of dating. Don't get me wrong, I love taking women out for dates. It's enjoyable to have another person to share an experience with. But after what felt like fifty first dates, I could only tell the same story about myself so many times before my sanity would come into question. After a while, it was practically necessary to tell a different story. I never lied, but sometimes I highlighted different parts of my life—you know, like the Facebook equivalent of talking.

The ability to have a conversation with pretty much anyone is a quality that I am not lacking. I would talk to my date about my current job as an educator or my previous position as a geologist. Sometimes I would tell her about the coral research I did in Australia during college or I'd just pick a current news story and learn more about how she felt regarding the topic. Once I got past the initial meeting period, and I confirmed that she wasn't a racist, bigot, or homophobe, then I could more accurately gauge if I genuinely enjoyed spending time with her. Even though I'm a Millennial, I still appreciate this archaic form of communication called "talking."

That's why, for me, one of the most challenging parts of dating a new person is trusting that she will actually show up for the date. We just met each other, she doesn't know me, and I don't know her, and we don't owe each other anything. Simply stated: she may not show up. I have been stood up many times in my dating history, both with and without explanation. A woman once told me the morning of a coffee date (after a week of talking and setting up the date), that she wouldn't make it because her "dog ran out of food."

When you've met someone that you really want to see again, someone who found a way to make you shed that first layer of defense, someone who makes you want to fall in love again—like how Jessa made me feel after spending many nights talking with her at the bar—then waiting for the other person to walk through the door is one the most excruciating moments in any new relationship.

Thankfully, Jessa did walk through the door for our first date, and the evening was great. I met a few of her friends and former coworkers, we shared a few shots, and we talked when we could between sets of the live music that was playing. After this first date, we both agreed that we should meet again soon. Her previous relationship had not gone well, and she told me why she had agreed to go out with me: she was finally over her ex. At the end of the date I dropped her off at her house. We kissed. We kissed a lot, but we didn't sleep with each other. In fact, we almost said in unison that we should wait on sex, as if we both knew there could be something more. I was not dating or sleeping with anyone else and I felt ready to be in a relationship again. I liked Jessa, and if her facial expression after we kissed meant anything, then I can assume she liked me back. This was why, for our second date, I was devastated when she didn't show.

❦ ❦ ❦

We had planned to meet and celebrate her birthday. She was going to introduce me to more of her friends, and it was supposed to be us taking the next step in what might be an awesome partnership. It wasn't like we hadn't confirmed the date. We had both texted several times to say how excited we were to see each other. Then, on Tuesday, September 20, 2011—the day before we were supposed to meet—I stopped receiving text messages from her. Her radio silence continued the following day (when we were supposed to have our second date), and she never again responded to my texts or phone calls. I even went to the place where we were supposed to meet and, of course, she wasn't there. After a few more texts and calls, I went from slightly concerned to just plain angry. And while I knew it was possible that there was a legitimate reason for Jessa standing me up, her absence and lack of communication hit me like a ton of bricks. After a few days, my anger turned to embarrassment (because I had told friends about her), which was followed shortly after by feelings of depression. It was similar to the feelings of depression I had when I was younger or when I was in California pining over Karla (the bridesmaid from Iowa).

I had been on and off antidepressants for a while at that point. A few months before my first date with Jessa, after enduring a series of disturbing dreams that always ended in a gunshot, I had decided to tell my doctor. The gunshot would never be directed at anyone, but after what seemed like a regular dream, all of a sudden there would be a gunshot—*Bang!*— and then everything would go black. This dream, which I had been having on and off since high school, now started happening while I was awake. It's hard to describe, but there would be moments during the day where my mind would check out for a split second, and in that second I would see the gunshot—*Bang!*

My doctor prescribed a daily dose of Citalopram after I broke down crying in his office while trying to describe the dreams. He was the first person I ever told that something just didn't feel right in my life, and that it hadn't felt right for a long time. Whether he knows it or not, that doctor saved my life, but not because of his years of medical training or the generic pharmaceutical drug he prescribed. He saved my life by merely listening to me that day.

For the week after I was stood up by Jessa, I was a mess. Although I had been feeling great for several months after seeing my doctor, being stood up was a huge blow to my psyche. My alcohol intake certainly didn't help anything. I drank a lot during that time and, just like alcohol tends to facilitate, the battle between anger and depression was ignited many times in my mind. As is usually the case with me, depression was winning. I guess I'm thankful my feelings decide to punch me in the gut as opposed to me punching someone else.

❖ ❖ ❖

Another week went by and, after some soul searching, I decided that I wanted some pie. I hadn't returned to Annie's since the evening that Jessa stood me up and I figured that if I was going to lose both a potential partner *and* my favorite late-night pie and coffee place, then I at least deserved a face-to-face explanation. I had no ill intentions for this meeting and I merely wanted to prove to myself that I could still be civil with Jessa.

Everyone is entitled to make decisions about their lives, and she had clearly made hers—at least, I thought she had.

When I arrived at Annie's, even though it was one of Jessa's regular nights, her coworker was working behind the bar. I looked around and Jessa was nowhere to be found. For a moment, I thought she might have switched her schedule to avoid me. I ordered a meal, and while I was waiting for my food, I decided it was finally time to start the questioning. I asked her coworker behind the bar, "So, where's Jessa tonight?"

The bartender, two other people at the bar, and another waitress who was walking by all stopped what they were doing and looked directly at me. The pause between my question and the bartender's response felt like the pause I felt when I was waiting for the officer to tell me my fate in that parking lot in Southern California. I will never forget the look of sadness on the bartender's face when he responded, "She died."

I have never felt more selfish in my life than I did in that moment.

After a few minutes of disbelief on my part, he explained that, on the Tuesday before our second date was scheduled to happen, she had been in an accident while getting on the light rail. Her arm got caught in the door and she was dragged underneath the train. That next day (the day of our scheduled second date), a day after she lost her life, I was developing a hateful and spiteful mental image of her because she was not responding to my text messages. A day after her family and friends lost a loved one, I was sitting in my apartment wondering if this horrible woman was ever going to call me back. A day after the world lost yet another beautiful soul, I was using her as a reason to be, once again, angry with women and dating in general.

Notwithstanding the previous few years in Denver, dating had generally not been a positive experience for me. Although I enjoyed the dates themselves, they never seemed to go where I hoped and, admittedly, I was getting a little impatient. Jessa not showing up had felt like the icing on the cake that pushed me toward deciding, for two weeks, that no woman deserved to be treated like a princess (as my mother had taught me in my youth).

So there I was at the bar, learning that Jessa had died and feeling like a selfish jerk. After the pause was over and everyone continued what they were doing, a simple Google search confirmed everything the bartender shared with me. It was all over the *Denver Post* and had been discussed on local news stations the evening she passed away. I had simply not watched or read anything for a few days because I was busy developing my own narrative to the story—one that demonized an innocent woman, a victim of a terrible accident. There are no self-help books or Hallmark cards for this scenario. Of all the life lessons a parent may bestow on a child, this topic is usually not one of them. I didn't know what to do or how to feel. I just felt sadness for Jessa's family and friends. It had been two weeks since she had passed away. The funeral had already happened. Was it appropriate for me to do anything? I only went on one date with this woman and it was a great date, but I didn't know any of her family and had only met a handful of her friends. I was so sad and confused at that moment for all of those reasons and more.

With a somber tone, I told the bartender a very truncated version of my relationship with Jessa. To my surprise, after explaining that I thought I had been stood up for our second date, he stopped me and said, "You were the one?" Apparently, she had been talking to others about me at work and had told them about our first date, and how she was very excited for the second. Hearing this was like having my emotions strapped to a medieval torture wheel, stretched to the edge of breaking, and made me feel even worse.

It's not revelatory to say that dating can be nerve-wracking largely because you don't know if feelings of attraction are mutual. I had told my friends about Jessa and, over the two weeks I was sulking about her silence, I had assumed she just didn't care about me or wasn't attracted to me. Instead, after talking with her coworker I discovered that, for the first time in a long time, I had met someone who felt the same way about me as I did about her. And now she was gone.

I decided that reaching out to any of her friends and family just wouldn't have been appropriate. During the days that passed, I was still confused as to how I should be feeling. We went on one date and then she died. I read the news articles multiple times and, finally, after another few weeks, the thoughts in my head started to clear. To this day, my deepest thoughts and condolences go out to Jessa's friends and family, and every day I hope that I can forgive myself for thinking such terrible things about a magnificent person. In her passing, Jessa gave me a gift that I will never be able to repay—the gift of perspective. The way we look at and evaluate the various happenings in our lives can, and does, affect the people around us. There is nothing more detrimental to our happiness than when we choose to view something through a lens of negativity. Although it'll take years to cement this lesson in my actions, I hope those who loved Jessa know that her passing has influenced at least one person to be a better person for this world—but I bet I'm not the only one.

CHAPTER 8

Appalachian Trail 2014
35 Days; 416 Miles

On the day I left Hot Springs, the weather was overcast and wet, and talk of a late-March snowstorm had surfaced in the local news. Although it was hard to leave such a great place, I begrudgingly hiked eleven miles to the first shelter outside of town, where I met a fellow thru-hiker, Penguin Man, who was already set up to stay the night. The one thing about this shelter that stood out, sadly, was how much trash and debris had collected inside. This was the case at many of the shelters and it was starting to become a little disheartening. Because I strive to backpack with a Leave-No-Trace mindset, it continued to shock me that, even though we live in a world where drones can deliver your morning breakfast, we still have people leaving trash in the woods.

Once, while departing from a shelter, I saw that a hiker had left behind a titanium pot, a spork utensil, and a nice headlamp, which all together was probably around fifty dollars' worth of gear. When I returned the items to their rightful owner at the next hostel, he merely responded with, "Aw, man, I was looking for those. The trail provides!" (No, the trail didn't provide—*I* cleaned up your trash.)

❖   ❖   ❖

While working as an environmental educator in Denver, I had many roundtable discussions with like-minded, environmentally friendly people. During these conversations, we would talk about innovative ways people could further promote sustainability in their everyday lives, like by installing solar panels, wind turbines, or water-catchment systems in and around their homes, or by using graywater systems to reuse dishwater and bathwater for flushing the toilet. However, what was not discussed probably as often as it should have been were the seemingly archaic topics of recycling and littering. (Who doesn't *recycle?*) There are various organizations throughout the United States that are promoting and advocating for better environmental policies and regulations, but a lot of these groups tend to highlight the more innovative technology that's available—the, dare I say, "sexier" environmental topics. Although graywater systems and solar panels may be more fun to talk about, and many of the organizations I worked with did phenomenal jobs of keeping the basic principles of waste management in the curriculum, my observations both in the city *and* in the woods show me that we still have plenty of work to do.

As stewards of our own environment, it's crucial that we all take a few extra seconds to ensure that we preserve the outdoors for other visitors, and most importantly, for future generations.

❦ ❦ ❦

So, on my twenty-sixth night of hiking the AT, when I arrived at Spring Mountain Shelter to find debris left by previous hikers spread over the entire campsite, I was really frustrated. My patience with picking up other peoples' trash and carrying it many miles out of the woods was beginning to wane, especially because I had just resupplied in Hot Springs and my pack was the heaviest and fullest it could be. The same was true for my other hiking companions for the evening: Ramen-Shaman and Cheez-It, and their Australian shepherd, Sheila, whose doggy backpack was also packed full of treats. Trash is not only an eyesore, it poses a real danger of attracting animals—and not just small rodents, I'm talking about bears. Even though there are people in this world who still feel it is okay to feed wild animals (which it is not), bears do not care who gets injured when they are searching for food—because they're bears.

Thankfully, someone, possibly even the culprits who left the trash, foresaw this problem and left a large trash bag in the shelter. We used the bag to pick up what we could, which included food and camping items like spent fuel canisters and half-full bottles of hand sanitizer. I packed a few items into my personal trash bag to carry out, but the rest of it went into the larger bag, which we then hung over a tree branch with some spare paracord from my pack. It wasn't perfect, but it was the best we could do with the resources available. My hope was that since we were only eleven miles from a trailhead, a trail-maintenance group with more resources would arrive soon to take the rest of it out of the woods.

❦ ❦ ❦

The next day, the weather was gorgeous for a fifteen-mile hike. I crossed over a ridgeline with drop-offs down both sides, left into Tennessee and right into North Carolina. This area was a bit rocky with plenty of bouldering, but it made for some magnificent views. I finished the day at Jerry Cabin Shelter, which was quite clean and had an indoor fire pit and tarps hanging down over the open side of the shelter. The next day was the supposed snowstorm that the meteorologists had warned me of, but after such a beautiful day, how bad could it be?

Really bad.

Penguin Man and I woke up to at least four inches of snow on the ground and more falling furiously as the wind blew sideways across the front of the shelter. His first words to me that morning were "I think we're stuck here for the day." I couldn't have agreed more with that sentiment.

Penguin Man was from Florida and probably in his late fifties or early sixties. He got his trail name because of the massive winter display he sets up in his yard that consists of many penguins, a few of whom even ride an active roller coaster that's hurtling and plunging around his house. (He showed me a video of this on his phone and it was quite the display.)

I had no intention of heading out in these conditions, especially because we were nine miles from the nearest road crossing. Although I had hiked in snow before, the howling wind that day was quite daunting. When I woke up that morning, Penguin Man already had a small fire going in spite of the wet weather—a valuable skill that would contribute to our survival for the next twenty-four hours. I immediately made some freshly ground coffee for both of us, which was the first time I had the chance to share my favorite morning luxury with someone else; most people were usually gone by the time I was grinding the beans for my first cup.

We talked about our options and it was clear that staying there and sticking together was in our best interests. As a Floridian, Penguin Man knew he needed to stay warm. While I can start and keep a fire going, I was totally impressed with his invaluable ability to do so despite the wet logs and twigs he had available. Being from Iowa, I knew exactly what you do with snow: shovel it. (With four able-bodied kids—three boys and a girl—buying a snow blower seemed silly to my parents. To this day, shoveling the driveway when I go home in the winter is pretty much an expected task, which may explain why I plan more summer trips back home.) So, I grabbed the small camp shovel that was left by a previous trail volunteer and started carving out paths.

First, I cleared the area in front of the shelter and then I made a path downhill to the privy (a small structure similar to an outhouse). After that, I moved snow aside so we could get over to the bear cables (a permanent sets of pulleys used to hang food bags that can be found at some dedicated campsites), and then finally finished with an uphill shoveling session to ensure we could reach our water source.

Before I was done, I had begun to sweat and even taken my jacket off as the snow continued to fall. The shoveled paths helped to prevent these areas from turning into ice luges as a result of us compacting the snow all day as we walked around to accomplish tasks at each location, such as gathering firewood, filtering water, and using the privy. We perfected a system of placing logs close to the fire to dry out and slowly shifting them into the embers when the used logs were exhausted of all their free carbon. Between the two of us, we kept a fire with wet logs continuously going for approximately thirty hours in a snowstorm.

Another survival tactic that proved useful was putting my fuel canister inside of my sleeping bag. Even though my mummy-style bag didn't have a lot of extra space, waking up with fuel that was easily combustible was well worth the extra discomfort I endured while sleeping. Two months before this snowstorm, I had serious sticker shock when I bought my new North Face zero-degree, Hungarian-goose, 650-fill down sleeping bag for over $400. But after many cold nights during my first month on the trail, that purchase proved to be the best decision I had made while planning for the trip. It was my cozy sanctuary from the cold at the end of each day. After my AT adventure, and especially after my two nights stuck in a shelter with Penguin Man, I am convinced that Hungarian geese are the warmest animals on the planet.

Brazenly, three other people braved the storm and joined us later that day at the shelter, and they were absolutely elated at the situation they came upon courtesy of Penguin Man and Batman. One of them was an older gentleman named Four-By-Six, and the other two were brothers who shared a joint trail name of the Jersey Brothers. The latter two were clearly disoriented from the storm and had smiles on their faces when they saw the fire. Their fuel was so cold that it wouldn't ignite, so I loaned them my pot to boil water. (The pot for their Jetboil cooking system could only be used with the stove that came with the system or else it would damage the individual parts.) As the day ended, I sat by the fire writing postcards and reading a few more chapters in my book, *1858*, a novel detailing the critical years leading up to the Civil War.

The next morning, the other three headed out before Penguin Man and me. We made coffee again and, knowing that I hiked at a faster pace than him, we said our goodbyes as I left. There was an unspoken sense of respect between us. I don't doubt that I would have survived in that shelter by myself, but it was Penguin Man's efforts and skills—and the wood-gathering contributed by the others during the second evening—that made my two nights in that shelter not just survivable, but downright enjoyable. Even the most purist readers of DC Comics would agree that two rivals, Penguin Man and Batman, made a pretty good team to protect Gotham City from Mr. Freeze over those two days.

❀ ❀ ❀

When I finally headed out, it was clear the battle with the weather wasn't over as there were still knee-high snowdrifts to deal with and the trail was hard to find. By the end of the day, my feet were again cold and wet. I caught up with Four-By-Six and the Jersey Brothers fifteen miles later after an ill-marked switchback errantly took me down a mountain on which I should have stayed on top. I convinced the Jersey Brothers to hike an additional three miles with me to a road crossing where I thought we'd find a hostel or hotel. I called the number for a place called Mother Marian's and, to avoid any hassle from their HOA, I'll just say that Mother Marian's was not a hostel but *was* a place with a wonderful family who offered us a dry, warm place for the night (for which we gladly offered some money in exchange for their kindness). This generous family showed us authentic southern hospitality for which we were very grateful. In fact, when the family's dog ate one of my forty-dollar, thermal, touch-screen gloves out of the laundry basket, Mother Marian politely refused when I offered to pay for my stay.

The following day, I hiked another eighteen miles into the town of Erwin, Tennessee, to join up with the lovely artist from Chicago I had met while I was in Hot Springs. Sometimes you meet people who you just click with, and Shannon was one of those people. She had agreed to pick me up in Erwin and show me around Asheville, where she was house-sitting for a friend. Asheville is a small college town with lots of microbreweries and a good vibe. We spent a day in the River Arts District and ultimately at the Wedge Brewery. Even though we knew our paths weren't meant to cross again for a long time, if ever, it was still hard to say goodbye when Shannon dropped me back off in Erwin. After admitting to her that it can be lonely some nights on the AT, she later sent me a computer-printout photo of Kathy Ireland in a bikini—the woman of my boyhood dreams—to keep me company on the trail. Some women just know the way to a man's heart, and Shannon found a humorous way in.

❧ ❧ ❧

I finally left Erwin, after meeting up with a new trail family, to start the trek toward Virginia via Roan Mountain, which is the last peak over six thousand feet until the White Mountains in New Hampshire. The climb was rough and the paths were icy on the way down, but the weather was the nicest it had been in over a week. I ended that day at Overmountain Shelter, one of the more epic places to stay along the trail. This shelter is an old red barn that was converted by its owners for use by hikers. The barn is located just off an adjacent trail that was historically used by fighters in the Revolutionary War, and it was also used as a backdrop for the movie *Winter People*. The view from the shelter of the nearby valley was spectacular, especially as the sun began to rise and a spectrum of red and orange began to illuminate the sidewalls of the valley. We had a late start the next day due to some post-sunrise morning thunderstorms, which I watched roll in with a cup of coffee in hand. Ultimately, we all hiked over Hump Mountain and finally down near the town of Elk Park. That section of trail was one of the most diverse in terms of changes of scenery and even included a few small waterfalls.

After a sixteen-mile day, my new crew of hikers and I found a cozy little spot called Black Bear Resort, a hostel with a

Approaching Overmountain Shelter after a long day on the AT

bunkhouse right along Laurel Creek. There were about fifteen people who stayed there, and we all meshed really well—nothing like a bunch of tired hikers, fun locals, and a few cases of beer to ensure an enjoyable time. Soon we would be in Damascus, Virginia, with terrain that we had heard was a little less drastic in terms of elevation changes. But, as you quickly learn while hiking the AT, subjectivity should always be considered when another person says, "it's all downhill from here!"

Two states and 416 miles down. Twelve states and 1,773 miles to go.

CHAPTER 9

Colorado 2011

In the weeks and months after Jessa's death, I made a real effort to carry forward the lessons her death taught me by viewing things through a positive lens, especially regarding dating and relationships. But other areas of my life, like my living situation, desperately needed attention as well. To say that my apartment on South Fairfax Street in Glendale, Colorado was less than ideal would be an understatement. In fact, I am talking *so deep* under the statement that you'd have to dig to the earth's nickel and iron outer core before you would arrive. The building was not government owned nor rent controlled, and I never saw a dead drug addict with crack sprinkled on him around the property. But there were a few observations I made while living there that would describe a less-than-ideal living situation.

Observation 1: I didn't own *that* nice of a car, but in that particular neighborhood, my 2006 Chevy HHR was like a gold-plated Ferrari. Within three weeks of moving into the neighborhood, my car was broken into. I woke up to a smashed passenger window and a ripped-out in-dash navigation system. This was the *second* time my car had been broken into that year, but this time, the vandalism caused not only the loss of my navigation system but also exterior damage to the door because the thieves used a crowbar. In both cases of vandalism, these criminal masterminds overlooked the DVD player that was under the seat and the LCD screen that was on the sun visor. The way I see it, if you're going to risk possible jail time, then at least do your homework and get everything. The worst part was sitting down with the special investigative teams from my insurance company. Instead of making sure I felt supported by a company to whom I had been making payments for many years, this "special team" sat me in a windowless room and grilled me for hours as to why this happened. The lead investigator later admitted that they often saw cases of fraud from my neighborhood, so they assumed I was just attempting to get the insurance money. After two $500-deductible payments and a downgraded car value due to a history of vandalism, I'd say the investigators were a little off track with their assumption that I wanted this to happen.

Observation 2: I once saw a handicapped man with one leg parallel park his wheelchair between my car and my motorcycle. Let me repeat: I saw a handicapped man *parallel park his wheelchair* on a paved city road. First of all, I'm pretty sure he didn't have a cane so I'm not sure where he was planning to go after he parked the wheelchair. Secondly, the wheelchair was there for more than forty-eight hours and yet I never saw a ticket. Handicapped or not, there are rules to be followed. If you can operate a motorized vehicle then you can obey the local parking laws.

Observation 3: The building itself was a shit box. (Full disclosure: I was the on-site manager.) To receive $200 off my monthly rent, I promised to keep the place clean. My duties included, but were not limited to, vacuuming, cleaning surfaces, picking up the laundry room, emptying trash cans, cleaning windows, and shoveling the sidewalks. My total rent was only $465 per month (another indicator of the almost-government-project status of these units), so after the rent reduction I paid a grand total of $265 per month to have a roof over my head. It was actually in a convenient location in the city, which made up for having to clean little kids' snot off the windows and pick up Play-Doh every day from the carpet. However, it was the very delightful night I came home to find human feces on the third floor that really made me want to move. It *literally* was a shit box.

❖ ❖ ❖

So why did I live there? I had been teaching environmental education with the Greenway Foundation for a few years and, although I loved what I was doing, money was tighter than when I was a geologist for the consulting firm in California. The average one-bedroom apartment in Denver at that time was probably around $700–$800 per month. With my reduced rent at that property, I was potentially saving $5,000 over the course of a year by putting gloves on, picking up some trash, and keeping the place clean.

Although my living situation during most of 2011 was less than desirable, it did serve a purpose. As a twenty-seven-year-old single male I didn't care if my one-bedroom apartment was the most conducive place to hold a dinner party. Not only was it economical, which allowed me to live a more comfortable social lifestyle, it was also close to certain amenities that helped to alleviate some of the negative aspects of my living situation. The property was within walking distance of the Cherry Creek Trail and was only a block away from a local bar called Prickly Pete's—home to the best chili cheese fries in Denver and a weekly poker night that attracted some big players. The best perk of my apartment's location was the walkable proximity to a King Soopers grocery store. It was nice to avoid the calamity of finding my keys, walking to my car, driving, finding parking, loading groceries, driving back to my apartment, finding parking again, and unloading groceries only to realize I forgot the butter to fully complete my evening's dinner of Kraft mac 'n' cheese.

My favorite aspect was the late-night grocery shopping as it was open twenty-four hours. It was a relief not having to fight the after-work crowd, not to mention also having the first pick of new "manager special markdowns" that employees would sometimes set out a night early. It was one of those late nights when I was shopping for some random item that proved to be a turning point in my life. I generally don't believe in fate, but I do believe in the ability to take advantage of opportunities that present themselves. So, although my apartment had its downfalls, if I hadn't lived in that particular location at that particular time, I would have never gone to the Glendale King

Soopers one evening in October of 2011—where I met Megan while walking down the Asian food aisle.

Megan and I had previously crossed paths at a local running club, but it was that evening at the grocery store near my apartment that allowed us to formally meet, chat, and exchange numbers. Over the next few months, Megan and I built a relationship that I can only describe as perfect. Our relationship progressed in a way that I had never felt before. Our first date was at my favorite pizza place: Sexy Pizza. Afterward, we went for a walk and ended up getting ice cream around the corner where, without any other information, I impressed her by guessing her exact birthday (month and day). I believe it's little things like that that can make relationships blossom. Finding someone with whom you can feel comfortable and happy is a wonderful experience that I hope every person can enjoy. Whether that person is a significant other or just a good friend, pursuing happiness (with other people) is one of those rights I feel our Declaration of Independence correctly describes as "unalienable."

As the next few months passed, I fell in love with Megan. Our relationship was a refreshing change of pace to how my dating life had been going for the past few years. It had been a time of exploration, a time of being single, and a time of trying something new and seeing how I felt about it. Although it was fun at times, after Jessa died it was clear I needed to find a new path forward in dating and relationships; it was clear I needed to hit a reset button on my feelings toward women, regardless of past experiences. Megan made me want to press that button.

After a few months with Megan my life felt like it was on the right track. I was in love, I worked at a job I felt passionate about, and I lived in a city that provided a fun lifestyle. All nagging feelings of depression and loneliness were gone, and I felt like I could start thinking about bigger, future life changes that previously seemed out of reach—like buying a house or having kids. Unfortunately, those thoughts and feelings only lasted a short while. A few days before Thanksgiving, my boss approached me while I was running an after-hours program at one of our regular schools. He informed me the budget had been set for the new fiscal year, and it didn't include my salary.

Well, shit.

CHAPTER 10

Appalachian Trail 2014
37 Days; 467 Miles

After leaving Black Bear Resort at the end of the Tennessee section of the AT, we took a nice walk to a heavily visited place called Laurel Falls. Day hikers, families, and even a geology class taking notes were there that day. After the falls, we encountered a relatively steep 1,500-foot climb, and then hiked down to a reservoir and a recreational area with a shelter and a campsite. There, that evening, I was reunited with Ramen-Shaman, Cheez-It, and my four-legged girlfriend, Sheila. Also in attendance were Owl and Doctor Scrambles, a couple of old college buddies who were hiking together. It was a relatively quiet night with talk of a possible rainstorm arriving the following evening.

The next day, although I hadn't set any plans (one of the perks to hiking through the woods is the freedom to make schedules on the fly), I woke up earlier than usual, so after coffee and breakfast I was ready to start hiking by eight o'clock that morning. At that point, I had no idea that I was about to hike forty-one miles in thirteen and a half hours, reaching the town of Damascus, Virginia, before the day was done.

❦ ❦ ❦

Another hostel located near the Black Bear Resort (where I had stayed the previous evening) is a place owned by the AT legend himself, Bob Peoples. Bob has a Chuck Norris–like status of awesomeness among the AT community. He is one of many volunteers who have helped to make the trail better through regular maintenance efforts and by building more shelters and privies. Thru-hikers began making it a challenge to hike the entire fifty-one miles from Bob's place to Damascus, Virginia, in less than twenty-four hours, a feat that's otherwise known as the "Damascuthon." By some accounts, Damascus is where the southern Appalachian Mountains "end," and reaching the town marks the completion of approximately one-fifth of the entire trail (assuming the hiker is moving northward). Because the terrain becomes more leveled out, these fifty-one miles from Bob's place to Damascus had, for certain hikers, become a race of sorts. As the story I heard goes, apparently, Bob was not pleased that hikers were blazing through the final part of Tennessee and not taking their time to enjoy his state. So, legend has it that Bob, a man believed to be capable of moving boulders and changing the weather, decided to change the route of the trail from one of flat terrain to one that requires a steep 1,500-foot climb (the one I mentioned previously), with the goal of crushing any fleeting spirits of hikers hoping to blaze those final Tennessee miles in a day.

However, in this day and age of lightweight backpacking and high-protein energy bars, hikers are still finding ways to accomplish this physical feat even after Bob's reroute of the trail. I hadn't heard of the Damascuthon until arriving at the reservoir—already ten miles past Bob's place—that evening with Ramen-Shaman and Cheez-It. And although I had no earlier intentions of attempting one-go at the remaining forty-one miles of such a ridiculous (not to mention unnecessary) physical task, that's precisely what I did.

❦ ❦ ❦

I can't pinpoint a single reason why I decided to hike forty-one miles in one day, but it most likely was a combination of many factors. I had heard there was a rainstorm approaching that evening and I really wasn't looking forward to a soggy couple of days of hiking. I also noticed my fuel was running low and I wasn't sure if it was going to last another two or three days, which is what I would have needed if I were to only hike ten or fifteen miles each day to easily cruise into Damascus. My waking at an early hour gave me a lot of daylight and my hiking pace had recently increased to three miles per hour, which allowed me to quickly reach waypoints that were farther north than I had expected. My original plan after leaving the recreational area was for a twenty-two-mile day, but my legs were feeling great after the morning hours passed. I was also meeting (and passing) many hikers I had met in the previous days, along with some fresh faces, including a couple of "section hikers" (folks who hike small sections of the AT over multiple days) who gave me a much-appreciated Snickers bar. All of this aided in my overall positive energy during the day and the miles just flew by.

Another goal was to catch up with some friends—Tree, Dorothy, and Wind Screen—who had started eight miles ahead of me that day. Those were guys I wanted to share a beer with once I hiked into Damascus. I met up with them after hiking twenty-two miles (my original goal), and we discussed our options while enjoying a late lunch at Double Springs Shelter. It would be a thirty-three-mile day for them to hike into town and they all seemed up for the challenge. This conversation marked the moment that I began considering the possibility of hiking forty-one miles that day. If I chose to hike into town it would include at least an hour of night hiking, if not more, which I had not yet done on this journey. Also, those final miles would be downhill, which I knew would be more difficult as my knees do not enjoy the angle and pounding of downhill hiking.

After we left the lunch spot, I noticed the clouds ominously getting darker, reminding me of the weather factor that was involved in this decision. I also had a pride issue: At that point, I had only met one other person (a professor from Portland with a trail name of Oil Stain) who was attempting to hike the entire trail while carrying an external-frame pack. I wasn't about to let my cumbersome, yet very loved, pack keep me from a physical goal I knew I could attain.

❦ ❦ ❦

There are generally two types of backpacks: internal-frame packs and external-frame packs. Internal-frame packs are usually lighter and designed to have a more ergonomic fit. They typically can't carry more weight than what they are designed to carry, and the straps and fabric can tear or break if an attempt is made to pack on more weight. If purchased new, they can also come with hefty price tags. External-frame packs have a basic metal frame that can have individual pieces (e.g., main compartment bag, sleeping bag, tent, etc.) strapped *onto* them as opposed to all of it fitting inside, like what's required by an internal-frame pack. External-frame packs create the cliché look of traditional hikers of old, are relatively cheap, and can typically carry more weight than internal-frame packs. (In fact, in the White Mountains of New Hampshire, the crews who stay and manage the huts throughout the park use vintage, wooden, external-frame packs to carry all the food required by the people who are staying at the huts each evening.)

It's very rare to see external-frame packs in today's hiking world, and no outfitter store that I visited along the trail offered even a single model. In fact, the only place I've seen these for sale in recent years is in the camping sections of local Ace Hardwares and military surplus stores.

I purchased my external-frame pack at a Gander Mountain store about eleven years prior to beginning the AT, and I've improved, switched, and modified the way I pack it many, many times—and I love it. Whenever someone sees my pack, they are sort of taken aback by this "ancient" hiking tool. (One younger hiker even exclaimed, "You're the dude with the homemade backpack!") But it allows me to carry about forty or fifty pounds of food and gear (including the luxurious food-preparation items I've mentioned), which is almost twice the amount possible for hikers using some of the lighter weight, internal-frame packs.

On average, I hiked around fifteen to twenty miles per day on the AT, which is a lot, but not compared to lightweight backpackers who typically average twenty to twenty-five miles per day. In my experience, it's usually someone who is "going lightweight" that tends to talk more about hitting schedules and goals versus someone like me, who is more concerned about having freshly ground coffee each morning. This is an ongoing debate among trail enthusiasts. Most hikers who concentrate on carrying as little as possible will always confirm that they are enjoying the trail just as much, if not more, as anyone else—and I'm sure they are. At the same time, however, I witnessed those same hikers leaving items in shelters because they didn't want to carry more weight. While this was not the case with all lightweight backpackers, it was something I observed along the AT.

The extra luxuries I carried on the trail—like a coffee grinder, a grill grate, and a cutting board—allowed me to prepare some intriguing meals. However, at this point along the AT, I also had people tell me I would "never make it to Maine" carrying that much weight, and some even made inferences that I should drop some items to do more miles in a day. To each their own, I suppose. The irony was that I was already hiking as many miles as some of these lightweight backpackers *and* I was eating much better meals (I actually gained weight during my journey), but I had not yet hiked a thirty-mile day. And although I knew it was not a race (there are no medals at the top of Mount Katahdin), my competitive mindset wanted to prove to myself (and to others) that I was physically capable of doing thirty miles in a day. So, I suppose it was no surprise that the day I woke up next to the recreational area turned out to be the day I would put my body to the test and attempt to hike not thirty, but forty-one miles in thirteen and a half hours, with a forty-pound external-frame pack, through the mountains, finishing in the dark.

❖ ❖ ❖

After another three hours of crushing miles, I caught up again with Tree, Dorothy, and Wind Screen (who had left the lunch spot before me) at the final shelter before a ten-mile, downhill ridgeline hike into Damascus. It was about 6:30 p.m. when we ate a quick dinner and met three new friends (Hayley, Indy, and Andy) who were hiking a smaller section of the AT. I had already hiked thirty-one miles that day, which would have been a momentous day for any hiker, but I knew the character-building part was yet to come. The description of it being a "downhill ridgeline hike" means that, just like a bear market–stock ticker, even though we were going down in overall elevation, there were still many intervals of uphill climbing. Whether your climb is mostly uphill or mostly downhill, or whether you're at two thousand feet or six thousand feet, a three-hundred-foot climb is *still* a three-hundred-foot climb.

I left the final shelter with nothing but pure adrenaline running through my veins. Tree and I took the lead and, knowing this would be a prime scenario in which I could hurt myself, I used the little bit of sunlight we had left to keep my eyes super focused on the terrain. Just after 8:00 p.m., the shadow of darkness had taken over and it was time to switch on my headlamp. At a time like this, regardless of your spiritual beliefs, you pray to whatever deity you worship that your headlamp stays at full glow for the next hour and a half because that's what it was going to take to get through the task at hand. (Or, in my case, just remember where I packed the extra batteries.) Tree and I talked about a range of topics in an attempt to pass the time and maintain a bit of sanity, at least whatever bit we had left.

We passed a few solitary campfires that were started by other hikers who had made the decision to not hike at night and to set up cowboy camps. In general, I don't think night hiking with a heavy pack is a safe backpacking practice, unless it's for survival or safety purposes. The occasional night hike to see the sunset or the stars is a magical experience, but hiking with a heavy pack and at the pace we were going, with tired legs, was probably not the greatest idea. I had rolled my ankles enough in the daytime and knew that limiting my field of vision at night wasn't going to make avoiding injury any easier.

We began to see the town lights with about three or four miles to go. The illumination was very encouraging and probably had the effect of increasing our pace. Also, right around that point, we came up to the state boundary sign between Tennessee and Virginia. Crossing into a new state that I had never visited before, at night, in the middle of the woods, was a bit surreal. We took some photos and videos and celebrated with some bromance-esque high fives. However, I also had the sneaking suspicion that if I stopped hiking for too long my legs would collapse and not work for three days. Needless to say, making it to Damascus was a necessity at this point—at least in my mind.

When we descended the final set of switchbacks into town, I was extremely satisfied with myself, and the feeling my body was exhibiting could only be described as euphoric. But, like many milestones along the AT, the experience a thru-hiker has when entering Damascus is one of utter confusion: we literally came out of the woods into some guy's backyard. Add in the fact that it was 9:30 p.m. and that Tree and myself were two bearded men scrambling around with large, weapon-like sticks (trekking poles) in our hands, one can see how the scene might

Enjoying some beers with Tree after our monster day of hiking

have been oddly perceived by the owner of that property (although I'm sure they were used to it). I turned on my phone to find the way to a place called the Blue Blaze Cafe, a much-discussed bar and restaurant that we were desperately hoping was still open and still serving food and beer—especially beer.

As we located the bar, a message popped up on my phone from Ramen-Shaman. He had called to inform me they had decided to take a shuttle at a road crossing into town to avoid the rain and get a warm meal. (My thoughts: *That's nice of them but they took a shuttle?!?!*) I had completely forgotten that I had started my day with them at the recreation area, and as the voicemail was ending, we opened the door to the Blue Blaze Cafe where the first people I saw were Ramen-Shaman and Cheez-It—with looks on their faces full of shock and awe. Their response was expected: "No way did you just hike here!" All I could do was nod and respond, "Are they still serving?" They were, and it was glorious.

❊ ❊ ❊

The next day, word had gotten out about the heavy miles we had completed the night before. (Trail talk is very much a real thing and stories tend to spread.) I went back to the Blue Blaze Cafe for lunch and continued to respond to inquiries about my forty-one-mile hike into town. I didn't do the official "Damascuthon," as that's technically fifty-one miles in under twenty-four hours, but I did hike those fifty-one miles in thirty-one hours, with forty-one miles completed in just thirteen and a half hours. I also only took breaks for an hour and a half, so I hiked forty-one miles in twelve hours for a net hiking pace of almost three and a half miles per hour—I was flying. Although there had been stories of other hikers who had completed the whole distance in twenty-four hours, our feat was just as impressive to almost anyone wanting to hear about it.

After a much needed zero-day, the next evening in town was a fun night of drinking pitchers of microbrews, playing good music, racking games of pool, and sharing stories with locals and other hikers. One trail angel bought a round for any members of the AT hiking class of 2014 who were in the bar. We had an enjoyable time and drank a lot of beer, which was probably not the greatest idea after completely draining my body of energy by hiking forty-one miles the night before. But, hey, sometimes you gotta put your balls on the table and just go for it, and I did just that.

Another hiker and I had challenged a couple of locals to a game of pool, and it was clear these townies were not pleased that all these dirty hikers were taking up space in their bar. There was a little smack-talk exchanged between the local duo and my team, but I don't remember very much because I quickly reached a point of inebriation where new memories became nonexistent. What I do remember, because there are photos and videos for proof, was that in the excitement of the pool game coming down to the wire, while attempting to psych-out the other team, I pulled my pants down, whipped out my genitals, and sat them directly behind the pocket in which our opponents were attempting to sink their next shot. Sometimes you really do just have to put your balls on the table.

❖ ❖ ❖

Alcohol has been the culprit in many a person's tale of debauchery. Sometimes those stories are funny, sometimes they're sad, and sometimes you can't even decipher what type of emotion a drunk story should elicit from an audience. Alcohol has had a major influence in my life, as it has for many others, and those experiences aren't always positive. However, on that night, with my testicles sitting directly on the side of a pool table, my opponents scratched on the eight ball and we won the game. On that night, alcohol had a sense of humor, but that's not always the case.

Three states and 467 miles down. Eleven states and 1,722 miles to go.

CHAPTER 11

Hawaii 2012

While growing up, I was given a lot of misinformation about the opposite sex. When I told my parents during my freshman year of high school that a girl had just accepted my invitation to the homecoming dance, my father's only response was to say, "Oh yeah? Do her parents have any money?" He belched out a loud laugh as he spoke. Due to the several adult beverages he had consumed I've since chalked up the interaction to my father's inebriated attempt at being funny. While I know there weren't malicious intentions behind his question, those were still the first words my father ever said to me about dating.

Then there was the time in the high school men's locker room, and I was listening in on a conversation between two upperclassmen whom I classified as "popular." These two young men were proudly reliving the time when, after a hard day's work detasseling corn fields (a common summer job for many young people in the Midwest), a girl on their work crew had asked them for a ride home. The young men agreed on the condition that the girl would give one of them a blowjob in exchange for the ride. The girl reluctantly agreed, and upon being dropped off at her house she said, "I don't think I'm gonna ride with you guys anymore." At this point in the retelling of the story, the guys laughed and high-fived. Both of these young men were on the homecoming court and liked by many people. As a young teenage virgin hearing that story, I honestly assumed that situations like the one they were describing were okay and just part of "becoming a man." I had no reason to think otherwise, especially because other (supposed) role models in my life confirmed this for many years of my adolescence.

Calling certain comments "locker room talk" is how millions of young adult males are taught to justify misogynistic remarks regarding the opposite sex, and unfortunately this is a learned behavior passed down by some school teachers, coaches, and other adults with influence. I do believe that, on some level, part of the problem isn't the flippant classification, but the locker room itself. And a lot of us, myself included, are actively trying to change our ways and the words we use as we become more educated on the subject.

This message is for all young men who may not be hearing the best information about women: if you feel confused, it's okay—so are a lot of others. It's taken me over thirty years to fully learn that some things are not acceptable to say to and about women, and I am still constantly learning. That learning curve may be steeper for some than for others, but my hope is that people continue to work on themselves as they adapt to better ways of thinking and communicating. Only *we* can change the locker room.

Although I started dating Megan as an adult, many years after the experiences I described above, it was only when we got together that I began to communicate effectively with women (or at least I thought I was). I knew I still had a lot of work to do, but at some point I realized I just had to take that leap of faith—the leap that involved treating Megan with more respect than I had given to any other women I had dated. That meant I had to wear my heart on my sleeve, but I knew Megan was worth the potential heartbreak.

❖ ❖ ❖

Like many of my colleagues in the education field, I had devoted a lot of love and energy toward my position, and it felt like the floor was dropping out from below my feet when I learned I would be losing my job. Although I won't say my job in Denver was my entire identity, I will say that it helped prop me up on a pedestal of confidence and happiness that most strive for in a career. In the few months since I had met Megan, I thought I had found what I was looking for in life. Everything was in place, or so it seemed.

After going home for Thanksgiving and speaking with Megan about my options, I decided to finally move forward with an idea that had been brewing intermittently for a few years: I was going to move to Hawaii. When I searched online and found a cheap ticket for the exact same date that my lease was to end at my Glendale apartment, I thought it was a clear sign I should take this chance, and Megan supported that decision. In fact, she supported it so much that she decided to shake up her own life a bit and finally go visit her sister who was living in Italy at the time, and do her own "*Eat, Pray, Love*–thing," as she said. She convinced her company to let her take a leave of absence to spend six weeks in Italy, after which we would decide what we wanted to do about "us."

Everything seemed perfect. So perfect, in fact, that her flight to Italy left the very same morning as mine did to Maui. On the morning of March 1, 2012, we kissed each other goodbye inside the terminal at Denver International Airport and flew to opposite sides of the planet.

❋ ❋ ❋

But just like with Karla (the bridesmaid at my brother's wedding), this proved to be another example of why long-distance relationships and I just do not mix. Even though Megan and I talked every evening and it seemed to be going well, I was finally put to the test when a new female friend on the island invited me over to "go running." My new friend knew of Megan, but she also knew Megan was eight thousand miles away. When I arrived at my friend's apartment, I quickly discovered there would be no running and she had instead planned for us to have dinner. As I was leaving after dinner, I found myself in a scenario for which I only have myself to blame: my friend and I kissed before I pulled away and quickly said, "I have to go."

The only thing I was concerned about was what I had just done to Megan. Although we were technically together, we also made it clear before we parted ways that we still needed to decide what our relationship was, and after that kiss with the other woman it was clear that I felt my relationship with Megan was worth keeping. So, yes, I told Megan about the kiss. Yes, she was shaken up by it. Yes, it almost ended what we had. But we continued to talk and when she returned to Denver from Italy, we both felt confident about our relationship. So confident, in fact, that Megan bought a plane ticket and arrived on Maui in June of 2012.

By then, I was living in a small one-bedroom apartment on the island and was working as a museum docent for the Lahaina Restoration Foundation. In fact, my one-bedroom apartment was historically the old warden's quarters of the town prison, *Hale Pa'ahao*, and I served as the caretaker for the prison museum inside the stone walls. The adjacent prison yard was complete with ample green grass, and banana, mango, and papaya trees, all for my taking.

After Megan arrived we did all the things this island in the Pacific had to offer: we went snorkeling, spent time at the beach, drove the road to Hana (a rainforest on the opposite side of the island), and even made love on top of a cliff looking out into the ocean right before getting blasted by a giant wave that crested the top of the rock face. Megan even got a job at one of the small shops on Front Street. I was living with a beautiful woman whom I loved in Hawaii. I thought everything was coming together, but I still had a lot to learn.

❊ ❊ ❊

Perhaps there were signs I didn't see, or perhaps she was just keeping thoughts and feelings to herself, but from my observations we were happy for the entire first month we were living together. But, I hadn't been sleeping well for a few weeks and I had been having disturbing dreams that involved Megan and I being in an airplane that would crash. Sometimes it would just be me on the plane and sometimes it would just be Megan. I'm sure any therapist would have a field day with these dreams, and they really bothered me. After arguing for a few evenings over trivial things, I finally shared the dreams with her and, apparently, they were the final straw for her and caused another fight. She woke early the next morning and left the apartment before I got out of bed. I thought she just needed time to think, so I went to work assuming we would talk about it later in the day. That would be the last day I would ever see Megan.

Thankfully, I took the back-alley route while walking home from work that evening. The bus stop was in the alley, and as I approached it, I saw Megan sitting on the bench with two bags packed. My heart stopped. I learned that, after I left for work, she returned to our apartment, packed her bags, and purchased a last-minute flight back to Denver. We sat at that bus stop for three bus-route cycles and talked as much as two people in that scenario could without causing a scene. I pleaded with her to reconsider. I pleaded with her to give it some more time so we could figure out what was wrong. Nothing I said changed her mind. In the end, I drove her to the airport. I felt my only choice was to support her decision, and just as many relationships reach an impasse, so did ours in the beginning of August in 2012.

In the following weeks, we still talked on the phone. We missed each other. That's what happens when you let someone else into your heart; you miss them when they're not around. It was clear we had unresolved issues on our minds that needed to be discussed, and our talks over the next few weeks were civil. Then the unthinkable happened: she agreed to come back to Maui. We decided that we still loved each other and that it was merely a lack of communication that was driving this wedge between us. With her on the phone, I bought her a plane ticket (a little bit bigger gesture than just a pint of Ben & Jerry's).

Although I was excited for her return, I could tell something was still on her mind, something that just wasn't being communicated every time we talked. The morning of her flight, she called to inform me she would not be getting on the plane. I never talked to Megan again.

❦ ❦ ❦

I still can't recall an exact thing I said, or an exact reaction I had to something she said, that could have set in motion the last few weeks of our relationship, but obviously something wasn't right. For whatever reason, I didn't have the ability or the knowledge to be the person she needed. If I was doing or saying something wrong, I wasn't a good enough partner to know how to identify it.

I went through an angry phase after Megan didn't get on the flight, but hindsight has a way of providing perspective, and the truth was that I just wasn't ready to communicate effectively with her. I wasn't ready to be a better partner, and Megan deserved better. I held on to the hope that, with enough time, our relationship could work again.

And then she married someone else.

CHAPTER 12

Appalachian Trail 2014
69 Days; 802 Miles

After spending two zero-days recovering from my forty-one-mile day *and* my hangover, I finally left Damascus and hiked through the Grayson Highlands, a state park where wild ponies still roam free, which gave me a memorable encounter with a pregnant momma pony who decided the sweat on my leg was a delicious snack to lick off as I walked past her. Upon arriving in the town of Pearisburg, Virginia, I found a Chinese restaurant and stuffed my stomach as full as the all-you-can-eat buffet would allow. Afterward, I headed to a small clearing above the city called the Rice Fields and enjoyed a relaxing view of West Virginia. (Although the AT traverses over five hundred miles through the state of Virginia, it only briefly crosses into West Virginia at a point farther north than where I was at that moment, overlooking the border between the two states.)

I spent that first night out of town with my fellow hikers Triton, Vegemite, and another hiker whom I had met before called Steady. Steady is a pretty incredible woman. She is a "triple crowner," which means she had already hiked the entire

Appalachian Trail as well as the entire Pacific Crest Trail on the West Coast *and* the entire Continental Divide Trail through the Rockies. She was doing this section of the AT again to get her legs back in shape for another hike she was planning to do in Scotland. She was the first person I heard utter the phrase, "If you're not sleeping, you might as well be hiking."

❖ ❖ ❖

The following night was my fifty-fifth night on the trail and was spent camping alone, which I hadn't done since my very first night when I was lost on Hawk Mountain in Georgia. On that first night, alone in my tent, I was admittedly a little scared about what the future of the trail held for me. Even though I had been backpacking for over ten years, I still knew that I had a huge learning curve ahead of me to fully know the AT. Fifty-five nights later, my legs were stronger, my pack felt lighter, and I was more mentally aware about what it was going to take to get me through living on a trail in the middle of the wilderness. However, it was still lonely when I realized that I was going to be the only person staying at the Bailey Gap Shelter that evening.

When I tell people about my AT experience, the first question I'm often asked is "Did you do it by yourself?" I usually respond with "I was never really doing it by myself," even though I was alone for most of the actual hiking itself. A handful of times, I was step-in-step with another hiker, but that was rare. But, at the end of many days, hikers often congregated at the shelters or at dedicated camping spots, so I rarely felt like I was totally alone.

To be honest, when I started my AT adventure, finishing the entire trail wasn't my primary goal. While I knew that being able to say I hiked the whole trail in one attempt would be awesome, for me it was more about taking five or six months to enjoy the wilderness and the hiking culture, and to explore the eastern states. Interestingly, according to employees at the Appalachian Trail Conservancy (ATC), although thousands of people start the trail each year with the intention of hiking the entire thing, only about twenty-five percent of people actually do so. Along with the thru-hikers who endeavor to hike the entire trail, there are also thousands of day hikers who come out for just an evening or maybe a few days. (Because this crowd is more concentrated on the weekends, and I didn't often look at a calendar, seeing more day hikers was a decent indicator of what day of the week it was.)

Although it was lonely, that rare solo night in the woods was one of the most thought-provoking evenings I had on the trail. And although meeting new people and sharing stories and conversations are some of my favorite pastimes, it dawned on me that even while living in the woods for few months, an evening of complete silence was a rare and beautiful thing.

There was nothing unique about Bailey Gap Shelter. The water source was about two-tenths of a mile away and the shelter itself was a simple, six-person lean-to built in the 1960s—and I had it all to myself. While there, I thought about the past few years and contemplated all the curveballs that life had thrown at me. My notes in my trail book about this evening merely include the names of some women from past relationships, the word "Family," and the word "Silence." I viscerally remember the feeling of clarity I had when I looked up at the starry sky and knew that things were going to be okay. There's a lot of noise in this world, and it's amazing what a few moments of silence can do to help clear the mind.

❦ ❦ ❦

There are over two hundred three-sided shelters along the 2,189 miles of the AT. Some are big, some are small, some are clean, some are dirty, some are right next to the trail, and some are not so close to the trail. Now ask yourself this: When planning your day, which might include hiking anywhere from one to fifty miles (one day I stopped after only two miles), would you rather hike only one-tenth of a mile at the end of that day to where you are sleeping, or would you want to hike another half mile or more? My answer to that question varied daily, but I usually preferred to stay at shelters that didn't involve too much hiking off the trail, especially after a longer day.

However, when hikers stay somewhere other than a shelter, the shelter is spared additional wear and tear, and the hiker who does stay there tends to reap the benefits of a beautiful, and often pristine, place to stay for an evening. I wasn't a fan of all the camping graffiti that some hikers felt the need to carve into the wooden walls of the shelters. I mean, part of me *really* wanted to know that "Stephanie Was Here" and some of the "art" was *really* inspiring—like my favorite piece of shelter graffiti, found in Maine, that simply said, "Nature Sucks"—except… not at all. It was always a treat to stay in a shelter that didn't have too many signs of human use (although I see the irony that the shelter itself represents human use), and I was grateful that the next two evenings I slept in shelters that were a bit off the trail and mostly unspoiled.

❧ ❧ ❧

At the risk of sounding like a realtor trying to sell a property, I want to share that Sarver Hollow Shelter could fit six people and had a vaulted ceiling and an overhang that even gave the picnic table some shelter from the rain. I stayed there with a weekend hiker who was backpacking alone for the first time. She went by the trail name Volleyball. Her only food source was a small container of bananas and granola. While I applaud someone taking the adventurous first step of going hiking on their own, I must say that bananas and granola might not be all the sustenance one needs for a few days in the woods. I offered to share some of my dinner with Volleyball, which was the least I could do since she already had a fire going when I arrived. As bedtime approached, we both began reading our respective books. At that point I had finished three books on the trail (Dan Brown's *Inferno*, Bruce Chadwick's *1858*, and David Mitchell's *The Reason I Jump*) and I was on my fourth book, Tom Clancy's *Command Authority*. I'm a slow reader but I really enjoyed using my Nook e-reader because the backlit paperwhite surface was perfect for reading at night while cuddled up in my sleeping bag. (No product pitch intended.)

Volleyball told me she was a substitute elementary school teacher, which turned our conversation toward discussing her teaching duties, including how she sometimes read to the children. I told her that I had met many hikers who read aloud at night (I had loved falling asleep to my good friend Coconuts expertly narrating *The Hobbit*) and that if she wanted to read aloud that evening, she was more than welcome. As the daylight continued to fall and we were preparing for bed, she asked if she could still read aloud and I happily agreed. Her soothing teacher's voice reading a Stephen King novel helped give me one of the best nights of sleep I had on the trail.

❦ ❦ ❦

Pickle Branch Shelter, named for the meandering nearby stream that served as the shelter's water source, was one of the best places I camped while on the AT; it was when I was off the beaten path that I truly felt like I was in the wilderness. I arrived there early in the day and after reading a bit and drinking some early evening coffee, I decided to dip my feet in the stream. There is nothing like a babbling brook and being alone with your thoughts in the woods. However, I smelled bad. Like, really bad. I hadn't showered in a while and when I caught a whiff of what smelled like microwaved leftover fish, my decision to put my toes in the stream quickly progressed to being fully naked in the water.

I went downstream as far as I could, took off my soil-splattered, turquoise Batman shirt, stripped off my overpriced dry-fit underwear, and dipped my naked body right into the water. This may seem like a good place to share some deep life revelations realized in this moment, but all I could feel was the freezing cold water and my balls shrinking up to the size of raisins. But I'll take shriveled balls any day of the week in exchange for serenity and a little bit of personal hygiene.

This is also one reason why people should always filter their water when hiking. Some hikers don't and it blows my mind. You never know what could have just been in that water source, like somebody's sweaty balls (and any accompanying bacteria).

❊ ❊ ❊

While at Pickle Branch Shelter, I had one of the most ridiculous bear bagging experiences of my life. Bear bagging is the practice of hanging your food, garbage, and other scented items from a tree so that animals who may be attracted to such items do not get your food or get too close to your camp. Even though this practice is called bear bagging it really is for all animals, most notably rodents.

This is another backpacking practice with disagreement surrounding its importance or necessity. Admittedly, most black bears are more scared of humans than humans are of them, but with a bear bag, just like insurance, you have it in place for that *one time*. That one time you run into a bear who was fed by humans and now, as a result, is aggressive. Or that one time a mouse gets a little too frisky and starts chewing its way through your backpack, even though you hung it from a hook in the shelter. For me, bear bagging is also a fun camping pastime. From finding the right tree to finding the right rock—these are

Even in the woods, there are still chores to be done after dinner.

enjoyable activities to do while camping. And besides, what else do I have to do? Here's how bear bagging works:

> Step 1: Find a rock to tie a rope onto that's shaped so the rope won't fly off it too easily. (Paracord is lightweight, durable, and relatively cheap rope. Fifty feet should be plenty.)
>
> Step 2: Find a sturdy tree limb. The ideal limb is parallel to the ground and high enough to keep the food away from the tallest bear in the world. Most recommendations call for the bag to be at least twelve feet off the ground and roughly six feet away from the main trunk of the tree. I also try to abide by the practice of

hanging the bear bag approximately one hundred feet or more away from my campsite.

Step 3: Tie the rope to the rock and throw the rock over the tree limb.

Step 4: Tie one end of the rope to the storage bag, pull it up with the other end of the rope, and tie *that* end to another tree.

Seems simple enough, right? Let me explain how I managed to make this not so simple.

I found my tree and rock, tied the rope to my rock, and tossed the rock over the limb. But instead of falling directly to the other side of the branch, the rock's momentum continued and wrapped the rope around the tree branch—twice. Not good. Many good paracords die a lonely death because their rock gets them knotted around a tree limb. Luckily, although the rope had wrapped around the limb twice, it wasn't tied up too badly and I figured if I could get it swinging back and forth, and if I pulled back with the correct timing and angle, I could get the rock to swing back over the branch one time without any further damage or loss of rope. Another factor, though, was that all of this was taking place at night and my viewing area was limited to the range of my headlamp's glow (which segues nicely into my advice that hikers should hang bear bags during the day, if possible).

I started softly pulling on the paracord to get the rock swinging back and forth and, just as the rock was at the back end of the pendulum, I pulled quick and hard, hoping to swing the rock back around the branch one time. My timing was impeccable because the rock wrapped back around the branch not once, but twice, thus freeing it from any connection with the tree limb and sending it hurtling back towards the origin of the rope—my hand. Furthermore, as the rock looped back around it hit the branch with so much force that the rock actually broke into two pieces. Of course, this all happened in a matter of seconds, and as I looked up into the dark with my limited headlamp beam to see what that cracking sound was, all I saw were two flying objects headed in the direction of my face. My reaction time was a bit slow, so I didn't even make a move until they were within a few feet of me. I hit the ground as quickly as I could and heard the two pieces of rock whiz past my head like two meteorites barely missing the earth.

I think it's moments like that when a person must laugh at the trivial things that life throws at us—even rocks hurtling **toward** our heads.

❊ ❊ ❊

There's a fine line between a being badass hiker and being the idiot who got struck by lightning because he was wearing a metal external-frame backpack in a thunderstorm. To avoid being that idiot, I decided to hitch a ride to the Homeplace Restaurant in the town of Catawba, Virginia, where fourteen dollars buys a fantastic experience at an all-you-can-eat southern-food restaurant. When I and three other hikers arrived, all we saw were other patrons entering the restaurant wearing what could only be described as their Sunday best.

This was drastically different from my usual hiking look of dirty-and-homeless, but when we entered the restaurant, we were treated no differently than any other customer. We proceeded to gorge ourselves on roast beef, fried chicken, mashed potatoes, green beans, and mac 'n' cheese—which is considered a vegetable in the South.

As we unconsciously shoveled loads of food into our mouths, we had no idea that a little bit of trail magic was brewing at the table next to us. A woman (and her daughter) had correctly identified us as hikers as her son had hiked the AT in a previous year. They graciously paid for our table's tab and when the waitress informed us of this our hearts were bursting with gratitude. It's amazing how hiking in the wilderness for days on end, and living off minimal resources and without modern conveniences, can remind you of what is important and how to identify pure goodness in the world. We were starving and soaking wet, and then felt like kings and queens when we entered the Homeplace, yet the moment we were told that our tab had been paid we were humbled once again by the kindness of these strangers. We exchanged contact information with the two trail angels, shared a few trail stories, and listened to the mother angel talk about her son's experience.

After our stomachs were full, we hit the trail for a few more miles before calling it a day. The next day we hiked to McAfee Knob, a vista with some of the best views in all of Virginia. The rock outcrop that makes up this area sits over a beautiful valley that was simply breathtaking. However, I and other AT hikers concurred that this was not necessarily a shoo-in

12: Appalachian Trail 2014

Obligatory McAfee Knob picture

for the most beautiful spot in Virginia, as later that day we also crossed a place called Tinker Cliffs. The biggest difference between these two similar spots was that Tinker Cliffs had a longer expanse of rock outcrops that also looked over the valley below. Interestingly, Tinker Cliffs *seemed* more beautiful because of my lack of expectations. It was here that I also had the high honor of being present for when Canary, a hiker with a beautiful voice, decided to sing, in its entirety, "Part of Your World" from *The Little Mermaid*. You never know what's going to happen on the trail.

❋ ❋ ❋

Later that day, my right leg started exhibiting symptoms of terrible shin splints and after ten miles of hiking I was in a great deal of pain. I soaked my shin in the nearby stream and took some ibuprofen. When it wasn't feeling any better the next day, I decided to hike another ten miles to get to the town of Daleville. I thought that if I could just suffer through ten more miles of hiking, I would then take a few days off and let it heal properly. I still don't know if this was the best decision, but staying in the middle of the woods with only a few days' worth of food didn't seem like a promising idea either.

The next ten miles were dreadful, but when I finally reached Daleville and found the hotel where many other hikers were staying, I couldn't have been happier. Better yet, the three days I decided to stay in town to let my leg heal also happened to be the three rainiest days of the previous two months. In fact, it seemed the entire country was on lockdown as the local news station reported tornadoes and thunderstorms across the nation.

I spent most of my three days in Daleville at Mill Mountain Coffee and Tea and Three Li'l Pigs Barbeque, and I didn't regret spending a single moment resting up and staying dry. After three days of rain, the weather began to clear. I packed my bag, said goodbye to the front desk clerk at the hotel, and headed up the hill. I packed out a pound of seasoned sirloin to grill on my first night back on the trail and once again felt like a king. There's nothing like eating rare-cooked steak on the top of a mountain to make you feel accomplished.

❖ ❖ ❖

My time in Daleville proved productive not just for my shin but also for some trip logistics. I had planned to take a break that

May not only to refresh my hiking spirits, but also to participate in certain events in my off-trail life. One of the biggest obstacles to doing an extended hike like the AT is missing out on other things likes weddings, birthdays, and graduations. Many seasoned hikers warn that taking too much time off the trail can make a hiker feel too reliant on life's little pleasures, but I knew it would have the opposite effect on me. I loved being around my family and friends, but I suspected that taking that small break would only make me crave getting back to the trail.

I was grateful for my time in Daleville that allowed me to organize the logistics to ensure that I'd return to the trail after my break in May. Although I had no clue what obstacles would present themselves after I returned to the AT, I couldn't imagine anything stopping me at that point. So, after hiking for a few more days, I left the trail and headed to California. I figured I could squeeze in a little quickie side-hike on the West Coast—the annual Memorial Weekend Death March.

Three states and 802 miles down. Eleven states and 1,387 miles to go.

CHAPTER 13

Hawaii 2012

When Megan didn't get on the plane, I was devastated. She was the first person I ever truly loved, and it took me a few months to realize that although my heart was broken, I wasn't. To distract myself, I devoted more effort toward work and planned small day trips around Maui. Megan was the first woman I ever lived with, albeit only for a few months, and although our relationship only lasted for ten months, it was the longest relationship that I had ever experienced. I was frustrated and angry with her after she left, but it wasn't my feelings toward her that were the problem, nor were they justified. Megan had done nothing wrong. It was my feelings toward myself.

For years I had wanted (or at least I thought I wanted) a committed relationship, notwithstanding a few stints of behavior that might indicate otherwise. That's what we're brought up to believe we should want; most children are taught to seek out that connection with someone, that partnership. However, when that doesn't happen, when we don't find that special someone with whom to have that connection, each person develops their own ways to not just survive, but in some cases, actually thrive while being single.

Therein lies the problem. When I was living in California and Colorado, I became really good at being single—and I mean *everything* involved in being single. I dialed in my systems for buying clothes and groceries. I really enjoyed deciding when and what I wanted to eat. I enjoyed the pace I walked from one place to another. Not to mention the topic of managing money. It's no mystery that a lot of these systems must change when you're with another person; I believe the word is "compromise."

I loved every second with Megan, even the bad parts, but for some reason I couldn't correctly manage some of the changes required when shifting from being single to being in a relationship. We actually had an argument one day about how fast I walked. Toward the end of our relationship, we had a ridiculous fight about lettuce.

It began as a conversation about finances, which led to the topic of shopping for groceries. She wanted the (better) romaine lettuce and I was okay with the (crappy) iceberg lettuce. The latter is ninety-nine cents and the former is usually around two to three dollars. I can't even remember the exact events of the day, but we had been disagreeing about something when we found ourselves at the grocery store. We were in the produce section and she picked up a bunch of romaine lettuce, and while holding it for a few seconds she looked over at me, smirked, and then set the bunch back onto the shelf and proceeded to shop without putting any lettuce in the cart. When we returned home, the argument from earlier in the day was reignited. I can see now how little events like that marked the beginning of the end of our relationship.

The point of this story isn't to defend the merits of iceberg versus romaine lettuce, but to say that I have no idea what the original argument was about. I know we were talking about finances, but beyond that I don't have a damn clue what was said. I know the lettuce fight didn't cause our breakup, but trivial arguments like that one kept me from learning how to be a better partner for her.

In hindsight, it's clear that the source of our breakup wasn't anything I couldn't have figured out with more time, but sometimes we run out of time. Maybe I could have controlled my emotions better, but I can't change that now. I can either be depressed or find a way to move forward and be better in the future. Now, whenever I have a conversation about relationships, I always recommend to "just buy the fucking lettuce."

※ ※ ※

Later that same year, I visited my college buddy Cameron who was living on Molokai, one of the smaller Hawaiian Islands with a direct boat shuttle that departed from the port of Lahaina (where I was living). Cameron was born on Molokai but moved to the small town of Wyoming, Iowa, and later found himself at Cornell College in Mount Vernon, Iowa, which is where we met. As I snorkeled around a little cove with other friends, he was fishing around the reef and pulled up a

Hawaiian Day Octopus. Localized ocean currents have isolated this species of octopus to exist only in the waters around the Hawaiian Islands (thus the name).

Octopuses are peculiar creatures. They hoard items they find on the ocean floor to build piles of debris (known as midden piles) around their den in hopes of concealing the entrance from opportunistic predators. They usually only come out to eat or reproduce, and due to their habit of gliding across the ocean floor, they're sometimes called "the birds of the sea." Each octopus exhibits its own set of personal traits, especially regarding mating habits, which can include so much variety that scientists have trouble collecting quality data on the species as a whole.

The male octopus has an arm that is also its penis, which makes me think that if these creatures were designed by a higher power, that deity had quite the sense of humor. This arm-penis, or hectocotylus, is responsible for ejaculating sperm directly into female counterparts. At the end of the hectocotylus is the ligula which, not unlike the human penis, contains erectile tissue and becomes larger with attraction. As one may expect, the females prefer a larger ligula. However, as males are usually smaller than the females, sometimes the female chooses to eat the male instead of mating with it—a similar practice to that of the praying mantis or the black widow. So, in addition to being self-conscious about the size of their ligulas, male octopuses also must avoid becoming that evening's dinner. For survival, the males have developed safety measures including, but not limited to, the following:

1. Sneaking their arm-penis into the den of an unsuspecting female from a distance that's far enough away that they could retreat if attacked.
2. Pretending to be a female octopus to avoid a fight with other (usually larger) male suitors, which allows them to get close enough to the female to deposit at least one packet of sperm, called a spermatophore.
3. Removing their arm-penis and leaving the entire appendage inside of the female—my least favorite of the options!

Unfortunately, even the males that succeed in fertilizing an egg and escaping with their lives are still doomed. After mating, the males will soon go through senescence, which is a period where they stop eating and become entranced in a dementia-like state of carelessness that includes aimlessly wandering around the ocean floor. This post-ejaculatory euphoria is not a good thing for the male octopus. This carelessness can become the reason why onlooking predators may make the typically reclusive octopus their own delicious afternoon snack.

❖ ❖ ❖

As Cameron walked toward the shore carrying the live octopus he had just caught, it squirmed around in his arms trying to escape back to the sea. Cameron informed me that the only way **to kill an octopus is to burst its brain cavity inside of its head.** Traditionally, Hawaiians burst the cavity by locating it beneath the soft surface of the bulbous head and biting it with their teeth. If done correctly, you won't puncture the skin of the head (thus avoiding any unwanted liquids from going inside of your mouth). After the brain has burst, the arms will slowly cease to squirm, the color will leave the pigments of the skin, and the octopus will lie at rest, ready to join in the circle of life.

When Megan didn't get on the plane I began to wander aimlessly. For months after that, though I had made efforts to put on a good smile for the world to see, I knew I needed to make some changes to avoid going down the path of negative thoughts and a lifestyle that could prove detrimental to my physical, emotional, and mental health. I knew these changes could take years to fully incorporate into my life, but I had to continue evaluating how I could be a better person, both for myself in that moment and for a potential partner in the future.

I didn't want to end up like the male octopus. I was tired of indulging in my own version of senescence after Megan left, and it was time for a change.

So, when Cameron asked the group for a volunteer to burst the brain of the octopus so we could cook it for that evening's dinner, I stepped forward. I took the cephalopod in my hands and, after a few moments of searching, I located the brain cavity, prepared my taste buds, and bit down.

CHAPTER 14

Los Padres National Forest 2014

I began taking part in the annual Memorial Weekend Death March in 2007, after receiving an invitation from my friend Dave (trail name: Coyote Dave), who grew up in Fillmore, California—right on the doorstep of the Los Padres National Forest.

The forest includes approximately 1.75 million acres of wilderness and coastline areas in Southern and Central California. The northern section of the forest includes California's famous Big Sur coastline and the southern part includes areas ranging all the way from San Luis Obispo to Ventura. It has ten designated wilderness areas, four of which I have had the opportunity to explore, including the San Rafael Wilderness, the Dick Smith Wilderness, the Sespe Wilderness, and the Matilija Wilderness. Thanks to the efforts of the Condor Trail Association, there is now a continuous thru-hike that traverses 421 miles through the Los Padres National Forest.

In early 2014 (when I was preparing to begin the AT), Coyote Dave's annual email to see which of the usual suspects would be joining in the upcoming Memorial Weekend Death

March also detailed a route including sections in both the San Rafael Wilderness and the Dick Smith Wilderness. After the expected back-and-forth email responses that happen among a group of grown men (most of which included references to recent advances in powdered-alcohol technology and shaming of those who couldn't join the hike due to legitimate family or work reasons), the final eight hikers were confirmed and plans were set. The roster for the Tenth Annual Memorial Weekend Death March included Coyote Dave, Kevin, Potter, Jared, Dirty, Goldie, Giuseppe, and Batman (me).

❖ ❖ ❖

We arrived at the Santa Barbara Canyon trailhead in complete darkness and under a cloudless sky full of stars. These trips typically kick off with a night of car camping at or near trailheads to allow us to begin hiking early the next day. After imbibing a few beers while sharing stories of past Death Marches, I was ready to crash for the evening. The next morning started with a pound of bacon and a pot of percolated coffee, and it was with these nutrients that we began our trek up the gated Big Pine Buckhorn access road until we reached Santa Barbara Portrero and the Judell Trail junction. Veering southwest onto the Judell Trail, we descended through the canyon to its confluence with the upper reaches of the wild and scenic Sisquoc River. The hike through Judell Canyon offered a mix of exposed dirt trails and pine-tree cover, and the trail meandered back and forth over a mostly dry creek bed.

Carrying a few cans of beer into the wilderness after a night of car camping is an age-old tradition, but this time it didn't work out so well for Potter, as one of the cans exploded inside his bag during this first part of the hike. This gave me the lovely visual of seeing a grown man naked in the backcountry as he dried off his entire beer-soaked pack, which was not the last time Potter would scavenge to find dry clothes that evening.

We arrived at Cottonwood Camp after approximately twelve miles of hiking and with plenty of daylight to spare. It had been nothing but clear skies all day that didn't show any signs of changing; however, the forecast did call for a *slight* chance of rain in the late afternoon. Most of our hikes in the Los Padres had proven to be rain-free; in fact, sometimes I wouldn't even pack a tent. But since I had been carrying a tent with me all year since beginning the AT, I figured I might as well bring it with me on the Death March.

I'm sure glad I did.

After setting up my tent and getting settled in for the evening, I started a fire as the cook for that evening had planned to make bratwursts. In the roughly thirty minutes it took to get a decent bed of coals going, ominous gray storm clouds quickly took over the skies that had been blue all day. Just as the clouds engulfed the area above us, the rain began to fall and it didn't take long for it to start pouring. Assuming this would be a quick storm, the four hikers without tents didn't immediately take action, but it didn't take long for reality to set in, which ultimately sent Kevin, Potter, Dirty, and Giuseppe scrambling to construct makeshift shelters with whatever natural materials they could find.

The rain began to pool in areas of our camp, and the shelter building quickly shifted to canal digging while using camp shovels and sticks as we attempted to direct the pooling water downgradient and away from food and clothes. Although I wasn't too worried about water seeping into my tent, I *was* concerned about moving the water (that had built up to a few inches in a matter of minutes) away from the fire pit. It was clear this was not a regular rainfall for the Los Padres, and that fact was reinforced when I noticed a small splash from what appeared to be a rock landing in my camp-tini (camp cocktail). In fact, it *was* a rock: a small rock of ice from the sky. It was hailing.

To keep myself occupied as the rain and hail continued, I made it my personal duty to keep the fire going. Considering the conditions, and the fact that all of our wood was now soaking wet, this task proved challenging and at one point downright impossible when I noticed a pool of water building up *inside* the fire pit! I had all but thrown in the towel, but I found inspiration in remembering when Penguin Man and I kept a fire going through a snowstorm in Tennessee earlier in the year. I knew a rainstorm was just another obstacle of living in the woods, and that I needed to figure out a way to overcome it. Also, the remarkable thing about a good bed of hot coals is that until the very last ember is extinguished, the possibility of reigniting a flame exists.

After a few minutes of seeing some smoke rise from the embers—and with a little luck courtesy of a decrease in the rain's intensity and a few dry twigs found under a tree—I blew ever so slightly on the embers and a small flame sprouted from the coals. I immediately began strategically placing wet logs around the fire ring in hopes of drying them out and making them usable. I continued rotating logs to expose wet sides to the flames for the entirety of the storm, and as the rain finally began showing signs of letting up, my fire really came to life. The instant the rain totally stopped and the larger logs ignited my first thought was akin to that of a caveman: *I HAVE MADE FIRE!*

Although most of my gear remained unscathed in my tent, every other member of our group seemed to have something that needed to be dried. As efforts began to hang a clothesline over the renewed flames we celebrated with a few more camptinis. We concluded that probably two or three inches of rain fell in about sixty to ninety minutes. And although it felt like an accomplishment to keep that fire going, an important reminder quickly presented itself, too. If I could keep a fire going through a rainstorm, I shuddered to think about how easily a fire could stay lit in dry conditions. This is why it's *critical* to always completely extinguish campfires.

❋ ❋ ❋

After a few more days and nights of stunning weather and the normal shenanigans that take place during our Death Marches, we reached Alamar Saddle and the trail junction that led down to Madulce Camp, where we'd spend our final night. Just before reaching the campsite, we passed a two-mile side trail (Madulce Lookout Trail) leading up to Madulce Peak, which sits at 6,536 feet of elevation. I had been eyeing this peak on the map for several days and decided I wanted to reach the summit even though it wasn't part of our planned route. A few people in our group had hiked the peak during the first year of the Death March and described the side trail as "an easy hike." Although no one else voiced a desire to join me this time around, I felt confident that I could knock out the four miles to the peak and back with little trouble.

The area we had hiked through until that point was almost entirely burned down during the Zaca Fire, which destroyed over 240,000 acres in 2007, and (at the time) was California's second-largest forest fire on record. Forest fires aren't disasters you normally see in Iowa. We're more used to tornadoes and hay barns burning down. Because the Zaca Fire started shortly after I moved to Santa Barbara in July of 2006 for work as a geologist, it left a lasting impression on my mind. Fast-forward seven years and there I was, hiking through the same area that was engulfed by those flames. It was incredible to see what a fire area looks like after a period of regrowth, but remnants of that disaster were still abundant in the form of black, charred tree trunks and piles of ash in areas that had previously been the trail.

It had been over ten years since the other members of the group hiked the trail up to Madulce Peak, and back then I'm sure it really was "an easy hike." But that day, because of the postfire overgrowth, felled trees blanketed the area, loose rocks abounded, and the trail had not been re-marked well since the fire, which meant that the four-mile, roundtrip hike proved to be one of the most challenging hiking experiences of my life.

I almost decided to cut my losses and turn around after getting lost because of numerous ill-marked switchbacks. When I finally relocated the trail I stopped, looked both ways, and had a moment of self-reflection. I was fatigued and mentally drained. I could turn right and return to the main trail, or I could turn left and try to make it to the top. *Left*, I thought. *It must be left.* Finally, after a few hours of clearing branches, climbing over trees, and walking across the very loose, steep terrain that resulted in me sliding down the side of the mountain on multiple occasions, I could see the top.

After another half hour of trying to identify remnants of cairns (small rock piles marking the trail and switchbacks), I found myself within a few hundred feet of the ridgeline. At that point, the only thing that could satisfy my wanderlust was seeing a great panoramic view from the top, and I was determined to get there.

I had decided to keep my entire pack with me on this "easy" side hike, instead of switching to a small day-pack to avoid carrying all my gear. This proved fortuitous because even though it added weight and, inevitably, made it a more difficult hike to the top, having my full pack also meant I had all my food items and therefore could indulge in the pleasure of gorging on a large lunch when I reached the summit, which is exactly what I did. Upon reaching the top of Madulce Peak, I snapped a few photos and videos and, as if my body was making all the decisions, planted myself on a rock and filled my stomach with salami and cheese wraps while looking over the Los Padres National Forest from an elevation of 6,536 feet. There really are no words to describe my feelings in that moment, and the photos don't do it justice, but what I *can* say with absolute confidence is that the view was totally worth all the work.

❧ ❧ ❧

The final night of a trip like the Death March is always a bit surreal. Months are spent planning logistics, but when the week finally comes the journey ends quicker than you could ever imagine. For most of the guys, that last night meant they were one day away from going back to work; one of them even revealed that he was one day away from spending a week with his mother-in-law, so I'm not sure who had it worse. For me, however, that last night meant I was one day closer to returning to the Appalachian Trail.

As we departed Madulce Camp on that final morning, we headed down a rugged, steep terrain known as Heartbreak Hill, and then continued hiking for approximately seven more miles through Santa Barbara Canyon until we reached our original starting point at the trailhead. As is our tradition, a cooler of ice and beer was waiting for us in one of the trucks. After completing such an epic adventure, nothing tastes better than a can

A selfie with the US Capitol before returning to the AT

of suds with some friends. With the addition of the Madulce Lookout Trail, I completed a more than forty-mile hike during my time in California. Just a "little quickie" away from the AT.

❧ ❧ ❧

When I arrived back in Washington, DC, I hopped on an Amtrak and headed back to Lynchburg, Virginia, where I ultimately caught a ride back to where I left the trail over a month prior. After being gone for that time, my resolve to see my Appalachian adventure through was even more hardened. Although I had already spent way more money than I had planned for, I told myself that I wouldn't let that be a reason why I didn't continue the journey. Interestingly, although completing the entire AT hadn't been super important to me at first, I was beginning to feel that finishing the entire trail might actually be a goal I *did* want to accomplish. I couldn't think of a better attitude with which to continue my journey. So, on the day I turned thirty—June 9, 2014—I was back on the AT, and loving every step.

CHAPTER 15

Hawaii 2013

Not long after I exploded an octopus's brain with my mouth, I began to work on another project with the Lahaina Restoration Foundation: renovating the top floor of a historical courthouse in the harbor to become the Lahaina Heritage Museum. Although I had no experience building museum displays, Maui is a remote place, so there weren't a plethora of experienced museum curators nearby (only Mike, who was the head curator already working on the project).

So it was just a matter of good timing and circumstances when, barely a year into working as a docent with a small historical nonprofit, I—a geology major—was asked to be an assistant curator for a Hawaiian museum. I knew I was lucky, and that there were likely thousands of former art history students (many with advanced degrees) pulling their hair out wondering why they couldn't find a job in their field. (Maybe they should have majored in geology and moved to Hawaii?)

My first project for the museum was cleaning and preparing a kerosene oven from the 1940s that was used in one of the sugar plantation homes. It was donated to the foundation from a local family and my only instruction was to "make a display." This may sound a bit slapstick since we *are* talking about a museum, but in the months to come, while reaching out to other small museums around the country (and even the Smithsonian), the common refrain I often heard was "Did you try it? How'd it work?"

After overcoming a small learning curve, I began to carefully scrape off flaking rust; treat existing rust to prevent further oxidation; preserve all evidence of the original paint; and, finally, cut, sand, and paint a wooden display stand on which to place the oven and other various accessories. Mistakes were probably made, and I'm sure a more accredited preservationist would rebut some of my decisions, but I wasn't about to let my inexperience stop me from trying to figure it out.

As the project progressed, I expanded my skill set with every new request from Mike. You know those exhibits at a museum where you can pick up a headset, press a button, and hear a recording about the artifacts in the case? I built one of those. Part of my education also included acquiring answers to interesting questions like "What is a yo-yo doll?" and "Why is forty-six inches a good height for hanging displays on walls?" (A yo-yo doll is made of various pieces of cloth bunched together on a piece of wire and forty-six inches is a good height because it's much easier for tall people to look down than it is for short people to look up). I was even forced to learn basic graphic design skills because I was responsible for developing all the signage for the individual pieces, which needed original graphics and descriptions.

The night of the museum's opening was an enormous success. Mike and I were honored at a lei ceremony by Hawaiian elders as a stylish crowd of locals and tourists looked upon our work. With music playing and hors d'oeuvres being served, I watched as people of all shapes, colors, and sizes—much like the displays themselves—toured the completed exhibits.

As the crowds continued to mill around the main room and Theo, the foundation's executive director, gladly handled conversations with many of the foundation's donors, I chose to get an adult beverage and escape out to the balcony of a local restaurant with a view of the harbor. I felt like celebrating. After all, I had just helped curate a Hawaiian museum. Me: A skinny freckled kid from Cedar Rapids, Iowa. A kid who thought for the first fifteen years of his life that his only viable career choice was to be a professional basketball player. A kid who didn't go to his first-choice university because he couldn't afford it. A kid who majored in geology, got a job in that field and, like many other college graduates, realized that he wanted to do something different. A kid who fell in love, screwed it up, and then decided to prop his head up in any way possible and move forward with his life. A kid who walked through an open door of opportunity to take on a new challenge and became a man with "Assistant Museum Curator" on his resume. Yeah, I'll have a drink to that.

But as I consumed that beverage and looked over the harbor, I remember feeling both satisfaction and loneliness. Although I had just completed something that I was really proud of, I had no one with which to share my joy. As I pondered my future on the island, it dawned on me that even though I had met some amazing people who had positively influenced my life, Hawaii wasn't a long-term match for me. I needed to make a change.

Whenever my life was in a rut, I had a tendency to ground myself in whatever tall peaks were closest. Whether it was La Cumbre Peak in the Santa Ynez Mountains north of Santa Barbara or Lair o' the Bear Park in the Rockies west of Denver or Haleakalā Crater, a dormant volcano that sits over ten thousand feet above the sandy beaches of Maui, these truly awesome natural formations have all helped me to refocus and move my life forward in a positive way.

This is why, while sipping on a drink overlooking the Lahaina Harbor, I found myself thinking about what mountain experience would best help to propel me into my next stage of life. An old idea resurfaced in my mind, an idea that would require months of planning and lots of money, but that would also provide me with a lot of head-clearing opportunities in the mountains to reflect on life. There was no doubt as to what I needed to do next: it was time for me to hike the Appalachian Trail.

CHAPTER 16

Appalachian Trail 2014
84 Days; 1,019 Miles

After my break in California for the Memorial Weekend Death March, I returned to where I had left the AT, in the small town of Glasgow, Virginia, to quickly resupply with food and fuel. I was itching to get back on the trail not only because I had been off the AT for almost a month, but also because it was June, which meant it was hotter and more humid, and that the overall "bug density" of the air was noticeably thicker than when I had left in May. Not only does a hiker have mosquitoes and gnats to worry about, but the ticks, no-see-ums, and moths are also all dying for an opportunity to attack the beam of a headlamp or crawl into a sleeping bag.

As I was unpacking my snack bag for a quick lunch on my first day back on the trail, I felt a critter crawling on the inside of my right arm and immediately felt the painful sensation that could only be a bug getting the better of me. I quickly swiped it off my arm and soon saw the smoking gun: the stinger so eloquently left behind—a barely noticeable thin black rod that looked like the leg of an ant but packed the one-two punch of a wooden splinter. I removed the stinger quickly and remember thinking, *Holy crap, I haven't been stung by a bee since I was nine!*

I was immediately transported back to the memory: A group of us were playing Wiffle ball in my neighbor's yard (a few years before the same neighbor didn't invite me to his party in middle school), and as I rounded third base to head home, a bee flew into my mouth and stung me on the *inside* of my bottom lip. As I squealed like a baby pig from the pain, my brother Derek smacked me across the face and the bee came flying out of my mouth. It was a pretty horrifying experience, and I hadn't thought about it for over twenty years until that moment when I was eating a snack in the Appalachian Mountains. It's amazing how something so simple as a bee sting can trigger an old memory.

❦ ❦ ❦

I spent that first evening back on the trail in a shelter with two new friends, Gnat and Hater Mug, and we shared quite an eventful night. The moment the sun went down, the deafening roar of rain, thunder, and lightning that proceeded to pound the top of the shelter's metal-lined roof was downright frightening as the break between lightning and thunder was nonexistent. The storm continued throughout the night and the aftermath was evident the next day in the form of felled tree branches, slippery rocks, and giant mud puddles. The forecast predicted even more rain for the next few days, which was a bit concerning since the next eighty miles in front of me was going to include traversing two 2,500-foot climbs. Although I certainly hadn't spent my break in California just sitting around, those first two days of climbing in the rain reminded me of what I was attempting to do: hike two thousand miles through the woods.

For the next two days, I walked through rain, mist, drizzle, and more rain. Even though I had replaced my old Columbia boots with new North Face boots that were supposedly waterproof, they were no match for the hours of wetness I was facing. Admittedly, at first the moisture offered a nice reprieve from the warm June weather, but when I felt that first *squish* of a wet sock rubbing against the insole of my boot, I knew I was in for a less-than-desirable journey.

The silver lining of those first few days back on the trail was found at a campsite that had a beautiful area with a large stream running directly in front of Harpers Creek Shelter. The trees and foliage beamed with a green vibrancy that only the simplicity of a coat of water can create. I quickly got my camp set up for the evening, put my swimming trunks on, and found a luxurious water hole to relax in until dinner time. A spa at the beach in Santa Barbara is nice, but it ain't got nothing on a water hole in the middle of the woods.

❖ ❖ ❖

After a pretty uneventful next day of hiking, I found myself four miles away from my planned destination of Waynesboro, Virginia—the base town for Shenandoah National Park. As I noticed the sun was going down, I also realized my water

A selfie looking through the trees over the Appalachian Mountains

bladder had gone dry. I was relying on information from a few day hikers about the location of a camping spot with a water source, but that didn't pan out as expected. To remedy this problem, I decided to hike down a steep access trail to a welcome center in hopes of finding some water.

The welcome center was closed, but thankfully they had a drinking fountain that was operational outside the building. It was clear that camping wasn't allowed at the welcome center, and even though they did have a few log cabins on site to represent what life was like in the late 1800s, I think they would have frowned upon me setting up my sleeping bag on one of the cabin front porches.

Near the welcome center, I met a group of five individuals having dinner at a picnic table. They offered me some of their food and friendly conversation as we watched the sunset over the horizon. I don't remember any of their names, but one of the gentlemen was wearing a t-shirt that had "Shift Happens" printed across the front. I immediately chuckled at the geology pun referencing plate tectonics; he and I became fast friends.

With the day's light dimming, I got my headlamp out, put my rain cover over my pack just in case the looming cumulus clouds decided to dump a little moisture on me, and headed north for the next campsite. The terrain was relatively flat, which minimized my concern of tripping over a protruding tree root that could be hidden in the darkness, but I still kept my eyes overly focused on where my feet were landing. However, one distraction made concentrating a bit harder, and that was the fireflies.

There, in the middle of the woods, at about nine thirty in the evening, were literally *thousands* of little, tiny firefly butts lighting up the night. Again, old childhood memories resurfaced in my mind as I remembered catching lightning bugs in a jar when I was younger. And as much as I enjoyed chasing them during my youth, the thousands of them that were surrounding me that evening on the AT was just short of perfect. The light show created by such simple creatures that were brightening the dark was absolutely breathtaking, as if the stars in the night sky had fallen to earth and stopped just before hitting the ground. Even though I was tired and desperately craving the comfort of my camping pillow, I had to stop, look around me, and let this pure form of nature consume my full attention. There was no entry fee, there were no 3D glasses, and there was nothing I could do to influence it in any way. It was just beautiful.

As I wandered through the firefly light show and neared the location of the next campsite, I caught a pair of eyes in the beam of my headlamp glaring back at me from only a few feet off the trail. When I switched to the red light setting I could make out the silhouette of a standing adult deer. But it wasn't her eyes that drew my attention. It was the two eyes right next to the doe that were merely a foot off the ground. Standing beside its mother, barely visible even with my light, was the smallest baby deer I have ever seen in my life. Although I was dehydrated and tired from hiking more than I had planned, I still had the energy to let out an audible "aaaaaawwwwwww."

❖ ❖ ❖

Shenandoah National Park was authorized by Congress in 1926. The lands acquired for Shenandoah were privately owned, so establishing the park was not without its share of opposition. In all, according to information available at the welcome center, 465 families were removed from their homes; some resettled peacefully but others were forcefully evicted. Skyline Drive was built as the major road that traverses the area today, and it meets up with the famous Blue Ridge Parkway at the southern end of the park. The AT crosses Skyline Drive twenty-eight times over one hundred miles before it exits the park near the town of Front Royal, Virginia. While in Shenandoah, hikers are never far from a road crossing, which can be good for some folks in case they need to exit the trail for any reason. However, some hikers (like me) do not consider this the best "wilderness" experience.

Thru-hikers seem to have love-hate relationships with national parks. We love them because they represent notable milestones along the trail and they usually have facilities that allow us to pick up items along the way, which can lower the weight in our packs. The portions of the AT that run through national parks are usually better maintained, offer relatively easier terrain, and tend to have much more wildlife than elsewhere because animals are protected from hunters.

We hate national parks because they usually have a *lot* more people on the trail, including day hikers and weekend hikers and overnighters who quickly fill up the campsites. Also, even though the wayside shops that sell food and drinks are convenient, they're more expensive than the regular grocery stores found in other places along the trail. And, because most of the great vistas are designed to be accessible by everyone (including those who are driving), it's not uncommon for a thru-hiker to finish fifteen or twenty miles—including bagging multiple peaks, and sweating profusely thanks to a heavy pack—just to finally reach the Sawmill Run Overlook and see three cars pull up with passengers who jump out, snap some photos, and then get back in their cars to race to the next viewpoint. Let's just say it can be a bit of a letdown.

Although this may sound like I didn't have a pleasant experience in the Shenandoahs, that couldn't be further from the truth. In fact, they showed me some of the most diverse wildlife

I had seen on the trail up until that point. I witnessed creatures ranging from wild turkeys to venomous snakes, from deer to colorful lizards, and I even encountered the one animal *everyone* asks about: bears. Before I entered the Shenandoahs, I had never seen a bear in the wild. By the time I exited the north entrance of the park, I had seen eight.

❖ ❖ ❖

My first bear sighting happened when a relatively large bear was scoping out my campsite from the other side of a creek bed. The fact that this bear didn't run away upon seeing me and my fellow campers wasn't good because we knew it meant that, most likely, the bear had been fed by humans before or at least knew that humans tended to leave food around. Not good. Here's the lesson: DO NOT FEED ANY WILDLIFE. Please. Regardless of what you see on social media, just trust me on this one. Wild animals should not be fed by humans.

Carrying capacity is the scientific term that describes how an animal species can only sustain their population in a given area if they don't exhaust the available resources. Put simply, a species can only survive if they don't have too many babies that eat all the food, drink all the water, and take up too much space in a defined area.

If a species reaches population numbers that are beyond the carrying capacity of an area, animals of that species will die. So if a generation of bears in the Shenandoahs learns that humans will provide them with an additional food source by leaving trash in the woods, then they may reproduce to a population level that assumes both natural and human-provided resources of food will always be available. But if one of those resources disappears, the bears will change their habits to ensure their survival. This means they may become more aggressive to avoid starving to death and it's quite possible that their aggression could be directed toward humans.

The worst part about feeding any wildlife and allowing them to get too comfortable with humans is that the humans always win. If a bear or any animal becomes too aggressive, especially in a federally funded national park, that animal will be put down. All it takes is for one cute deer to get frustrated that he isn't getting more food from the six-year-old kid who is feeding it; if that deer endangers the child in the slightest way, the deer will be killed. Humans tend to have a zero-tolerance policy for aggressive animals, regardless of whether they're wild or domestic, and we also tend to ignore *why* those animals are so bold—usually it's because we've unwittingly taught them to be that way.

Although we all want a unique nature or wildlife experience, we need to resist that urge and find a way to be content with simply observing the animals from a safe distance. Even I am guilty of this: I've fed wildlife before prior to this journey, but I've since changed my habits as I learned how detrimental this can be to the animals.

While in Shenandoah National Park, I encountered many "overly friendly" wild animals: Five of eight bears ran away immediately, including two very cute cubs (which meant momma wasn't too far away). But three bears did not scamper upon seeing me, including the one I mentioned above, another one who was equally as bold, and a third bear that not only didn't run, but charged at me.

❦ ❦ ❦

I crossed a picturesque water source at a switchback in the trail and readied myself to gain a few hundred feet in elevation. Just as I was about to crest the hill and head toward Pinefield Hut for lunch, I saw the large black animal off the trail to my left, no more than twenty-five or thirty feet away. His proximity to the trail startled me and immediately brought me to a standstill. He was staring right at me. He didn't even blink. There was no reinforced plexiglass wall or a sunken gap of concrete like you might see separating visitors from animals at a zoo. It was just me, in the woods, with a bear.

In those few seconds that we stared at each other, a torrent of thoughts went through my mind, including what my reaction would be if he became aggressive. Any wilderness guide will tell you that you should never run away from a black bear. They are fast and will catch you. Instead, you'd be instructed to make yourself look big by waving your hands in the air while making a lot of noise. I was not without the contemporary thought, *This would make a great Facebook profile photo,* but intelligently left my camera in its case. All these thoughts took place in a matter of seconds before the bear made his intentions clear.

I heard a sound that would best be described as a snarl. Then, as if he was unsatisfied with my response, he charged. The large black animal got about ten feet closer to me before my reaction kicked in: My arms flew into the air. My trekking poles shot up over my roughly six-foot frame and the only thing that instinctively came out of my mouth was a loud and deep-voiced "HEY!" This initial "HEY!" was followed by a few more—"HEY! HEY! HEY!"—as if I was yelling to a dog who had just escaped from a yard. A really *really* big black dog. With huge teeth.

Between my drastic change in size and the loud noises coming from my mouth, the fully grown black bear stopped his charge but didn't retreat, which would have made me feel a lot more comfortable. Instead, he just stood there, continuing to stare me down. I took the break in his movement to slowly, without breaking eye contact, move my way past him up the trail. We bird-dogged each other until we were at least fifty feet apart when he finally turned and continued to rummage around the forest. I eventually felt safe enough to turn my back toward him and continue on my way to my spot for lunch—as opposed to being his.

When I arrived at the next shelter, I discovered an entry in the logbook that described a similar experience that had happened to another hiker the day before I got there. Clearly this bear hadn't had good experiences with humans and had become aggressive toward us. Unfortunately, I knew that it was only a matter of time before word would get out about an aggressive bear in the area and, once again, humans would win.

My final days in the park were wet. A downpour of rain blanketed the area on my second-to-last day, which included over six miles of hiking in pure whiteout conditions. The sun showed its sharp face on my final day in the Shenandoahs, which helped dry out my clothes, but my boots were still quite damp. I finally came across a small sign marking the end of the park; however, there were still about three miles remaining before I would reach Front Royal, Virginia. Even with the struggles with the wildlife and the weather, having walked the entire length of another of our nation's most visited and beloved national parks brought me a great sense of accomplishment.

❅ ❅ ❅

The Mountain Home Bed & Breakfast is located right off the trail near Highway 522. Owners Scott and Lisa (who share the joint trail name Anything's Possible) had taken on the task of restoring this pre–Civil War home. When I passed through, they still had a long way to go on renovating the main house, but they had converted the old slave quarters into rental accommodations for six to eight people. I took a zero-day and accepted an invitation to tour the main home, which included a unique history of the original owners. The town of Front Royal also allowed me to indulge in the luxuries of relaxing in a coffee shop with Wi-Fi and putting down a few pints of beer at the Lucky Star Lounge.

At the coffee shop, I Skyped with my friend Catherine from Canada who I had met three years before when our tour bus broke down in the middle of Peru. It's great having a Canadian friend to remind me of all the terrible things America does. (And then, when I remind her that our version of bacon is better, I always win the debate.)

After getting a week's worth of supplies in Front Royal I made the final push into Harpers Ferry.

❦ ❦ ❦

Loudoun Heights sits to the right and Maryland Heights is to the left.

This is the view one has while looking down High Street toward the historic town of Harpers Ferry in Jefferson County, West Virginia. Reaching Harpers Ferry represents a huge milestone for AT thru-hikers not only because it's home to the Appalachian Trail Conservancy Headquarters, but also because it represents the spiritual halfway point between the southern and northern parts of the trail. (Because the trail can change every season, the actual mileage halfway point also can vary year to year.) When I arrived in Harpers Ferry, I took refuge in a quaint little place called The Town's Inn where I enjoyed some delicious food while sitting on a balcony that overlooked the main street and the confluence of the Potomac and Shenandoah rivers.

Four states and 1,019 miles down. Ten states and 1,170 miles to go.

CHAPTER 17

Iowa 2014

As I watched the West Maui Mountains disappear into the horizon through the airplane window, my mind was a tidal wave of sand grains with each speck posing as a to-do item that needed to be addressed before late February, when I was to leave for Georgia to start the AT. It was December of 2013, so in addition to the wardrobe change that was necessary for me to leave a tropical island and dive straight into Iowa's "polar vortex" (which would dominate the midwestern weather media for most of that winter), there were many other logistical pieces that needed attention before I could find my way to the AT. Most of these pieces were fairly simple and included things like booking flights, evaluating my gear, and setting up automatic bill payments.

However, these logistics were small when compared to what would be my biggest headache of the entire year—bigger than hiking thousands of miles, bigger than running into bears, and bigger than moving my entire life from an island to the middle of the woods. On January 1, 2014, I was required to sign up for the Affordable Care Act (ACA), known more commonly as Obamacare. Let's just say the government's health-care website didn't have a box to check that would encompass my "2014 Life Scenario."

❆ ❆ ❆

I'm very aware that I'm within a demographic that will garner very little sympathy (nor do I seek any) when it comes to health insurance woes. In 2014, I was a healthy nonsmoking male in my late twenties with no children, no wife, and no pre-existing conditions. I was fortunate to have good genes and I know that being healthy is a luxury that not everyone enjoys. Despite this position of privilege, I stand firmly in the belief that health care is a basic human right and I support universal health care. So, although I was thrilled to have Obamacare as an option, as with most things in Washington, politicians screwed the pooch on the implementation piece—especially for someone who was planning to hike the AT and maintain health insurance while doing so. (Something that, surprisingly, many hikers didn't make a priority.)

Obamacare addressed problems that needed fixing by wiping out insurance policy clauses related to pre-existing conditions and doing away with lifetime maximums. Both of those changes directly affect my sister, Dawn, who was born with an immune deficiency disorder. Having had more surgeries than I can remember, she has already surpassed the traditional one-million-dollar maximum offered by most health insurance policies and she's not even in her thirties. And, although she is an incredibly hard worker, those caps would have severely limited her options in life and made it a legitimate risk to her health if she were to ever have a lapse in coverage.

Of course, there are many anecdotal stories on both side of the health-care debate, but as someone who has been on Obamacare since its inception (because that was my only option as someone who was not offered health insurance through an employer), I can honestly say it became immensely better in its implementation once a few kinks were worked out. But, in the beginning, they sure found a way to make it as confusing as possible for someone like me.

❖ ❖ ❖

The underlying theme behind my frustrations with the government's health-care website and its administrators was this: miscommunication. The biggest problems came from various health-care entities being on very different pages and having conflicting information. For example, I learned after the fact that I didn't even *need* to go through the ACA. I should have been able to call any insurance company and buy insurance directly through them, but after speaking with multiple people at three different insurance companies, I was repeatedly told that I had to sign up through the government's website. I suppose I could have asked more questions, but after three phone calls you tend to believe the people on the other end of the line.

There was also the question of whether or not I had to change my insurance plan every time I hiked into a new state. Considering that I would be entering these new states in the middle of the woods, what would I do if, for example, I broke my leg in Tennessee and had to go to a doctor in the nearby town of Damascus, Virginia? Would I still be covered? Although this may seem like an improbable scenario, that's the point of insurance: we get it for the unlikely events. If we knew exactly when and how we would get sick or injured, insurance agents would have a difficult time reaching sales goals.

Although neither I nor the Obamacare representatives knew it at the time, if I had health insurance in one state, it *would* cover me in another (for emergency purposes). This was all figured out seven months later after many phone calls. Let me clarify: it took *seven months* for me to acquire full coverage health insurance in 2014. That's absolutely ridiculous when compared to the experience I had five years prior in Denver when purchasing health insurance. I made one phone call that took around thirty minutes, my first month's premium was charged to my credit card, and temporary insurance cards were emailed to me immediately.

I began the process of signing up for health insurance on the day that I returned to Iowa from Hawaii: December 18, 2013. After seven months of making numerous phone calls, sending multiple emails, and mailing a stack of documents to a facility in London, Kentucky, a letter *finally* showed up at my Iowa address informing me that, at long last, I had health insurance with full coverage. That letter was dated July 17, 2014, and I wasn't even there to receive it; I had already been hiking the AT and in the Los Padres for five months.

Given the life-changing events that were to occur that August, just a few weeks later, the arrival of that letter in mid-July was cutting it *very* close.

CHAPTER 18

Appalachian Trail 2014
105 Days; 1,341 Miles

After departing Harpers Ferry, I had over 320 miles to hike before reaching the small town of Unionville, New York. (To put that in perspective, the entire distance along Interstate 80 from Davenport to Omaha—the entire width of my home state of Iowa—is 306 miles.)

I hiked those 320 miles, which were mostly through Pennsylvania, in twenty-one consecutive days without a single zero-day. While a few of those days consisted of hiking as few as two miles, there was not a single day in that period that I was not without the task of setting up and tearing down my home, bed, kitchen, and living room, and strapping it all to a metal external-frame on my back—such is the process of long-distance backpacking. A fellow hiker put it in these simple terms: "You gotta fall in love with the process." Life is full of logistics, not all of which are glamorous, but they're necessary to accomplish certain goals.

❈ ❈ ❈

Some people who currently live in the eleven states that seceded from the Union during the war that took place in America between 1861 and 1865 refer to that historical event as the War of Northern Aggression, and many of those same people believe this war was only about an egregious attempt by the federal government to take away states' rights. To *everyone else in the United States* this event is known as the Civil War and it represents our country's turning point where we moved away from the ignorant path of accepting slavery and toward the direction of freedom and independence for all. I was shocked to meet more than a handful of people along my AT journey who preferred the former description.

It took me just a few days to traverse the small portion of the AT that goes through Maryland and as I crossed the Mason-Dixon Line—an invisible historical border dividing the states that did and didn't support slavery during the Civil War—and entered Pennsylvania, I found myself thinking about these different points of view. I was also looking forward to meeting up with my old college buddy, Marshall, and traveling the fourteen miles off the trail to one of our nation's most historically important places: Gettysburg.

Although he was living in Ohio at the time, Marshall expressed a willingness to drive the six hours necessary to pick me up. To make the timing work, I hiked almost sixty miles in forty-six hours to reach our meeting place at a road crossing on Highway 30.

I met Marshall in our Speech Communications course at Cornell College in Mount Vernon, Iowa. The college is situated on the historic Lincoln Highway, which is a meandering road that runs from New York to San Francisco and, coincidentally, includes many sections that are concurrently Highway 30. I could have never dreamed that eight years after graduating college and over eight hundred miles east along the same road that housed our school, the guy in my first college class, who would now be a great friend, would be picking me up so we could visit Gettysburg together.

Even though the AT travels through many small towns, Gettysburg is, surprisingly, not one of them. Because of its distance from the trail, many hikers don't end up visiting, but I couldn't have been happier that Marshall and I had made these plans. Admittedly, neither of us knew much about the actual town and expected to just see "the battlefield." Therefore, we were surprised to learn that the battle took place over three days and covered a wide expanse of Pennsylvania countryside, all of which encompasses the small town of Gettysburg. I'm assuming if I had paid more attention in my US History class in high school, I would've known that. (Sorry, Mr. Schenkelberg.)

Though we could have spent multiple days exploring battlefields and reading historical plaques, we just didn't have time. We did, however, visit Gettysburg National Cemetery where Edward Everett, a politician from Massachusetts, delivered a two-hour introductory speech on November 19, 1863, before Abraham Lincoln shared a few remarks that barely lasted two minutes. We now know Lincoln's remarks as the Gettysburg Address:

> Four score and seven years ago our fathers brought forth on this continent, a new nation, conceived in

Liberty, and dedicated to the proposition that all men are created equal.

Now we are engaged in a great civil war, testing whether that nation, or any nation so conceived and so dedicated, can long endure. We are met on a great battle-field of that war. We have come to dedicate a portion of that field, as a final resting place for those who here gave their lives that that nation might live. It is altogether fitting and proper that we should do this.

But, in a larger sense, we can not dedicate—we can not consecrate—we can not hallow—this ground. The brave men, living and dead, who struggled here, have consecrated it, far above our poor power to add or detract. The world will little note, nor long remember what we say here, but it can never forget what they did here. It is for us the living, rather, to be dedicated here to the unfinished work which they who fought here have thus far so nobly advanced. It is rather for us to be here dedicated to the great task remaining before us—that from these honored dead we take increased devotion to that cause for which they gave the last full measure of devotion—that we here highly resolve that these dead shall not have died in vain—that this nation, under God, shall have a new birth of freedom—and that government of the people, by the people, for the people, shall not perish from the earth.

Lincoln changed the world with a two-minute speech. After standing where Abe stood and reading Abe's words, I can't

Marshall and I in front of a battlefield at Gettysburg

imagine a better way to truly understand the sentiment of that time in America's past. I didn't devote a lot of time or energy to understanding this part of our American history when I was in high school, but I sure do appreciate it now.

Marshall and I rounded out our Gettysburg bromance by imbibing a few local brews—most notably a few Yuenglings from America's oldest (official) brewery—while watching the FIFA World Cup and sharing college stories. I was grateful for the opportunity to understand this important historical place more deeply and to share the experience with an old friend.

❦ ❦ ❦

After Marshall dropped me off back at the trail the next day, I made my way to Pine Grove Furnace State Park, so named because of its rich history housing a large iron manufacturing facility from 1764–1895. The park serves as a major recreational area for visitors and is home to the Appalachian Trail Museum, which offers a collection of hiking artifacts ranging from old mess kits to an entire wooden shelter that had been constructed by Earl Shaffer, the first person to hike the entire AT in one season.

The park also includes a hostel known as the Ironmaster's Mansion. This beautiful home that was once the residence of the owner of the iron manufacturing facility was converted into a hostel with a large porch looking toward a forest canopy out in the distance. It also is rumored to have been part of the Underground Railroad, secretly housing slaves on their way to Canada. Even though Pennsylvania was a free state, the Fugitive Slave Act of 1850 allowed southern slave owners to pursue stolen and runaway "property" in the northern states and bring them back to the South, likely with harsh punishments for the escapee. One piece of evidence to support this rumor is the large crawlspace beneath the Ironmaster's Mansion that was accessible only by a staircase with an entrance that was hidden in a closet.

When I was there, the innkeepers of the Ironmaster's Mansion were Roger and Kathy, a married couple who took the position to be closer to their grandchildren living in the area. Thanks to inheriting the gift of gab from my mother, I had an enjoyable morning of conversational banter with Kathy. Roger provided some great history of the area, but he disputed the claim about the building being used as a part of the Underground Railroad. In fact, there is little hard evidence tying the property to such a history, and he believes the hidden crawlspace was likely used as a food or general storage cellar. Graciously, when my curiosity got the best of me and I requested to see the space in question, Roger was more than happy to let me enter the hidden entryway to the crawlspace.

Its only entry point was a flush, almost invisible access panel in the floor of a small closet that opened to reveal a wooden ladder leading down into the dreary opening. The small dark space beneath the main floor of the house had a dirt floor that was approximately ten feet by twenty feet wide, with barely three feet of head clearance. Whether or not the rumor was true, spending a few minutes in that space made the reality of that terrible past seem all too real. Although I will never know the fear that slaves faced while escaping to the North, that brief experience in the Ironmaster's Mansion allowed me to feel more compassion for those who suffered during that horrible time in our country's history.

❧ ❧ ❧

During my AT journey, I crossed over trails used by soldiers of the Revolutionary War and Civil War, and I passed cemeteries, solitary tombstones, and numerous small memorials. On the day I hiked over the Mason-Dixon Line, I began a new book: Solomon Northup's *Twelve Years a Slave*. This jaw-dropping account of a free black man being kidnapped and forced into slavery for twelve years absolutely tore at my heart strings, especially because I had the added influence of hiking through parts of our country that were near where some of the history in the book took place. Northup's candid accounts of individuals who were given no more respect than a head of cattle because they were given equal cash values made me question what it really meant to "have a bad day."

While I'm certainly not comparing my journey to that of a fugitive slave seeking freedom, it was an eye-opening experience to walk a path that was geographically similar to the Underground Railroad while being acutely aware of the history around me. However, as a white man in my thirties who has a passion for backpacking and history, and who seeks solace in the wilderness, I did find myself wondering, *Why are most of the hikers white?*

In addition to books and maps, the Appalachian Trail Conservancy also puts out a publication called *A.T. Journeys*. The issue that came out near the beginning of my hike in 2014 featured a cover photo of an African American hiker kissing the summit sign on Mount Katahdin, a common photo of thru-hikers. This magazine was available at most of the hostels, hotels, and outfitters I encountered during my first few months on the trail, and it was my buddy "M" who finally pointed out the elephant (or lack thereof) in the room with a simple observation: "This is the least diverse activity I've ever been a part of." He was spot on. Regardless of what that cover photo may have implied, in over thirteen hundred miles of hiking, I had yet to meet a single black person attempting to hike the entire trail. In fact, it wasn't until I was just a few days out from Unionville, when I came across a group of Outward Bound students, that I finally saw *one* black person with a pack on (indicating that he was doing a multi-day hike).

It was not just black hikers who were missing, but Asian Americans, Latino Americans, and people of *all* colors. There just wasn't much diversity and I couldn't help but observe that most of my fellow backpackers were white. Once I noticed this, I found myself thinking about why this was the case. I wondered if there was an inherent difference in culture that made outdoor experiences more accessible to certain groups of people or if perhaps the lack of diversity was due solely to a socioeconomic reason. While I never learned the (likely very complex) answer to those questions while on the AT, the lack of diversity bothered me.

Wilderness and outdoor experiences have provided me with so much needed solace and peace in my life that I would hope everyone, regardless of race, would be given the opportunities and mentorship to know about these options. Whether it be a long-distance backpack trip, a weekend car-camping trip, or even just a walk through a local city park, outdoor and environmental experiences of any magnitude should be, in my opinion, some of the most inclusive and accessible activities available. This lone observation is far from a researched hypothesis of what can be done to make backpacking a more inclusive activity, but hopefully it can help continue the conversation.

❖ ❖ ❖

Fun fact: due to the presence of ice caps on our planet's North and South Poles, we are, according to the scientific definition, currently in an ice age.

Approximately thirteen thousand years ago (give or take a few hundred years because geology isn't an exact science), the earth was colder. During that time, singular light-weight oxygen isotopes properly paired with two hydrogen atoms had evaporated from the ocean into the atmosphere and precipitated as snow onto seemingly endless landscapes of ice around the North Pole. These monstrous platforms of crystallized water, known as glaciers, flowed south like one may observe in an antique stained-glass window after years of gravity pulling the colored pieces of quartz slowly toward the ground.

The glaciers moved through preferential pathways like river valleys and low saddles between mountaintops. They would occasionally be slowed due to a lack of precipitation or perhaps a mountain around which there was no easy path. Nevertheless, they persisted, and with enough time they proceeded in their southerly direction away from the polar ice cap, grinding up rocks, trees, and any natural objects that didn't have the locomotive ability to save themselves from the slow but destructive glacial paths.

As global temperatures increased, the advancing glaciers halted their slow migration south and, without warning or declaration, naturally began to retreat to their provenance until an equilibrium of natural factors was met that allowed the sheets of ice to remain in a consistent location. As the ice began to melt, the rocky debris held within the glaciers fell out of their cold grips and was left behind. Depending on future glacial conditions, a terminal moraine of debris like this may be the only evidence that such destruction ever took place.

Such was the case for what is now Pennsylvania. Multiple glacial advances containing a diverse amount of rock and debris from Canada now make up areas that we call the Poconos. Although the broader mountain range has an orogeny (a geologic term describing a mountain-building event) that is just as intricate and exciting, suffice it to say the above description of retreating glaciers is a primary reason why the ridges of the Appalachian Mountains that traverse eastern Pennsylvania are covered with endless oddly sized, nonuniform piles of rocks.

Or… God put them there.

Regardless of which explanation makes the most sense to you, the portion of the AT that runs through Pennsylvania was one of the most difficult sections of the whole trail. This is not because it has massive elevation changes (the tallest peak along the trail in Pennsylvania has an elevation of barely over sixteen hundred feet), nor is it because there are long stretches between towns or resources (in fact, it was just the opposite), but because of 230 miles of soul-crushing, sole-tearing rocks.

❦ ❦ ❦

One shining example that illustrates how the AT never ceases to surprise was when I hiked into Wind Gap, Pennsylvania, after my one hundredth night on the trail. After leaving the town of Palmerton much later than I planned, I realized the sun would be setting before I would arrive at the Leroy A. Smith Shelter. As I continued hiking through the darkness, I noticed I wasn't all that tired, so when I reached the shelter in the early morning hours, I decided I could make it to Wind Gap—which was another five miles or so—before my body would really need a break. Also, a very important part of this story was that Google Maps had informed me that Wind Gap was home to a Dunkin' Donuts. As much as I love making coffee and breakfast while camping, Dunkin' Donuts sounded *really good* while hiking through the woods in the middle of the night.

I made it to Pennsylvania Route 33 at about five in the morning and headed to the other side of town to claim my prize of two bear claws and a blueberry donut. As vehicles were waiting in the drive-through queue, I walked into the air-conditioned entryway and unloaded my gear onto a table in the corner. I was enjoying my three servings of sugar-glazed delight when a gentleman, who I can only describe as looking exactly like Guy Fieri from the Food Network, approached me.

He informed me of his Native American heritage and said how proud he was of me for making this journey through his ancestors' lands. As he continued to tell me about the history of the area, I must admit that I found it a bit difficult to swallow that this white guy with beach blond hair was part–Native American. Still, we never can know a person's history by the color of their skin alone (a great characteristic of living in America) and I appreciated the unique conversation—especially at a Dunkin' Donuts before seven in the morning.

Before we parted ways, he told me to wait inside as he went to his car to retrieve something. He returned holding a two-foot-long, approximately five-pound, sharpened machete blade. By that point, a line had formed inside of the Dunkin' Donuts, and the Guy Fieri look-alike who was entering the building carrying a gigantic metal blade drew more than a few stares. The gawking then shifted in my direction as he held the blade on top of both of his palms as if to pass on the task of guarding the Holy Grail and said, "On behalf of my Native brothers and sisters, I present you this knife as a thank you for enjoying and protecting our lands."

Everyone in the Dunkin' Donuts stared in my direction.

Although I recognized the symbolism behind his gesture, the only thing going through my mind was *That looks so heavy!* After a few attempts to politely decline the gift, it was clear he was standing by his offer and I finally accepted the machete. You can never fully prepare yourself for the surprises the AT might present.

After the gentleman left, I pondered what the hell I was going to do with this giant heavy blade. It was nice, and I figured that on some other adventure it could even be considered a suitable piece of gear to carry, but not on the AT. Reluctantly, and full of bear claws, I strapped it to my pack and carried it into the woods.

❦ ❦ ❦

Even though Pennsylvania proved challenging, I can say I hiked every mile of it, albeit with aching joints. The biggest perk accompanying the hike out of Pennsylvania was the Delaware Water Gap National Recreational Area. Northern New Jersey, especially along Kittatinny Ridge, was gorgeous. I spent a few more days in New Jersey before beginning a ninety-mile

Enjoying coffee at the hiker cabin on the property of
Jim Murray (AT '89), just outside Unionville, NY

stint hovering close to the New Jersey–New York border. I enjoyed a couple of sunny days, which allowed me to easily make it to Unionville, New York, where I enjoyed a few IPAs at Wits End Tavern on the outskirts of town. Life was good.

Eight states and 1,341 miles down. Six states and 848 miles to go.

CHAPTER 19

Iowa 2014

Backpacking and the outdoors haven't always been big parts of my life. As I prepared for my AT journey in my home state of Iowa during the first couple months of 2014, I found myself reflecting on past outdoor experiences and was reminded of the ultimatum my parents gave me in second grade: I could either continue as a Cub Scout and quit playing organized basketball, or vice versa. We didn't have the money for both. It was an easy choice because the Cub Scouts offered cake-baking contests and wooden boat races, but basketball offered Michael Jordan. 'Nuff said. I never once regretted my decision, as my years playing for the Salvation Army Amateur Athletic Union (AAU) basketball team gave me some of my fondest childhood memories. The truth is, although I've met several Scouts as adults who loved learning wilderness survival skills while they were young, my experiences fell a bit short and left me with a fairly rudimentary understanding of the outdoors. I knew that a worm on a hook could catch you a fish and that Walmart had the cheapest twelve-person tents. That was about it.

I really began honing my outdoor skills during my college years when I started traveling and camping with my study-abroad classes. If you want to study modern carbonate marine systems or active plate tectonics you have to fly to places like Australia and New Zealand—and my small, private Iowa college gave me incredible opportunities to do just that. Camping on rock bluffs on the western coast of Australia and snorkeling to collect coral sediment samples opened my eyes to what "roughing it" really means. I will forever cherish that experience, especially because it helped jump-start my heart into a love of the outdoors.

❊ ❊ ❊

My first major backpacking experience came when I visited my college friend Julia (the same Julia I would later visit in Albuquerque on my road trip after leaving California) at her family's ranch in Montana right before I moved to Santa Barbara in July of 2006. We hiked about twenty-five miles through the Rocky Mountains in the Absaroka-Beartooth Wilderness up to Horseshoe Lake. It was there that Julia introduced me to backcountry cooking with an Esbit stove, a simple metal chamber that can hold a small fuel tablet and boil water with amazing efficiency. We stayed for two nights and climbed a rocky ridge to one of my first mountaintop vistas. It was beautiful. For a kid from Cedar Rapids, where the tallest landmark in town is a compacted pile of trash, hiking to the top of a mountain in the Rockies was surreal.

❊ ❊ ❊

After my trip to Montana, I moved to Santa Barbara to pursue my post-college career as a geologist. I immediately took interest in the many hikes in the front country (found on the south-facing slope of the Santa Ynez Mountains) that were within a few minutes' drive from where I was living. From Rattlesnake Trail to La Cumbre Peak to Gaviota Pass, I took every opportunity to traverse these short day hikes that offered impressive views of the Pacific Ocean. Some friends and I even started a small hiking group called the "Ramas," named after a pizza place located on the mesa in Santa Barbara where we would eat after our weekly hikes. The apex achievement of this group was a one-day hike that was approximately eighteen miles long through the entire front country of Santa Barbara. At the time, I thought, *Wow, I will probably never hike this far in one day ever again.*

I was wrong, and my backpacking skills continued to evolve after multiple Memorial Weekend Death Marches and many short weekend trips. Moving to the Front Range of the Rockies in 2009 allowed me to continue to hone my abilities by exploring many trails, including sections along the Colorado Trail—an almost five hundred mile thru-hike that traverses the Rocky Mountains through the White River, Gunnison, Rio Grande, and San Juan National Forests.

❀ ❀ ❀

In 2011, I traveled to Peru to hike in the famous Sacred Valley of the Andes Mountains. Although it wasn't a multi-day backpacking trip, I drew the confidence to plan numerous solo day hikes in a South American country from my ever-increasing knowledge and curiosity of the outdoors. This trip included a very early morning hike up to Machu Picchu—the same climb that explorer Hiram Bingham ascended one hundred years prior in 1911, when he was introduced to the ruins of the former Incan city by local indigenous farmers, and that he later introduced to the world. Witnessing a sunrise over a South American rain forest while climbing a mountain to see one of the new Seven Wonders of the World is something I will never forget.

❖ ❖ ❖

After leaving Denver for Maui in 2012, I brought my backpacking gear with me as the ocean isn't all that island has to offer. Haleakalā—the now-dormant volcano that sits at just over 10,000 feet of elevation and makes up a majority of the landmass on the southern bulb of the island—offers an intricate network of backpacking trails inside the crater. Unlike stratovolcanoes (the more common one-peak, large-eruption type that comes to mind for most humans when they think of volcanoes) like Mount Saint Helens or Pompeii, Haleakalā is a shield volcano with a broad area that includes many smaller eruption sites within the shield. Haleakalā and all of the Hawaiian Islands were formed because of the stagnant hot spot that sits underneath the Pacific tectonic plate, which is continuously moving westward.

Geologically speaking, all the islands are fairly young in age. Maui is only a few million years old and, if we're being liberal with our definition of the word "age," the Big Island is technically still being born. In fact, Lō'ihi Seamount, located about twenty miles off the south coast of the Big Island, is only a few thousand feet from cresting the ocean surface and becoming the newest Hawaiian Island.

The system of trails through Haleakalā includes a few cabins and a handful of tent sites, one of which is on the southeast side of the shield and overlooks the top of the Hana rainforest on the backside of Maui. I was fortunate enough to take two long trips in the crater, one with my friend Kaori from Japan and the other, wouldn't you know it, with Julia, who was visiting for an archaeology conference in Honolulu. I was thrilled to take Julia trekking through this unique Hawaiian landscape as she had done for me in Montana so many years before, and it was an incredible privilege to share a sunrise with her in a volcano crater while looking over a rainforest.

❦ ❦ ❦

As my moment of reflection about my past outdoor experiences subsided and my thoughts were brought back to the present task of planning for my AT journey—researching campsites and trail towns and organizing my camping cookware into a more streamlined set—I felt a little surge of confidence beat in my chest. From Australia to Montana to California to Colorado to Peru and finally to Hawaii, these experiences helped mold my backpacking and hiking skills and inspired me to decide in early 2014 to hike the Appalachian Trail. I had read books, blogs, and websites, and with hundreds of backpacking miles under my proverbial belt, I finally felt confident enough that I could handle everything a two-thousand-mile journey through the woods could throw at me. I knew there would be struggles along the way, but I figured lessons learned from my previous trips would provide an adequate skill set for any obstacle I might face. I knew there would be roadblocks both seen and unseen that could be thrown in my path, but I wasn't about to let that stop me from embarking on this adventure. Sometimes you just have to pack your bag and go.

CHAPTER 20

Appalachian Trail 2014
123 Days, 1,546 Miles

When chances we take meet our expectations, we fall asleep at night with the satisfaction of knowing we've made the right decisions, but how can we really be certain that's true? During the time that I spent on the AT in 2014, I found myself frequently thinking about the topic of "expectations."

When I started hiking the trail, my expectations of the people I'd meet, the cities I'd visit, and the nature experiences I'd have were quite different from what I actually encountered. I'm not saying they were negative, but just that I never expected certain events to occur the way they did during my first 123 days on the AT—especially toward the end.

❖ ❖ ❖

After leaving Unionville, New York, I crossed into New Jersey and began a twenty-one-mile day of hiking that started off just like any other. I deflated my sleeping pad, stuffed my sleeping bag into its sack, and rolled up my tent. After some pavement walking where the trail traverses a road for a few miles (due to an inability to gain permission to continue the AT through private property), I found myself in a marshy area that is part of the Wallkill River National Wildlife Refuge. The flat access road that served as the trail and circumvents a small portion of the refuge area was one of the most beautiful sections of the AT that I had seen, mostly because the wet marshy environment was very different from other areas I had previously walked through. Witnessing great blue herons and egrets flying over large swaths of cattails and prairie grasses provided a setting of bliss and calm.

The rolling hills of Pochuck Mountain State Forest provide a natural landscape that even Claude Monet would have struggled to recreate. Who knew that walking around a flat cattail marsh would have such an effect? Maybe it was because after constantly climbing up and down mountains, a piece of flat land was a pleasant change of scenery. Or maybe it was because I finally had a chance to look *up* at the mountains instead of down from them. It's hard to argue for one form of beauty over another due to its vastly subjective nature, but I can tell you I would've never expected that one of the most memorable views from hiking through the Appalachian Mountains would be from flat ground.

As I approached the top of a climb beyond the refuge area, I heard some noises that I assumed were from other people nearby as I was close to a road and had also passed a handful of hikers coming down the hill. As I got closer, however, I realized the sounds were not people, but rumbles coming from the bushes. It didn't take long to determine that what I was hearing was actually a very large black bear. This momma bear was rummaging around and flipping rocks to find bugs and other critters to eat while her two cubs scavenged nearby. My body froze, and I immediately went into an overly cautious mode. She was only about fifteen or twenty feet away from the top of the climb where a trail registry box was located. Although she didn't seem to be alarmed by me in that moment, I knew that could change quickly. One of her cubs was close to her but the other was on the opposite side of the trail, probably about fifty or sixty feet away from her, which put me right in between them. Although there is a lot of variance in hiking methodologies, one thing that is unanimously agreed upon is that you should never get between a momma bear and her cub.

The separated cub slowly started walking in my direction. I didn't feel any increased threat at that moment, so with my camera already in hand from an earlier photo, I snapped a few shots of the little guy when he was still at a safe distance (at least what I thought was a safe distance). Because other cubs that I had encountered while backpacking seemed generally quite scared of humans, I assumed he would dart up a tree if he caught sight of me. But this little guy showed no signs of retreat and continued his path right toward me—not a good thing with momma close by. When he finally got within about twenty feet of me, just on the other side of the trail, he apparently was done with his adventures for the day. With his ears up and his eyes staring right at me, this cute little bear cub made a very loud cry, darted off down the trail, and scampered up a tree about thirty feet away. I don't speak "bear," but I assume whatever that cub cried out was something along the lines of "MOOOOOMMMMM!!"

Within seconds, momma bear came running. From her position behind me, she charged through bushes and felled trees—it sounded like a dump truck plowing through old cars at a demolition derby—and she came to stop right on the trail about twenty feet from where I stood. She stared right at me, snarled, and very prominently stood her ground between me and her cub. My entire body stiffened up as I held still. She never directly charged at me, but her intentions were clear. Again, I'm just assuming, but her snarl probably translated to something like "Leave my cub the fuck alone."

Part of me wanted to remind her that it was all his fault, but something about her body language told me that she didn't care about my side of the story. After a staring contest that ended with me raising my trekking poles and getting loud and big, she slowly worked her way back into the trees while keeping an ever-so-cautious eye on me. She never got more than ten feet away from the trail, so I decided against Leave-No-Trace practices and walked through the trees and brush on the opposite side of the trail to get some distance between me and momma.

After safely reaching another bend in the trail about one hundred feet farther north, I decided that with my adrenaline pumping and the remaining daylight I would try and make it to New York's state line, which lies just before the town of Greenwood Lake. (The AT crosses back and forth over the New Jersey–New York border; the trail near Unionville, New York, is actually still in New Jersey, so I had to hike off the trail

Baby bear right before his cry for help from mom

to reach that town.) The day ended in typical fashion with my finding a campsite with flat tent surfaces and ample tree limbs to hang a bear bag. I woke up the next morning to see the entire area was surrounded by wild blueberries ready to be picked, which meant my usual oatmeal breakfast was supplemented by a couple of handfuls of ripe blueberries that nourished me as I made my way into a new state.

❊ ❊ ❊

Although the scenery was beautiful, the best and most memorable experiences from my AT journey were made of one thing: the people, both on (and off) the trail. In Greenwood Lake, I got a room at a waterfront bed and breakfast on the lake. Although it was a bit pricey for a hiker's taste, I had decided it was time to splurge a little bit and enjoy the evening with a shower, a place to clean out my gear, and a view of the lake right out my window. Inevitably, my dinner plans took me to Emerald Point Restaurant, the one place in town with an outdoor patio. Since this was a "fancy" place I put on my best outfit, which consisted of a Larabar t-shirt that I got from my friend Stacy (who worked for the company at the time) and swimming trunks.

I met two separate couples at the restaurant, each at very different points in their lives and whom I will likely remember forever. The first was Ryan and Bobbi—a lively couple around my age who clearly looked at life with a glass-half-full point of view. They met when Ryan was tending bar at a local establishment, and they lived in Bobbi's childhood home on the lake. Bobbi worked in retail and sold (in her own words) "shit handbags," but did so with such sarcasm and vigor that I was almost convinced to buy one. Ryan worked for the ski resort on the other side of the mountain, building terrain parks during the winter and doing other jobs necessary to maintain the resort through the summer.

After Ryan and Bobbi left, an older couple by the names of Joe and Cynthia took their seats. They had just returned from an RV trip spent exploring the national parks of the western United States. Cynthia was from Germany. Her daughter had just been married in America but was planning to have a second ceremony back in Germany. Although they had just returned from their RV trip, they were already planning the trip back to Germany for the second ceremony (a fact that definitely got an eye-roll from Joe). It was wonderful to meet people with stories to share. Although I loved telling people about what I had been doing for five months on the AT and the West Coast, it was a nice change to have them tell *me* all about their road trip. Watching Joe and Cynthia banter back and forth like a couple of teenagers gave credence to a life plan that involves a partner in crime. Joe continued the storytelling that evening with some of his travel adventures from when he was a bachelor, which helped validate some of the craziness of what I was doing at the time.

❦ ❦ ❦

A few days after leaving Greenwood Lake, I had planned a reunion with an old high school friend, Julia (a different Julia than the one from Montana), and her two beautiful children.

We met at Lake Tiorati where—because it was the weekend, which I had forgotten—picnic tables and grills were packed with families flocking away from the concrete jungle of the city to enjoy some outdoor time. Although neither Julia nor I knew there was a swimming area, it only took a few minutes before her kids realized they didn't care about wearing wet clothes and promptly got in the water while their mom and I caught up on life.

Unfortunately, after leaving Lake Tiorati and returning to the woods to begin hiking toward the next shelter, something unexpected occurred that would soon prove to be very detrimental to my journey's future: I felt a quick fluttering feeling inside my chest. Being a runner since early middle school, I am very in tune with how my body functions and operates, especially my heart. The fluttering occurred for a mere three- or four-second episode, but it was enough to make me stop in my tracks. After assuring myself that it was a fluke event, I continued walking into the evening and arrived at the William Brian Memorial Shelter where I got a very surprisingly good night of sleep. Little did I know, that would be the first of many fluttering feelings to come.

❦ ❦ ❦

I met a very important person during my time in New York. Her trail name was Mourning Dove and she began her hike at the New Jersey–New York border with plans to go all the way to Maine. As a newbie to the hiking game, she had the usual complaints that most hikers do in their first few days of a trip (pack is too heavy, straps don't fit right, etc.). We camped together for a few nights before I took off on a marathon day (literally twenty-six miles) to make it to Pawling, New York, where an MTA Metro North train would provide me transportation into the city. Mourning Dove and I were in relatively similar life scenarios before we started our respective hikes—we were both in our late twenties with jobs we enjoyed, but we knew something about our situations needed changing. We exchanged numbers and vowed to meet up again after I returned to the trail from the city.

❖ ❖ ❖

Because New York City is pretty much the exact opposite of a significant nature experience like hiking the AT, the sensory impact of going from being among a sparse number of people in the woods to the densely populated metropolis is unmatched. If you think coming across a momma bear and her cubs in the woods is a sticky situation, try taking the "L" subway line from Brooklyn to Manhattan on a Friday morning—"sticky" takes on a whole new meaning. When I arrived at Grand Central Station in Manhattan, I was hurtled into a frenzy of New Yorkers switching trains, running upstairs, and making other efforts to get somewhere as fast as possible just to stand in line again.

My main reason for making this stop in the city was not to remind myself of what the inside of a cab smells like, but to meet up with my college friend Joe. I met Joe on the football field when he was a junior defensive back and I was an incoming freshman receiver for the NCAA Division III Cornell

College Rams. Joe had lived on the East Coast since he left Iowa and was a part of New York's acting scene along with various other freelance ventures, including forming an acting group called *The Mad Ones*. Although my timing wasn't the greatest (Joe had *just* rented out his place because he was set to be out of town for a few months), we made the best of our time together.

You can't go wrong with a day that starts out in Central Park and is followed by drinking at a bar that lays claim to being the oldest continuous business in the city. In operation since 1864, Pete's Tavern remained open as a "flower shop" during America's failed attempt to curb alcohol distribution—the period that spawned the forefathers of today's organized crime networks and that we now call "prohibition." With a great beer selection and cool history, I'd say this watering hole was worth stopping in for a quick nip.

It had been about twelve years since my last visit to the city when my mother and I took a trip after I was accepted into Fordham University in the Bronx. (To put timing into perspective, when I last visited New York I had printed out my directions from MapQuest.) It was 2002 then, and my mother and I explored the city that just a few months before had been the target of one of the most devastating terrorist attacks in our nation's history. The towers were gone and most of lower Manhattan was still closed because clean-up efforts were underway. While taking a boat ride to see the Statue of Liberty on that visit, I remember the tour guide gave a very chilling description of the events of 9/11.

Twelve years later, when I visited Ground Zero after parting ways with Joe, I reflected on what those moments would have been like when the mayhem was taking place—to witness the chaos, to not know if loved ones were coming home—and it hit me once again how truly horrible the terrorist attacks of 9/11 were not only to the country, but especially to the individuals that were closest to it.

Mourning Dove, who is from the Bronx, would later share with me her experience of 9/11 and further validate this outlook. She described the moment that she heard the news over the radio, which happened while she was at a magnet school building away from the main campus, and how she was subsequently instructed by the principal to not tell anybody because an announcement had not yet been made to the rest of the student body. Approximately one thousand miles away, while sitting in Dot Pospischil's Western Civilization class on the second floor of Prairie High School in Cedar Rapids, Iowa, I watched in horror a video of the planes crashing into the buildings. I don't mean to downplay the effects that 9/11 had on people in the Midwest, but my experience paled in comparison to Mourning Dove's, who remembers seeing a female classmate begin to cry because her uncle was working in one of the towers.

These were my thoughts that day in 2014 as I took in Freedom Tower—standing in the center of it all, hovering 1,776 feet over lower Manhattan—a pillar of America's resolve after those tragic events. Below the tower are the reflecting pools that frame the footprints of the original two buildings and that house, according to the memorial's website, the largest man-made waterfalls in North America. I spoke with a police officer on duty at the memorial that day, and twelve years later the tone of his voice was still respectfully serious as we both talked about our experiences during those moments when the planes crashed into the towers. Although I didn't expect to spend part of my wilderness journey standing in a populated city next to man-made waterfalls, I am forever grateful I took the opportunity to visit and show some respect for this tragic event and the people who lost their lives that day. My journey was about exploring America, so visiting places like Gettysburg and the 9/11 memorial absolutely had to be included in the itinerary when the opportunities presented themselves.

❦ ❦ ❦

On my final day of walking through the streets of downtown Manhattan, my body was trying to tell me something. Out of the blue, my heart was beating in a way that I had never felt before and I was constantly finding myself short of breath; it felt similar to what I experienced when I left Julia at Lake Tiorati, except that the sensation was happening more consistently. *Should I call a hospital?* I wondered. *Of course not. I'm only walking. What could be wrong?*

I returned to Pawling where I purchased provisions and planned for another four or five days on the trail (I even got a haircut before leaving town), even though the odd physical symptoms in my heart continued. At that point, I still didn't think it warranted medical attention. I had the mentality of an athlete: *I can do it, coach.* In fact, I even knocked out two consecutive hikes of over twenty miles in the days following my departure from Pawling as I walked into Connecticut. Unfortunately, during those days another physical ailment began to influence my hike, and that was a tightness and swelling in my left knee every time I would stop for more than twenty minutes. I immediately (and incorrectly) attributed this to a swollen IT band, which is the ligament that runs down the outside of the hip and over the outside of the knee, helping to stabilize the knee during physical activity. I figured it was just an old college track injury acting up again and I had no reason to think my heart problems and swelling in my knee were related.

The tight knee, the shortness of breath, and the irregular heartbeats continued to prove problematic until I reached Falls Village, Connecticut. This very small town with a relatively upscale restaurant and a hotel named Falls Village Inn is where I met Ashley, who worked at the nearby Isabella Freedman Jewish Retreat Center. The center sits on a beautiful piece of land and the main building was next to a very picturesque pond. Ashley had invited me to visit the center the following day for breakfast. It was there that I admitted to Ashley that I wasn't feeling well and that mentally I was very "checked out" when it came time to hike the trail each morning. I thought my mental struggles were directly affecting my physical woes (not the other way around), and if I could just get over the mental impasse, I would be fine. *I can do it, coach.*

Ashley allowed me to stay at the retreat center for the morning, which reminded me of being at Camp Wapsipinicon near

Anamosa, Iowa, when I was younger, a fond memory. I took advantage of the comfortable couches in the main gathering room to read a book I had been carrying in my pack since I bought it at a town library sale in Palmerton, Pennsylvania: Ernest Hemingway's *The Old Man and the Sea*. Maybe it was fate, maybe it was coincidence, but I thought there could not have been a more analogous story to the situation in which I had found myself.

Hiking had become less fun for me since leaving New York City. It started to seem like a job that I had to do, a job in which I felt like I was trying to meet someone else's expectations. I couldn't decide if I was continuing because I truly wanted to or if it was because of some other reason. Although I had encountered many highs and lows along my journey, until recently it had always felt like it was something I was doing because I *wanted* to do it. I had been hiking the Appalachian Trail for almost four months at that point. I had gained amazing experiences, but my body was tired, and it was telling me something was wrong.

In Hemingway's book, Santiago (the old man of the title) goes many days at sea without catching a fish, yet he continues to go out every day because it is his passion, it is his love. Hiking was something that I loved and was passionate about. However, because of what my body was telling me—because my heart wasn't working correctly—it wasn't fun anymore.

After leaving the retreat center, I found my way to the town of Salisbury, Connecticut, where I met back up with Mourning Dove. Although I didn't know at the time whether I was fighting just a mental block or an actual physical problem, I felt I had experienced what I was looking for in this journey and I was ready to be done. I had undertaken many physical activities in my life, and while hiking over fifteen hundred miles through the mountains was certainly strenuous, I knew I could handle the physical requirements of this challenge (which is what made it mentally challenging). But my body was telling me through an annoying shortness of breath and a constant stretch of irregular heartbeats that I had reached an impasse in my journey.

❦ ❦ ❦

Although I was almost certain I'd be leaving the trail soon, I approached Mourning Dove with an idea about us sticking together for the next few days and she agreed. I kept hiking because I didn't know what else to do. Hiking had been my entire life for most of 2014 and the idea of not hiking just seemed so foreign. I figured if I kept walking, I would reach a town with more resources in a few days and that I could make more decisions then.

Mourning Dove and I started our joint hike into the beautiful, yet mosquito-infested, state of Massachusetts. We planned to complete around fourteen to fifteen miles of hiking each day. These distances were very doable and although I didn't experience any additional physical problems, my heart symptoms remained. In fact, after another few days it was overbearing. My heart wasn't racing, it just wasn't beating correctly. Even though I wouldn't describe what I was feeling as painful, it definitely didn't feel good. I could feel my heart beating in ways

I had never felt before. I began to get headaches, my shortness of breath continued, and, as if I had just hit a brick wall, an overwhelming sense of fatigue soon consumed my whole body.

At every road crossing for two days I would turn on my phone and look for places to stay. Both mentally *and* physically, I was done. Amazingly, though, a sliver of hope existed that I might only need a few days off the trail to rest; I still didn't think I needed to see a doctor. Thankfully, a random series of events caused me to finally seek out professional help for what I was feeling in my heart and led me to the place that I would call home for the next nine days: Berkshire Medical Center in Pittsfield, Massachusetts.

Ten states and 1,546 miles down. Four states and 643 miles to go.

I can do it, coa… I can't do it, coach.

CHAPTER 21

Georgia 2014

It had been over two months since leaving Maui for the mainland, and in spite of my troubles securing health insurance, it was great to see my family and friends. After making it through the holidays back home in Iowa, I traveled west to Denver, where a trusted crew of college friends resided and where I spent my last three weeks before beginning my AT journey.

I was grateful that the Mile High City was home to several of my friends who knew the struggles I went through when Megan left me in Hawaii. Once again, I was reminded how I'm always surrounded by good people in my life. These friends—Andy, Evan, and Ross—were all there for me when I needed to talk with someone while trying to move on from the breakup. They have all heard me cry when things weren't going well in my life. Although I'm not married, all of these guys have taken turns being my best man at times when I needed them most, so it was wonderful to spend time with them in early 2014—not crying or being sad—but being elated about what I was about to attempt: hiking the entire Appalachian Trail.

Even though I probably should have focused my financial resources in the months before I left for the AT more on food and logistics for the hike than on hanging out with my buddies, time spent with people who inspire me to be better was worth way more than any bottom line of a trip budget. (And, truthfully, REI, North Face, Dick's Sporting Goods, and Sports Authority got plenty from me in the final weeks of preparing to hike the AT.) Besides, drinking a few beers while playing in a city league Skee-Ball tournament doesn't cost *that* much money.

❖ ❖ ❖

I left Denver and arrived at Atlanta's Hartfield-Jackson airport a day before I had arranged to have a shuttle pick me up at my hotel and take me to the Springer Mountain Trailhead to begin the AT. The night before my shuttle was to pick me up, I went shopping for my first week of provisions and then found a small Irish pub in an Atlanta suburb where I pulled up a seat at the bar. I ordered a Guinness and some dinner, and it was there that a little bit of anxiety finally hit me. *What the hell am I doing?* I thought to myself.

Although I was excited for what was to come, it finally dawned on me that I really had no clue what I was doing. I had backpacking experience, but I hadn't ever hiked more than fifty miles at a time and I was about to attempt two thousand! I had bought the proper gear, and I had researched the trail enough to put me in a good frame of mind to start my first thru-hike. I had packed and repacked my stuff to find the optimal set of equipment (or at least what I thought was optimal) for a two-thousand-mile hike. But in spite of all this, it was there at that small Irish pub in Atlanta that a wave of emotions came over my whole body. It was there that I finally admitted to myself that I was little scared about what was to come over the next few months.

Back at the hotel that evening, I repacked my bag a few more times and ultimately decided to mail a few items forward as I didn't have enough room in my pack for all the food I had just bought at the grocery store on that first night in Georgia. This would be the first of a handful of times I would write *Dustin Waite, AT Hiker, General Delivery* on a USPS flat-rate box holding a random assortment of perishable items that I would later pick up in another town. The next morning, I handed over the package to the hotel manager who agreed to ship it for me, and I waited in the lobby for my shuttle. Although there were plenty of concerns I could have let bother me in those final hours prior to beginning my thru-hike—like the fact that I hadn't yet received any confirmation of whether my Obamacare application had been approved—I chose confidence instead.

February 26, 2014, was the day I began hiking the Appalachian Trail. I had all the gear, food, and adrenaline I needed. What could possibly go wrong?

CHAPTER 22

Appalachian Trail 2014
123 Days; 1,546 Miles

Here's what went wrong.

The provenance of Lyme disease in its bacterial form dates back millions of years. It was misdiagnosed as cases of rheumatoid arthritis as early as the 1970s, primarily in children who lived near and played in wooded areas. Most of these cases included children reporting a tick bite in an area of their body that also exhibited a rash that seemed to appear around the same time as the arthritis. By the 1980s, researchers made the connection between the disease and the patients' tick bites and identified the small deer tick as the common vector. Doctors began calling the disease "Lyme" (*not* Lymes) due to the many cases reported with a close proximity to the town of Lyme, Connecticut.

Ticks are classified as arachnids and are a close relative to spiders. A tick's legs are slightly curved and look like those tiny plastic parts on a piece of Velcro; this is their primary method of locomotion. If someone is in an area that has ticks, it's almost impossible to avoid those legs from wrapping around the fibers of a piece of clothing or a strand of body hair. Once attached, a tick will crawl around until it finds a place to sink its head below the skin's surface layer.

After finding its spot, the tick will begin to consume the host's blood and expose potentially infected fluids to the host's system, *but not always*. Near the area of the bite, a small rash can begin to form, *but not always*. This rash is commonly known to have a distinct bullseye appearance with a red dot in the middle of a larger ring, *but not always*. Sometimes the rash will remain in one area of the body, *but not always*. Sometimes the rash will spread to form other rashes around the body, even if the patient was not bitten in those areas, *but not always*. Headaches and fevers may be common within a week or two of being infected, *but not always*. Elevated levels of fatigue can set in, causing the infected person to drastically cut down their physical activity, *but not always*. If left untreated for a long period of time, the disease can cause muscle aches, cramps, and temporary arthritis, and some cases have shown that Lyme can hide within new blood and skin cells even after administering antibiotics, *but not always*. In rare but severe cases, the disease can spread to the heart, causing an irregular heartbeat, arrhythmia, and total heart block, *but not always*. (Total heart block occurs when the electrical signal from the atria, or upper chambers, of the heart is improperly sent to the ventricles, or lower chambers.) If treated properly, Lyme disease may leave the body completely, *but not always*. If left untreated, or if the case becomes severe very quickly, it can be fatal as the heart may cease to function due to operating at such a decreased level of efficiency, *but not always*.

The theme of this lesson is that depending on the person, the situation, the geographic area, the specific tick, or any number of other reasons, Lyme disease can affect an individual in innumerable case-specific ways. So, regardless of what your Aunt Mavis says happened to your Uncle Marty when he got bit by a tick last autumn, Lyme disease will affect every patient differently.

❖ ❖ ❖

I arrived at Berkshire Medical Center in the afternoon of August 4, 2014, only eighteen days after a letter dated July 17, 2014 was delivered to my Iowa address that stated I had health insurance with full coverage. I was diagnosed with third-degree, or total, heart block. I learned that a third-degree heart block meant that with *every* beat, the upper and lower chambers of my heart were not communicating and, like an engine with worn-out spark plugs, it had been misfiring for quite some time—except this would cost much more than a few dollars to fix. A blood test confirmed the presence of three forms of Lyme antibodies in my system, and thus the official medical diagnosis for my condition was Lyme Carditis.

But let me back up a bit.

❖ ❖ ❖

While still on the trail and before being admitted to the hospital, Mourning Dove and I reached a road crossing near the town of Lee, Massachusetts, that was only about a tenth of a mile away from the Berkshire Lakeside Lodge. I had every intention of getting a room there, but upon learning they were all booked for the evening I called a cab to take us into Lee where a Super 8 hotel became our resting place for the night. While in Lee, I stopped by the nearby outlet mall and actually bought new insoles, socks, and Merrell hiking boots because I thought the new gear might help encourage me to continue my AT journey. Instead, I became the proud owner of $150 in hiking apparel that would never see one step on the Appalachian Trail.

The next morning, I decided to seek medical help and saw on Google Maps that there was a doctor's office across the street from the Super 8; however, the waypoint wasn't updated and no office existed at that location. There was another doctor's office a few miles down the road, which at least gave me the opportunity to break in my new boots. Forty minutes after leaving my hotel room, I walked into the local family medical practice just as they unlocked their doors for the day.

To my dismay, they informed me they were all booked up and couldn't see me, even though the waiting room was empty. After pleading with them to reconsider because my heart was not feeling right, and telling them that I had insurance, they reluctantly said I could quickly see a nurse. Unfortunately, the nurse insisted that she was not going to provide any medical advice except to recommend that I find another doctor or urgent-care facility. The closest facility was a one-hour bus ride away, and to get to the bus stop I had to walk two miles back to the hotel. Despite knowing that I didn't have a car and that I had literally walked out of the woods to this doctor's office, the nurse just printed me out a bus schedule and simply said, "Good luck."

Let me break this down: an out-of-state patient walked into an empty doctor's office with complaints of heart problems and shortness of breath, and the nurse's only advice was to give the patient a bus schedule and tell him to leave the office, walk two miles, and take a bus to another town almost an hour away. Let's just say I definitely gave them a bad Yelp review.

When I returned to the hotel, I was so displeased with what had just happened at the doctor's office that I almost decided to head back to the trail. Thankfully, after discussing it with Mourning Dove, we decided to keep the hotel room for another night and take the bus to Pittsfield, Massachusetts, where the 510 Medical Walk-In facility was located. When we arrived there the next day, I was a bit leery of what they might say due to my last experience, but Jaimie, the physician's assistant, immediately showed great concern for my situation.

Although I had never seen a bullseye rash anywhere on my body, I was starting to exhibit other red rashes on my chest as well as a few small ones on my legs, and my right foot was swollen and numb. Jaimie asked if she could bring in Ashley, a physician's assistant student, to observe what Jaimie described as a classic case of "multiple bullseye syndrome" (even though the rashes didn't look like bullseyes) that was consistent with Lyme. The best thing that Jaimie did was listen as I described what I had been feeling during the previous few weeks.

Although Jaimie's bedside manner was excellent, I remained worried about my heart because that was the *real* reason why I sought out medical attention. (I likely would've kept hiking if I had only been having sore joints and muscles.) Showing what I thought was extreme humbleness for a medical professional, Jaimie admitted that she didn't have much experience in cardiac issues resulting from Lyme and brought in Bruce, another physician's assistant. After a few short seconds of listening to my heart he knew something was wrong. Bruce ordered the EKG, and Doctor Fribush (the head doctor at the facility) confirmed everyone's suspicions that my heart was broken. They called the emergency room of the local hospital (Berkshire Medical Center) and informed them that I would be arriving soon. That phone call marked the moment when I finally accepted that I would not be hiking the AT again anytime soon.

Although I was sad that my journey was coming to an end, I was actually relieved to hear this news—not because my heart was broken or because I wouldn't be hiking any further, but because this diagnosis gave me a concrete reason to explain what I had been feeling over the past few weeks. I think I would have gone insane if they had said, "Nope, everything seems fine to us." Instead, I felt validated in my belief that if this disease hadn't consumed my heart, I would've been able to continue my trek. *It wasn't my fault that I wasn't going to finish the AT.*

They performed another EKG at the hospital, the readout of which spurred my immediate admittance to a room where a barrage of wires were connected from my body to various machines as other specialists entered and exited the room. Although I'd heard from others on the trail that Lyme disease can affect your heart, until that very moment I didn't realize the full extent to which it could. My cardiologist at the hospital was the first one to utter the phrases "Lyme carditis" and "total heart block." Hearing those words made the situation a little more real for me; there was a severe problem with my heart.

The (many) other doctors on the scene quickly told me that when a patient's heart exhibits a total heart block the patient is usually barely able to stand and often passes out because of the lack of heart function, let alone able to hike miles through the woods and over mountains. More times than not, heart block patients are elderly or overweight and need surgery to implant a pacemaker. Even though I was young and healthy, according to my doctors it was a very strong possibility that I would need a pacemaker. I couldn't believe what I was hearing.

They gave me forty-eight hours until they would ultimately decide if they needed to put me into surgery and install the device. The urgency of this potential outcome heightened my sense of the seriousness of the situation, even though having a pacemaker is not necessarily that bad. A lot of people have them put in for non-life-threatening reasons and, contrary to what Hollywood movies might suggest, if a person's pacemaker stops working, they don't immediately die. However, to most people, myself included, "pacemaker" is a buzz word that definitely catches your attention, especially when, as one of my doctors said, "You are a young, healthy, very attractive thirty-year-old." (Her words, not mine. Thanks, doc.) Thankfully, within the forty-eight-hour period, the intravenous antibiotics did their job of killing the Lyme bacteria and my heart

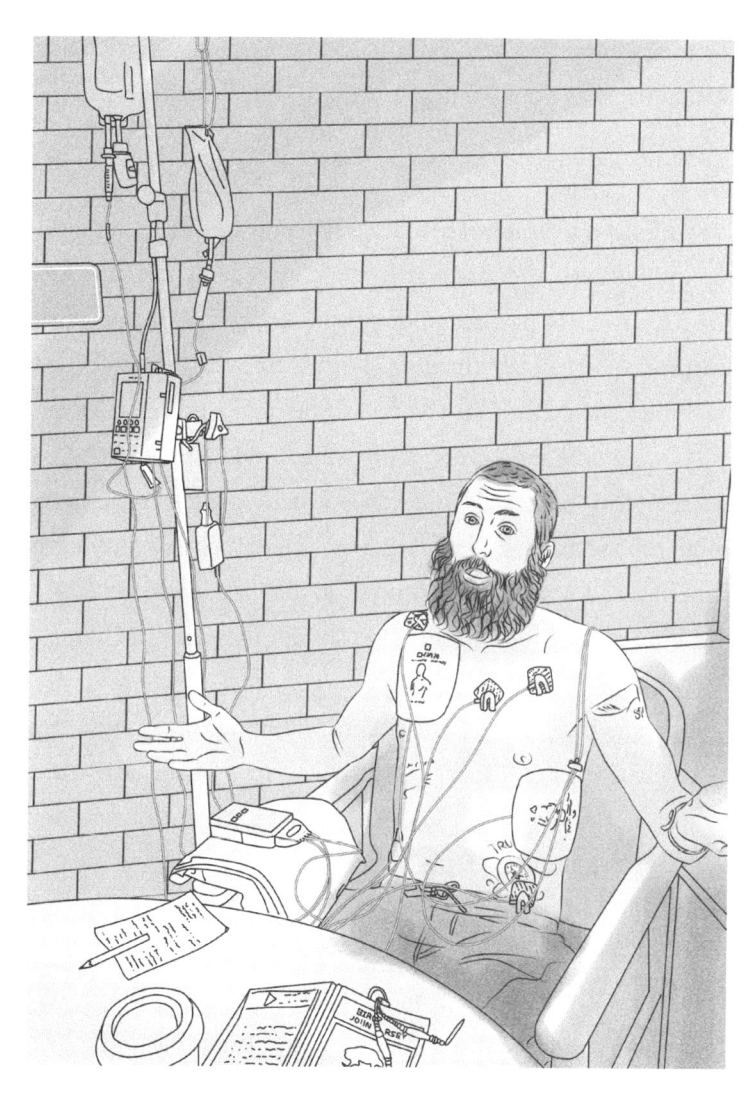

My heart wasn't working, but at least my beard was pretty epic.

telemetry monitors responded such that the electrical block was, albeit slowly, beginning to show signs of recovery.

❖ ❖ ❖

Describing my time spent in the hospital would be like depicting the excitement of watching an episode of VH1's *Where Are They Now?* if past appraisers from *Antiques Roadshow* were featured—not exactly thrilling. For nine days, I was confined to the telemetry unit on the fourth floor of Berkshire Medical Center. The only other reference I could call upon regarding the term "telemetry" was while watching a television show about robotic automation. Unlike that giant robot arm, though, I merely had a small heart monitor that was connected to a machine twenty-four hours a day (except for when the battery needed to be changed).

The small devices connected to my body transmitted my heart's readings to a computer that was constantly garrisoned by a troop of nurses in the central nurse station that was situated in the middle of the hospital floor. The nurses would record my vital signs two or three times each day and run an EKG every morning. Breakfast would come around eight, lunch between noon and one, and dinner always before six. Every morning, when the doctors would grace me with their presence, I endured the seemingly eternal verdict of "we'll see what happens tomorrow." That was my routine for the duration of my stay. To overcome the monotony of this schedule I made a habit of walking around and talking with nurses and other visitors who were there to see family members, and even enjoyed the company of an emotional support dog that visited the floor one day.

Thankfully, Mourning Dove changed her plans for a few days to help get my belongings from the hotel to the hospital. She even stayed with me in the hospital room for a night, but after we knew my condition was stable and I wasn't going to die, she decided it was time to continue her journey. I don't have many regrets in life, but I do wish I had said "thank you" more times to express my gratitude for all she did in the weeks leading up to my stay in the hospital. Just having someone by my side during that challenging time was so appreciated, and I am forever grateful for her help and support.

Although my shortness of breath and heart palpitations did show signs of improvement shortly after starting the intravenous antibiotics, they didn't disappear completely. The third-degree heart block remained until the fifth day of my stay when positive news came pouring in from the nurse's alcove. I had officially entered the realm of, wait for it… *second-degree* heart block. Carpe diem! Essentially, my heart was still broken but not *as* broken. Nonetheless, this was good news and it gave the doctors (and me) hope that everything was healing as expected. Though episodic palpitations and shortness of breath continued, my body was overall feeling better. *I think I might be able to do it again, coach.*

By the eighth day, my hospital routine was almost automatic. I had even curried favor with the inner circle of nurses and convinced them to reserve bottles of real Coca-Cola for me from the cafeteria, as opposed to that horrible caffeine-free alternative soda. It turns out another one of the rarities that my case presented was that, despite the Lyme, the underlying condition of my heart was actually pretty strong. My heart was healthy; it just had faulty wiring.

After years of running, playing basketball, and hiking thousands of miles through the woods, I had a very low resting heart rate. In fact, it was so low that for three consecutive evenings the nighttime nurses burst into my room to make sure I was alive because my heart monitor was showing readouts of extreme bradycardia. When I would fall asleep, my heart rate would drop into the twenties—which is dangerously low (sixty is the normal rate for healthy adults)—but that's just how my body was recovering from the Lyme. My heart was trying to reach a healthy equilibrium and slowing down to a crawl at night was the path it was taking. It definitely jars the senses when a stranger wakes you up in the middle of the night and abruptly says, "Mr. Waite, are you awake? Get the defibrillator!" The upside was that my doctors agreed I could begin consuming a *little* caffeine, which felt like a big win.

❊ ❊ ❊

My mother and sister kindly drove out from Iowa to provide me company and a much-needed change of clothes. Despite having lived in the woods for four months on the AT, I was starting to get a bit ripe even for my taste. I was very grateful to have family nearby and their visit was timed perfectly as we all received the good news that I would soon be discharged. Although my heart was still in second-degree heart block, the small yet consistent improvements that my monitors showed over a three-day period were enough to convince the doctors that I would be okay to leave and continue my antibiotics orally instead of by IV. My sigh of relief at the sound of this news was barely audible as I knew I would not be returning to the AT then, and maybe never.

Another reason for my lack of fanfare was because I was being discharged with a big unanswered question: Would my broken heart fully recover? The doctors hoped that because I was a healthy individual my heart would continue to heal itself. So instead of leaving with a finite answer, I was released knowing there was still a long uncertain road ahead. One thing was sure though: the road began with a sixteen-hour car ride back to Cedar Rapids, Iowa. Without a doubt, this was the most frustrating day of my AT journey.

Ten states and 1,546 miles down. Four states and 643 miles to go. *Still.*

Eternal

Part II

CHAPTER 23

Iowa 2015

After I was released from Pittsfield Medical Center and taken back to Iowa, it soon dawned on me that I was thirty years old and living in my mother's basement. Part of the reason for this arrangement was that my doctors encouraged me to not be alone for long periods of time as we continued to monitor the pumping function of my heart, and another part was that I hadn't worked in almost a year and was lacking the necessary credentials for a property management company to see me as a viable tenant. Returning to Iowa after my AT hike was not part of my plan, but after my stay in the hospital it was clear that my options were limited.

However, one positive constant in my life was Erica. She was one of the first people I met in college because she was on campus early for work study and I was there for football. Back then, we took long walks along the newly finished brick pedestrian mall through campus and, almost like a Ouija board, both of us seemed to guide the other to the same spot after each stroll: the bench next to a small pool of water known as Ink Pond.

After receiving a Facebook message from Erica while still on the AT—when I was at the Isabella Freedman Jewish Retreat

Center reading *The Old Man and the Sea* and contemplating what I would do with my life if my heart issues proved to be serious—we began exchanging long, catching-up messages. Soon, our conversations progressed to shorter daily messages that included details like what she'd eaten for breakfast. It was nice.

By the time I was messaging her from my mom's basement toward the end of 2014, I had known Erica for twelve years, and for almost every one of those twelve years either she or I had been in some sort of relationship with another person. So, after being confined to the fourth floor of a hospital and then living in my mom's basement, there was no doubt in my mind that I needed to make the efforts necessary to see if there was something more between Erica and me. It was all I had. Unfortunately, there was one small obstacle: she was living in Sri Lanka. I was confident, though, that after my months of reflection while in the woods, *hopefully* making myself a better person, I finally had the tools to make this relationship work.

❖ ❖ ❖

After my return to Iowa from the hospital in Massachusetts, I began working as a server at a new local brewery. I was hired with the understanding that my position would evolve into a more involved one, including building the distribution of the brand. But because that position hadn't been developed yet, I spent my time taking orders and writing a few blog passages that would ultimately make it into this book.

My relationship with Erica truly began when she returned home over New Years to visit family and I traveled to

Milwaukee to be with her. Once she returned to Sri Lanka after the holiday, the glue between us was composed of daily Whatsapp conversations and weekly Skype chats that could last for hours. Although there were eight thousand miles between us, and Sri Lanka's time zones were separated by half hours (which was tricky when scheduling communications because our time difference was ten and a half hours), I loved her, and the effort was absolutely worth it.

In June of 2015, Erica returned to the states from Sri Lanka to the same emotions that had I possessed since the moment we reconnected almost a year before. I spent time with her family and she did the same with mine. It was wonderful. We traveled back to our alma mater in Mount Vernon, Iowa, and walked around the campus. We even went back to the old bench next to Ink Pond. Sitting with Erica on that bench again was a moment that I never thought could be possible. After so much time had passed, I had almost entirely written off the possibility of this ever happening. As we were sitting on that bench looking over Ink Pond, together at last, I almost couldn't believe that I had been given a second chance to date Erica. It turned out this visit was even more special because we had decided that when she returned to her job in Sri Lanka, I was going with her.

Life was good.

❖ ❖ ❖

Even though I truly believe I was in love with Erica, I was still new to love. Erica was only the second person to whom I ever said and meant the words "I love you." (I had said it a third time while I was living in Colorado, to a woman named Tiffany, but that was more of a practice run than anything.) When Erica and I were planning my trip to Sri Lanka, I should have just quit my job and moved there permanently to be with her. That may sound extreme, but I knew that one of the things preventing our love from reaching the next level was the physical distance between us. Although I know people who have successfully navigated long-distance relationships, those examples had foundations before the separation and even *they* say they wouldn't wish that on anyone; and after my previous experiences with long-distance relationships, I wouldn't either.

But, instead of moving to Sri Lanka, I decided to only visit for ten days so I could return to my job where my title had evolved into Head of Sales and Distribution for the entire brewery. My position had grown into helping build the brand of the brewery from almost the ground up and, given the number of sales I was closing, I was doing a damn good job and thoroughly enjoying it. Because Erica was unsure of how long she would continue to live in Sri Lanka, I thought it made sense to stay in Iowa and have an established position in place for when she returned. In hindsight, it's clear the distance was getting to me and had ultimately become too much. Although we can never be sure of the "what ifs," I think moving to Sri Lanka would have helped Erica and I stay together.

The second big mistake I made was that I opened my big stupid mouth. I need to give some context so as not to sound like a completely terrible person, but make no mistake, I am aware that what I said was awful.

While I was visiting Sri Lanka, Erica and I began drifting apart, and in retrospect I can see that it was definitely me who was drifting from her. Whether it was because the distance was getting to me or that I knew I wasn't moving to Sri Lanka (this was still a possibility at the time, but we hadn't had "the talk" yet) or whether it was because of something else, I don't know. What I do remember, though, is feeling uneasy in our first few days of the trip, like I was trapped in a corner, especially as Erica continued to ask, "What's wrong?"

I can't remember any of the details or specific things that took place in the first few days of the trip that led me to say what I did, but while wading in the pool of our resort near Mirissa Beach on the southern coast of Sri Lanka, I said these irrevocable words: "I don't know if I'm attracted to you like I thought I was."

I am a fucking asshole.

You can never take a comment like that back or, as I learned in the seventy-two hours following that moment, even explain what you meant in a way that can salvage the situation. To be clear, when I said that comment (and still to this day) it had nothing to do with physical attraction. Erica is, was, and always will be one of the most beautiful women I have ever known. However, after discussing this with family and friends, I now know that those words, no matter how they're said, will always be heard by the recipient as "I don't find you physically attractive."

Regardless of how strong willed a person is—Erica was one of the strongest—that is never good to hear. I apologized many times to her, and I explained that what I was trying to say was "There are a few things about my feelings for you that are on my mind."

There's no doubt in my mind that this comment was a wedge in the block of ice that our relationship became after that moment. Even after I apologized, and the wedge was removed, the ice continued to melt. Three days after the words were said, we were still traveling through beautiful parts of Sri Lanka and were staying at one of the many national parks in the country. We saw elephants, exotic birds, and even had the entire place to ourselves as we were the only people staying at the lodge within the reserve. Even though social media allowed me to show that we were having an enjoyable time, it was a sad cover for yet another time in my life that I had to learn from a mistake. I should've taken more time to think about my feelings for Erica and, more importantly, how to communicate them more effectively.

The final mistake I made with Erica (or, at least, the final one I'm going to explain) was that when I returned to Iowa from Sri Lanka, instead of doubling down on my efforts to maintain my communications with Erica, I became complacent. We continued our system of communicating: we talked via Whatsapp every day *or close to it*, and we Skyped at least once a week. However, it was the "or close to it" part that I let get out of hand and, ultimately, I never fully accepted how big of an impact that had on Erica.

I felt I was constantly messaging her and, in fact, it bothered me how my life was being affected by the increased amount of time I was spending on my phone. But she felt like it wasn't enough. Although one may take my side and agree that in addition to communicating, we also needed to have our own space, I have since concluded that didn't matter. If I loved her, then I should have shared my feelings regarding our communication schedule while concurrently supporting her needs as well. Although at the time I felt like I was giving her every second of my life outside of work, if she needed me to give her that, especially while she was alone in Sri Lanka, then that's what I should've done. But I didn't do that. Instead, I stood my ground in favor of *my* feelings and, as one may expect, the block of ice continued to melt. Our Skype chats turned into arguments, which in turn affected my efforts and desires to communicate further. Perhaps if I had just set aside my feelings and sent a few more messages each day that would have helped, but who knows.

Just as time gave me more perspective on my breakup with Megan, time once again allowed me to see that I just wasn't ready to be in that relationship with Erica. Once again, I made mistakes. Once again, I was wrong. We are all, with some exceptions, good people who sometimes get things wrong, but we can't let that keep us down. I've made *many* mistakes, and I will make many more. It's not a matter of if, it's a matter of when and, more importantly, how I respond when I do. It's clear that in order to be a better person, I have more work to do.

CHAPTER 24

Appalachian Trail 2016
Total on the AT:
134 Days; 1,726 Miles

As I stared out the window while approaching the tarmac at Albany International Airport, I knew I couldn't dillydally at the baggage claim for too long once we landed. Although it was a smaller airport than JFK or La Guardia, I had never been to Albany before, and I knew it would take me a while to complete everything I needed to do before nightfall. When I scheduled my flight out of the Santa Barbara Airport, I thought I had allowed enough time to make it to the L.L.Bean in Albany and still catch the bus that was heading east toward Pittsfield, Massachusetts. If I had miscalculated things, I'd be forced to delay my return to the AT one more day, which was simply not acceptable at that point.

I had just spent the summer of 2016 back in California, and after some hiking, thinking, worrying, planning, and a chance encounter with a childhood crush, all I wanted was to get back to the trail and finish the thing that was taken away from me two years before when my heart was broken. Although the possibility that my heart condition could act up again was very much a concern, I had placed those thoughts in the back of my mind. Finishing the entire Appalachian Trail may not have been a high priority for me when I began my hike in 2014, but it was clear that I needed to this time around in 2016. I wasn't about to go back home again without a photo of me next to that wooden sign.

❈ ❈ ❈

The oversized-baggage counter located near the pickup carousels in the airport is usually where I find my fourteen-year-old, external-frame backpack after a flight. It may look larger and less comfortable than some of the newer options, but after years of throwing that thing around my shoulders with anywhere from twenty-five to sixty pounds loaded onto it, I've become accustomed to knowing the most efficient way to move it around with little resistance. However, airline baggage handlers have not. This means that every time I place my loaded pack on the scale at the airport check-in counter and watch it carried away under the wavy black plastic flaps, my heart skips a beat knowing that when I pick it up at the end of my travels, it may not include everything with which it started. Regardless of how well the individual pieces are secured at the beginning of the trip, it's sure to have things out of place at the end. I've lost straps, had handles ripped off, and even had an entire tent disappear. (How can they lose a *tent?*) In fact, when I landed in Albany on August 1, 2016, if it had not been for one very lucky strap, I would've lost a $200 sleeping bag!

Backpackers are probably one of the few groups of people who feel comfortable unpacking every single thing inside their bag onto the airport floor just to inventory items and repack for the non-airline portion of the trip. For example, trekking poles are not exactly the most carry-on-friendly items, however, having them strapped to the outside of my external-frame pack isn't where I want them when I begin hiking. After commencing this airport ritual and accounting for everything, I found my way to the L.L.Bean outfitter to purchase isobutene fuel for my camping stove (another not-so-airline friendly item). Then, I hopped a few buses to Dalton, a town with an AT trailhead that was only a few miles from where my journey ended previously at Berkshire Medical Center in Pittsfield, Massachusetts.

After a planned evening with Thomas, a trail angel who allows hikers to stay on his property, I hit the trail running. Not literally of course, that would be a terrible idea, but I did begin hiking with a burst of energy that was almost equal to when I first started the AT on Springer Mountain in Georgia two years before. Except this time, I didn't get lost.

The weather was overcast and drizzly, and the trail was a bit muddy from rainfall in the previous days, but none of that concerned me. My pack was a bit heavy and my clothes got kind of wet, but I didn't mind. I was passed by other thru-hikers, but that didn't bother me one bit. Hell, even when I summited Mount Greylock, the tallest peak in Massachusetts, to discover there was absolutely no view because of the weather conditions, I didn't care. All that mattered to me was that I was back on the AT—just being there was something I wasn't sure would ever happen again because it was unclear if my heart would ever again be able to handle hiking hundreds of miles through the woods. The truth is, I still didn't know, but I was about to find out. I had decided that I didn't want to live the rest of my life resting on a crutch, blaming my heart condition for not achieving certain life goals. I didn't want to spend the rest of my life wondering where my physical capabilities ended or where my mental ability to take on new challenges began. I just wanted to act.

I didn't mind the bad weather conditions and in spite of my diminished physical capabilities, by the time my adrenaline subsided and I decided to call it quits for my first day back, I had logged just over twenty miles and put myself within a one-day hike of the Vermont border. I didn't mind that at all.

❊ ❊ ❊

Constructed in the early 1900s, the Long Trail is one of the oldest long-distance hiking trails in the United States. Its 272 miles provide a path for hikers to walk from the southern border of Vermont to the southern border of Canada. The AT shares almost 105 miles of trail with the Long Trail (mostly through the Green Mountains) and, upon diverging, the AT veers east toward Hanover, New Hampshire, while the Long Trail continues north. After spending the summer in Southern California, which was in a constant state of drought, Vermont in the early fall seemed to be the antithesis of that and was bursting at the seams with moisture like an overfilled waterbed. Although the state is nicknamed "Vermud," and I definitely

The fire tower on Stratton Mountain

encountered a plethora of muddy patches on the trail, one thing is certain: Vermont is beautiful. Saying that Vermont is "very green" is an understatement. If it were possible to imagine every shade of green in the world, as if Bob Ross had just painted a forest of happy trees, that would *maybe* begin to capture the lushness of what I experienced.

At the top of Stratton Mountain, which sits along a shared section of trail, hikers come across a plaque that explains the origins of the Long Trail:

> It was here, in 1909, that James Taylor conceived of the idea of a "Long Trail" extending from Massachusetts to Canada. Then, in 1921, after construction of

Taylor's Long Trail had begun, Benton MacKaye—Forester, Author, Philosopher—further expanded that concept into a footpath linking all the scenic ridges of the entire range—and the Appalachian Trail was born.

Although there were days when I wished Benton MacKaye had decided to skip a few of the ridges (not all of them are scenic), I'm glad his dream has provided many souls a path on which they can take a few days, months, or years and think up a few dreams of their own. At least, I hope that's what a few of us were doing out there.

❦ ❦ ❦

"Are you hurt or are you injured?"

This was a common question posed by my high school football coach and was meant to imply that a player could play if he was hurt, but not if he was injured. Essentially, if you're injured, medical attention is needed, but if you're merely hurt, you can play through the pain. It was this question I was asking myself after hiking almost sixty miles in my first three days back on the AT. More specifically, it was my knees asking the question.

I've had sore knees before, but what I was feeling after those first three days was the most excruciating knee pain I had ever experienced. It was clear that if I wanted to continue for another six hundred miles, I needed to alter my hiking strategy—which, until that point, had mostly been based on two cups of fresh ground coffee and the positive adrenaline that comes with knowing my job description was "enjoying nature."

My first three days back on the AT mostly consisted of waking up to beautiful sunrises (especially the one visible between the mountain clearing at Kid Gore Shelter) and retraining myself to ask my fellow hikers for their trail names, but it was also obvious that I needed to pay more attention to how my body was feeling each day. A twenty-mile day meant nothing if I didn't take the time to enjoy the scenery, but due to rocky and muddy descents my knee pain was becoming my primary focus.

I was confident that I was merely hurt, not injured, but just in case I decided to take a zero-day in the town of Manchester Center, Vermont, to ice and rest my legs (and consume a hefty dose of ibuprofen). I found myself at the Green Mountain House Hiker Hostel—one of the best hostels along the trail—which is run by a lovely gentleman named Jeff. He and his wife operate Green Mountain House as a retirement project and primarily reside in Ohio. Because of climate differences between Maine and Georgia, both northbound and southbound hikers come through Manchester Center around the same season, so Jeff only operates his hostel for three months each year. Jeff told me that he enjoys it very much and said, "There are no zero-days in the hiker hostel business along the AT." For that, I was very grateful.

❈ ❈ ❈

While I was still dealing with my heart recovery back in Iowa, I agreed to serve as the officiant for a friend's wedding that was going to take place on September 17, 2016. I knew that in order to complete the trail with enough time to get back home and prepare, I had to apply some *Moneyball*-style calculations to my mileages each day. I crunched the numbers: I began hiking in western Massachusetts on the first of August, which gave me approximately six weeks to walk over six hundred miles to northern Maine and arrive back in Iowa with at least a few days to plan a wedding. (Okay, all I really needed to do was prepare a few remarks and make sure that no extended relatives interrupted the ceremony or got too drunk, but it was still an important role.)

At first, I hit my original goal of fifteen miles per day, but since I needed to increase my mileage because of my days off recovering from the knee pain, finishing the trail in time for the wedding wasn't going to be a cakewalk. My schedule was further complicated by my plans to meet up with my friends Kevin and Sarah in Rhode Island. While I knew these were definitely first-world problems, they were nonetheless important details that were churning in the back of my mind and needed to be factored into my planning.

Most hikers have at least some sort of schedule in mind to accommodate other obligations ranging from financial to familial, from occupational to social, and everything in between. While on the AT, I met people who had just finished high school, just retired, just lost a job, just bought a house, just got married, just had a kid, just got a new job, and nearly every other life scenario one could imagine. There will *always* be complicated logistics that can cause someone to not embark on a journey, so it really just comes down to this: How badly do you want to do it?

To say that I had not conceived of some outline of a plan prior to my recovery time at the Green Mountain House would be misleading, but while I was there, I took a hard look at a calendar and flight schedules, and at what my body was telling me about my health. I still wanted to maintain "enjoying nature" as my first priority while on the trail, but I also knew I had to find a good balance between enjoying nature and the necessary logistics involved with walking through it.

❋ ❋ ❋

Right before I was admitted into the hospital in 2014, I had met an older gentleman who went by the trail name Slow-Runner. After he asked me what I thought the "purpose of the trail" was, I responded in very vague terms (because I thought it was a very vague question) that the trail was "a journey" and that it was "a different journey for everyone." I thought this was a good response, but as soon as I was done speaking Slow-Runner spun around to confront me with body language that radiated with disapproval. "It's not a journey, it's an endurance challenge!" he insisted. Slow-Runner then informed me of what I was doing wrong with my hike and showed me his calendar with the mileages he planned to achieve each day.

**Drying out the gear at Green Mountain
House before hitting the trail**

I guess in some ways his description of the trail being an "endurance challenge" was correct, but I would respectfully disagree with that being an all-encompassing portrayal of hiking in the woods. In fact, I think it's downright ridiculous. However, I will withhold further judgment and say I hope Slow-Runner stayed healthy, made his mileage goals, and completed *his* journey.

❖ ❖ ❖

As I was sitting in the living room of the Green Mountain House with bags of ice on my knees, I realized that I needed to apply a few of Slow-Runner's tips after all. If I didn't finish the trail this time around, I wasn't sure if I'd have the energy for a third trip to the East Coast. A third attempt would mean cashing in on time and resources that I knew could be devoted to other trips and life experiences, so if there was ever a logical time for me to reach Mount Katahdin, it was now. I *had* to finish the trail.

After two nights of rest at the Green Mountain House (and ingesting more than the recommended dose of ibuprofen), my knees were feeling better—not perfect, but a far cry from the feeling of pins and needles being shoved into the bottom of my knee caps that I had been experiencing with every step prior. I gathered the confidence to pack up five days of food and hit the trail again. I also held in mind a tentative hiking schedule to get me to the top of Mount Katahdin with a few days to spare before the wedding. I owe the bride, Laura, an award for appearing to be completely chill about the whole thing. When I informed her that I "*should* be back in time," I was surprised the phone didn't open up like in a cartoon with a giant hand to slap me in the face.

❦ ❦ ❦

After a few colder evenings in the woods, including one at a makeshift shanty town of tents when a bunch of hikers stayed at the former Qu's Whistle Stop restaurant, I hitched into the nearby town of Rutland to a hostel and restaurant called the Yellow Deli, which is owned and operated by a religious group known as the Twelve Tribes. There are many religion-affiliated groups that help hikers along the trail, and many of them do just that—help. Although some hikers may have dissimilar experiences, I never felt pressured by any group that was offering help along my journey to agree with or join any religion. In fact, the kindness shown by these groups usually made me feel more compelled to spend time discussing the members' beliefs, even if I didn't agree with some of the major tenets.

Although all the bunkbeds were reserved at the Yellow Deli for that night, I was reassured over the phone that there was space available on a covered back porch for me to roll out my sleeping bag. Even though I'd rather sleep in the mountains most nights, after a few nights of living in the wilderness, a shower, a nice meal, and some good company was the best medicine to replenish my waning wanderlust. However, when I arrived at the hostel the back porch wasn't quite as covered as advertised. Although a tarp hung from the wooden rafters surrounding the porch, it definitely didn't protect the entire wooden platform. The staff at the Yellow Deli felt terrible that they didn't have enough beds for all of us, but I was grateful to just be surrounded by good people. As the rest of the hikers retired to their beds for the evening, the four of us outside on the porch set up our sleeping bags and hoped for the best.

At about four in the morning, I felt the first drops of rain. The tarp did what it could to divert the precipitation away from our bags, but soon the storm hit with a fury and those first drops of rain were nothing compared to the drainage that began flowing off the tarp toward my sleeping bag (and the rest of my gear). There were about fifteen feet between me and the door to the communal area of the hostel; however, that was fifteen feet of uncovered patio that I would need to traverse with my gear through the storm. As the water crept closer and threatened to completely saturate everything I owned, I quickly unzipped my sleeping bag, rolled out the right side, and, in one big swoop, picked up everything I had and darted for the door. Miraculously, I didn't drop a single item, not even a sock, as I entered the dry hostel.

As I sat and watched my sleeping bag twirl around in the hostel's dryer in the early morning hours, I thought it was humorous that even when staying in town I had to scramble to keep myself dry. I suppose it could have been the trail's spiritual way of telling me to stop slacking and get back to hiking, and I was glad to accept whatever life lessons the trail threw my way.

After my sleeping bag was dry, I packed up and left the Yellow Deli to catch a bus back to a lodge that was aptly named the Inn at Long Trail. With just over forty miles remaining in Vermont, I figured a nice quiet breakfast of bacon and eggs at the Inn was my way of reminding the trail that there are no rules to this whole thing. Mount Katahdin isn't going anywhere. *Hike your own hike.*

❖ ❖ ❖

Hiking the final twenty-five miles into Hanover, New Hampshire, was miserable. Temperatures reached nearly one hundred degrees and because of a lot of trail magic, my pack was heavy with enough food for almost three days when I had expected it to be nearly empty as I walked into town. However, if one of my major concerns was that nice people kept giving me food, I figured my life was okay.

Mile marker just before hitching into Rutland for a soggy evening

The final trail angel along that stretch was a woman who owned a house in West Hartford right on the trail, and she only had one rule: if you stay at her bunkhouse you must jump off the West Hartford Bridge into the White River. After enduring the heat and a stretch of trail that was more exposed to the sun's blinding rays than others (because it contained fields of prairie grasses rather than tall trees), I was most compliant to the one and only rule.

Some may look at the lifestyle of living in the woods and call those people "poor" or "homeless." But after hiking in sweltering heat and humidity, and then feeling the cool water of a flowing river rush over my body as I splashed down from twenty feet above, this is one experience I'll be poor and homeless for any day of the week.

Although I wasn't even two weeks into my second round of hiking the AT, when I reached Hanover, I was going to take a little break. My friends from California, Kevin and Sarah, were bringing their kids to a beach house in Narragansett, Rhode Island, and that was all the reason I needed to rent a car and spend a few days at the ocean with good friends and some Del's lemonade.

Twelve states and 1,726 miles down. Two states and 463 miles to go.

CHAPTER 25

Iowa 2015

My relationship with Erica consumed most of my energy for the first part of 2015. The year was full of other things, too, such as multiple echocardiograms, EKGs, and Holter monitors as my heart, although improving, continued to exhibit signs of defect like erratic palpitations and spontaneous rapid beating, which scared me every time they happened. As for work, I continued to grow the distribution of the brewery. Just as I devoted more time to museum projects in Maui after my breakup with Megan, once Erica and I went our separate ways I put my energy toward developing my position with the brewery into something I could be proud of, and I was. We grew from ten locations to over fifty, and we made some waves in the beer community in eastern Iowa—when your product starts replacing Budweiser and Miller Lite in a few local bars in the Midwest, people start to notice.

Because my degree from Cornell College says "Geology," to make a sustainable living selling beer I once again had to reinvent myself, and I really enjoyed doing so. Although it may sound counterproductive for a brewery sales manager, I used my role to advocate for more responsible drinking habits. (After all, most alcohol companies recognize that responsible drinking is key to long-term growth because consumers need to be alive to buy their products.)

Except for a handful of times, I didn't drink much alcohol until college. When I say a handful, I mean like the time when I was around six years old and I chugged a glass of what I thought was grape juice. After swallowing the last drop, I saw a look of horror on my mother's face that can only manifest when a mother watches her first grader slam a glass of wine. (So, technically, it *was* grape juice.)

Beginning in college, drinking played a major role in my social life, but in the years since graduating it had become clear that I should reduce my habit a bit. There are many positive experiences in my life that involved sharing a pint in a responsible manner (like when I met up with Marshall in Gettysburg), but there had also been plenty of moments where alcohol proved detrimental (doing donuts in a parking lot across the street from a police station comes to mind). Ironically, selling mass quantities of beer as the Head of Distribution for a brewery made me more conscious of a desire to reduce my alcohol intake.

❖ ❖ ❖

With any residual energy I had left after breaking up with Erica and working at the brewery, I dove headfirst into expanding my working knowledge of small, four-stroke combustion engines. Shortly after returning to Iowa, I found a 1979 Honda CM400T on Craigslist and purchased it from a guy named

Wes in a CVS parking lot. I had completed various maintenance tasks on previous motorcycles that I had owned, but on this bike, I finally cracked open the carburetors and began to work on their jumbled mess of tiny pieces, each of which could seemingly cause the entire bike to choke up and die at any moment.

As my knowledge about carburetors grew, so did my confidence in just about everything else that was going on in my life. However, unlike in my relationships, the bike never left after I made a mistake while working on it. When I screwed up in my relationships, the women never stuck around to see what I learned or how I changed. With the motorcycle, however, I could make a mistake, watch a YouTube video, fix the error, and show the bike what I learned. (It was like having another chance to sleep with the woman to whom I lost my virginity my freshman year at college and showing her how much better of a lover I had become.)

It was toward the end of 2015, after I had rebuilt both front and back brakes and completed multiple carburetor rebuilds (a few of which were done just to see what certain adjustments would do for engine efficiency) so I could embark on a long test ride to my cousin's wedding in Dubuque, Iowa, when I discovered that a circlip that holds the rear sprocket on the wheel hub can snap off, causing the sprocket, chain, and tire to fall off. Translation: my tire fell off while going sixty-five miles per hour on a motorcycle. I later discovered this was likely due to a problem with the alignment. Thankfully, when the tire fell off it got caught in the chain, and that allowed it to at least stay within the rear swingarm of the frame. I kept the bike upright during the initial wobble, and I was able to slow down to a speed at which I could control my skid to a stop and finally get my feet down to stabilize it, so the body of the bike never touched the ground.

Much like my learning curve with communicating with women, I now know to check the alignment before riding a motorcycle for a lengthy distance. However, continuing to learn from my mistakes doesn't guarantee that things will always be better in the future. (Like during my junior year of college when I actually *did* have another chance to sleep with the woman to whom I lost my virginity, but I wasn't any better of a lover the second time around.) I am constantly learning, and I'm okay with that.

❦ ❦ ❦

By September 2015, although I had moved out of my mom's basement, I had merely moved into my sister's basement, which didn't even have a working sink in the bathroom. I had dated a beautiful woman from my past who I previously thought was unattainable, only to watch that fade away. I had bought a thirty-six-year-old motorcycle that was constantly disassembled and not operating. I had developed a good group of friends and business networks in eastern Iowa through my efforts with the brewery, but I never felt like that job was going to sustain itself over the long term. This objective view of my 2015 is probably like how many other people might describe any year of their lives: full of highs, full of lows, full of lessons, and full of new goals. But, in the end, there was still work to be done to be the person I wanted to be.

I had hiked over fifteen hundred miles through the woods, and even though inspirational books might suggest that such big adventures will produce a definitive life lesson with which to move forward, unfortunately, at least for me, my first fifteen hundred miles of hiking the AT hadn't quite done that. I was living in my sister's basement with a broken bathroom sink. Where's the definitive life lesson in that?

❅ ❅ ❅

The question I was asked most frequently during my recovery time in Iowa was "So, are you gonna go back and finish the AT?" By the end of 2015, I still hadn't planned to return to the trail. As for a definitive life lesson, well, I learned that I needed to learn more. I needed to continue to manage my expectations. I needed to continue to set goals. I needed to continue to strive for the improbable, but I also needed to remember that some life-changing epiphany might not happen while achieving those goals.

Perhaps my mindset was different when I hiked the trail in 2014, but my mind in 2015 was coping with the fact that although I acquired great life experience during my months of hiking the AT, it didn't pay the rent. With the future of my heart condition still unknown, and no plans for returning to the trail soon, I set my expectations on what I could control: increasing the distribution of the brewery, finding a new rear swingarm for my motorcycle, and building a bathroom sink for my sister's basement. Essentially, I did what many people strive for every day—even if they didn't just hike up a mountain—which is to be happy with the positive things in my life. Although my breakup with Erica was difficult, I learned to redirect my efforts toward the things I could control, rather than focusing on those that I couldn't.

CHAPTER 26

Appalachian Trail 2016
148 Days; 1,890 Miles

The city of Münster is located in the northwestern part of Germany and has a colorful past. It is where the Treaty of Westphalia was signed in 1648 to end the Thirty Years' War. This series of wars escalated after Roman Emperor Ferdinand II tried to forcefully impose Catholicism on his domains, which angered the Protestants, and others alike, and started one of the most disastrous times in European history. The subsequent famine, disease, disrupted economies, and relocation of inhabitants caused drastic changes in people's livelihoods; pregnancies were likely postponed and families torn apart. It's amazing that even fifty percent of the population made it through this grim time.

Almost three hundred years later, the Bishop of Münster spoke out against World War II, which resulted in the city being heavily fortified by the Nazis. In fact, visitors today can still visit one of five large barracks in the city that housed the Sixth Military District of the German Army. As part of a major Allied campaign to destroy Nazi oil reserves, the city was massively bombed on October 25, 1944, almost destroying it entirely.

In the decades that followed after the war, Münster began to rebuild. As postwar construction efforts helped to bring it into the modern world, families began to move back into the area and the population began to recover. Secondary schools and universities helped drive students to the area and the city now has a population of around 300,000—which is amazing considering its devastating past. Clearly the people who live there now have many historical reasons to embrace life for all it can offer. Perhaps this rocky past in Münster's history is why, when I woke up in the Trapper John Shelter outside of Hanover, New Hampshire, the woman in the sleeping bag next to mine was a sixty-four-year-old woman named Red Tortoise who was a resident of Münster, Germany. She was maybe five feet tall and probably didn't weigh more than a hundred pounds. Yet at sixty-four years of age, this inspiring woman was hiking the entire Appalachian Trail.

Whatever sequence of historical events led to my chance meeting with Red Tortoise in the middle of the woods, I am very grateful the universe made it possible. Although she moved a little slower, she had hiked everything that I had up until that point. On the morning we woke up in the same shelter, we shared a few stories from the trail, and she told me about Münster and her life back home. She was trying to finish the trail before her six-month visa expired, which would be a great goal for anyone, but especially for someone who was *twice* my age. I also introduced her to Pop-Tarts, a staple trail food especially when all you have is a gas station at which to resupply. When I said they were "breakfast food," Red Tortoise's response was simply to say, "Breakfast is very different in America."

❦ ❦ ❦

We had just hiked over Mount Moosilauke and down a long steep slope of rocks when a group of hikers and I decided to head into the town of North Woodstock, New Hampshire, to find a room for the evening. When it appeared that all the rooms in the town were booked, we did what any group of people with limited resources would do—we scavenged. Some went to a Chinese restaurant, some to a local brewery, and some to a market to resupply. I was in the latter group, and although they didn't have anything particularly unique at the market, they did have grapes. I *love* grapes.

With my pack loaded with the delicious fresh fruit, I walked into a nearby bar for a cheeseburger, fries, and a locally brewed brown ale before heading back to the trail. There was clearly some sort of wedding function happening in the bar because there was a woman wearing white and a group of ladies all dolled up hanging out in one spot—the tell-tale signs of a bachelorette party. Before you go assuming some kinky story takes place next, I should explain that there were also multiple men and lots of babies. Apparently, this was one of those joint bachelor/bachelorette/rehearsal dinner things. My first thought was *You have a baby—in a bar.*

I started a few conversations with various patrons in the establishment, and before I realized it, it was nine thirty and dark outside. This is not the greatest scenario when you are in a strange town in the middle of the mountains with no place to stay. Astonishingly, I did the impossible (for male hikers at least) and found a hitch back to the trailhead (female hikers notoriously have an easier time finding a ride). The smart decision would have been to quickly find a campsite for the night, and there were many right near the road, but I wasn't that tired so I started hiking instead.

As I mentioned before with my experiences in Tennessee, Virginia, and Pennsylvania, I'm usually not a big advocate of night hiking. It's not that hiking at night doesn't provide a wonderful experience, but just that it adds one more element of risk to walking through the woods. If something does happen to go wrong, the darkness complicates the logistics involved if others were needed to come help. That being said, a little night hiking under the right conditions can be good for the soul. Hikers just have to determine their comfort level and accept responsibility for such a task. Like all wilderness experiences, taking a moment to evaluate your risks and abilities can go a long way toward reducing the chances of creating a much larger problem. For this night hike after leaving the bachelorette party, I saw on my map there was a campsite seven miles north and I figured I could make it without much trouble.

I figured wrong.

From the road, the terrain was almost straight up and rocky and with a full pack of food my pace was slower than usual. As midnight crept closer, my body began to ache with every step and there was only one thing on my mind: grapes. I decided to take a break, sit down, and enjoy my recent purchase. I picked a spot near some water, found a rock for a seat, and pulled a few grapes off the top vine in the bag. Before the first handful reached my mouth, I heard a terrible sound. It was like what you might hear when you disrupt a ground hornets' nest, which is funny, because that's exactly what I had just done with my right foot.

Almost immediately, they swarmed around me and my pack. I dropped my handful of grapes, threw my pack around one shoulder, began swinging my trekking poles around (as if that was going to accomplish anything), and, with my headlamp swaying from side to side like in a low-budget horror film, I ran away up the trail with two fresh stings on my legs.

After what seemed like an eternity of running up a rocky trail at night, I finally came to a stop. I pulled out my GPS and tried to get my bearings. I was near a viewpoint close to the top of Mount Wolf, but in the dead of night a viewpoint doesn't really provide the same heightened excitement one might find in the clear of day. After catching my breath, I found a giant granite boulder and scrambled to the top of the rock. With adrenaline still flowing thanks to my great escape from the ground hornets, I tried to gather my thoughts under a night sky that was well lit from a full moon. Still panting like a dog, I reached into the top of my pack, grabbed my bag of grapes, and, for the next hour, ate every single grape while sitting on top of that rock. It was the best bag of grapes I have ever eaten.

❖ ❖ ❖

For over eighteen hundred miles, I had heard the AT community rant and rave about the awe-inspiring peaks of the White Mountains of New Hampshire and the death-defying climbs that are required to see them. However, there was a point when I became sort of numb to any descriptions of upcoming climbs, because the reality was that I was going to hike it anyway, so I didn't see the point of bothering myself with the details. The major peaks through the Whites range from four to six thousand feet in elevation, with the tallest (Mount Washington) peaking at 6,288 feet. In fact, there are forty-eight peaks above four thousand feet and it has become an informal challenge for individuals to summit them all. Although the elevations are not necessarily extraordinary compared to other mountainous areas, the composition of the landscape is a different story. A very rocky story.

As I've mentioned, as glaciers advanced and retreated over time, they crushed up rocks from the north and pushed them south, which left pieces behind as they melted during their journey back toward the North Pole. The pieces that fell out of the melting glaciers make up most of the very steep, rocky ledges on which one must climb to summit most of the peaks in the White Mountains, and you can be sure the AT does its best to find the steepest route.

These rocky climbs and descents made hiking through the Whites more logistically challenging than even the ranting and raving led me to believe. One might assume hiking downhill

Descending Mt. Washington in the Whites

means having a faster pace, but that's not the case when the downhill is scrambling over wet mossy rocks while enduring winds at 70 mph. (Mount Washington holds one of the highest wind speeds on record at 231 mph, which is proudly stated at the small museum that sits atop the mountain.) Planning for daily mileages and camping spots wasn't easy either. Even though there are large huts that may seem like lovely places to stay, they are actually lodges that are constantly booked up in advance for $100 per night—not exactly in the average sleeping budget for the typical AT thru-hiker.

At some point, the mantra "It's about the journey, not the destination," became very real to me. That was fine because I think this is how a backpacking trip should be. The decreased ability to plan my days in the Whites reminded me to take my time, enjoy the beautiful views, and take advantage of meeting some new friends. Except for one day of extreme winds and rain (which resulted in a very intense five-mile hike along a ridgeline), my experience through the Whites fulfilled at least one description everyone shared: awe-inspiring. I did experience my fair share of scrapes, bruises, and ankle rolls over those seven days, not to mention trying to avoid being blown off the rocks in high winds (there were 90 mph gusts when I was there), but regardless, the Whites lived up to the hype.

❊ ❊ ❊

As I approached the final state through which the AT travels, I had already met many individuals who I am honored to call friends. Surprisingly enough, I also met up with several other friends who I hiked with in 2014 before my heart complications took me off the trail. It's amazing that someone I met on a trail two years before in New Jersey could randomly show up at a campsite in New Hampshire, but that's how the AT works. Coconuts, Spice Kit, and Blitz, all hikers who I had met in 2014, were on the trail again in 2016. Sharing stories with old friends is one of my favorite pastimes and I was thrilled to see these familiar faces.

My favorite reconnection story took place atop Mount Garfield. When I stopped at the summit for a quick snack, I ran into another hiker. Although I couldn't pinpoint the exact memory, I knew I had met this person before. After learning my trail name was Batman, her eyes widened and a large

A view from inside Gentian Pond Shelter only a few miles from the Maine border

grin formed across her face as she proudly exclaimed to everyone within earshot at the top of that mountain, "You made out with my cousin!" It was true. In 2014, her cousin was a trail angel outside the town of Palmerton, Pennsylvania. Suffice it to say that her cousin provided me with more than Little Debbie snacks and soda that evening. Apparently, what happens on the AT stays on the AT, even two years later.

Although my legs were tired, my shoes were getting worn, and my heart was exhibiting intermittent little palpitations (especially during times of extreme heat when dehydration was an issue), I felt strong enough to continue after I walked the final few miles of flat ground that marks the exit path out the north end of White Mountain National Forest. My mileage math was working out in my favor and it appeared I might actually be able to pull this thing off *and* finish in time to officiate Laura's wedding. As long as I could buy enough Pop-Tarts, it was looking like I'd be fine.

Thirteen states and 1,890 miles down. One state and 299 miles to go.

CHAPTER 27

Iowa 2015

"I'm just trying to take race out of the conversation." This was one of many phrases I heard (or read) repeatedly throughout 2015 as our nation's conversation about racial inequality intensified, and as people tried to define what it meant to be racist. As I've spoken with individuals around the world about this, I've found that, depending on a person's background or experience, racists often justify their insensitive comments by claiming they're "just rhetoric" or "just fact" or that they're "just telling it like it is." (I heard KKK-member Avery say many racist comments while staying with him down in the Florida panhandle, but I will always remember one in particular: "The blacks are just destined to be criminals—that's a fact!" Wow.)

It's incredible how various phrases, quips, or statistics are twisted by their speakers to fit their agendas which, unfortunately, sometimes means that these people feel justified in stating their racist opinions openly—even around the very people they're alienating. Regardless of their provenance, many of these statements are shrouded in very grey clouds of a discriminating past.

❋ ❋ ❋

While I was growing up in Iowa, racism seemed liked an archaic atrocity that was only practiced by terrible people in history books. My classmates and I all agreed that racism was bad, and that individuals guilty of being racist took part in reprehensible acts like slavery, cross burnings, and lynchings. It seemed almost an indisputable fact that we were *good* white folks in Iowa, and, as members of a Yankee state during the Civil War, we were definitely not racists.

As I've grown older and asked more questions and visited more places, however, it has become clear that I was exceptionally predisposed to not being racist because of our alarmingly low population of non-white residents, and I imagine I wasn't the only one. It's easy to be blissfully unaware of potentially racist comments when there are no people of color to remind us that a comment might be offensive. To say there were *no* non-white people in Cedar Rapids in the 1990s would obviously be false, but the fact remains that the lack of diversity (especially as compared to other major cities) likely skewed the perspectives of many Iowans. I know for me it did.

❋ ❋ ❋

In elementary school, there were two black kids on my AAU basketball team and both were fantastic athletes. Unfortunately, I realized in my later years that I treated them both in ignorantly racist ways. For example, when we were discussing how high we could jump (because the ability to touch the net or the hoop's rim was constantly used to gauge awesomeness at that age), I proudly proclaimed to the other members of my team that "black people have extra muscles in their calves and that's why they can jump higher." When I made the claim, I remember the look on Courtney's face (one of my two black teammates), and it was a look of pure shock. Thankfully, I have since learned that all humans have the exact same number of muscles in their calves. I stupidly said this not because I had empirical knowledge of human anatomy, but because I heard it from someone else: an older (white) kid from another team—who had heard it from his father. I did no fact checking and blindly believed every word (though I would later learn it was part of a racist joke referring to black people being stronger because of their ancestors being slaves). In the mid-90s in some parts of the country, before "fake news" was a catchphrase, bad information was already being distributed and it was largely going unnoticed.

❖ ❖ ❖

My family and friend group in Iowa is quite diverse. I have three black and one Alaskan Inuit first cousins who were adopted. One of those black cousins has a black child (my second cousin). One of my white cousins married a Mexican man and they had three biracial children who are my second cousins. Another white cousin has three children with three different mothers and his kids (my second cousins) are all biracial. One of those biracial children (my second cousin) has since been adopted by his white grandparents (my aunt and uncle), which makes him now legally my first cousin. My group of friends is equally diverse. Ironically, the diversity among those who I spend time with doesn't stop the racist and discriminatory remarks because, as I said before, some people believe their comments are "just telling it like it is."

Many things have been said between family and friends while hanging out in Cedar Rapids that could be analyzed for years by social scientists, but it was my friend Jayme's comment during a Thanksgiving celebration in 2015, only a few months after Erica and I stopped talking, that will live in infamy. About ten of us were sitting around the table at a house party playing a card game, coincidentally called Mexican Crazy Eights, when the topic of discussion turned to the school to which our friend of Mexican heritage (who wasn't present) was choosing to send their daughter. (She had dropped out of her previous school and was thus enrolling in the local "alternative" school option.) As Jayme searched through her cards, she calmly said, "I've seen photos of kids from that new school and I don't think it's a good school." A few us raised our eyes from our cards as she said those words, and another friend asked for clarification: "Oh, you saw *photos*? Tell me, what was in these photos that makes you think it isn't a good school?" While that follow-up question was never answered, what happened next included an argument that blew up in a way that no game of Mexican Crazy Eights ever should.

I don't believe Jayme ever expected her original comment to garner as much debate as it did, but I also don't think she felt there was anything wrong with her comment in the first place. Now, if she had clarified that she "saw photos of those kids and *they were all carrying hypodermic needles and automatic weapons"* then possibly I would be compelled to agree with her that the school might not be suitable for our friend's daughter. But her comment (which was left unclarified) would likely be offensive to many people. What could she have possibly seen in those photos that would make her believe the students at the school were so bad? One assumption was that she saw people of color. People who, for whatever reason, she believed "looked" like they might have been bad, dare I say, *hombres*. For she provided no other information about those students than what could be seen from the photos.

As with all of our tiffs, with time, this event eventually became water under the proverbial bridge as we are one of those odd friend groups who are able to remember we love each other and move forward in spite of past hurts. About a month later, though, another comment was made that wasn't as easy to move beyond.

❦ ❦ ❦

It was Christmas Eve, and a group of us were engaging in what has become an annual Christmas tradition: drinking at a bar before going to Christmas Eve mass. We were at a bar right by Veterans Memorial Park—home of the Kernels, which is a minor league baseball team in Cedar Rapids.

Although we had previously celebrated the birth of Christ at more classier establishments such as Tornado's Grub & Pub, that year we chose to imbibe at a bar near the stadium where I once caught a foul ball and had it signed by Mike Sweeney, who would go on to join the Kansas City Royals Hall of Fame (he was playing for the opposing team that day). Because of the stadium's proximity to the bar, that area of town now not only represents cherished childhood memories, but it's also the place where my friend Abby once said, "The blacks have moved in so my housing value has gone down."

I almost spit my drink out.

"What did you just say?!" was my response.

Just as I assume ignorant innocence was behind Jayme's Thanksgiving comment, Abby clearly didn't think her statement was going to cause a reaction, and I bet she even expected me to nod my head in agreement. (I didn't.) Instead, I responded with some questions.

Me: "Why do you say that?"

Abby: "Well, I just got my appraisal back and the value of my house is lower."

Me: "What did the appraisal say?"

Abby: "Well, it actually said that people don't value split-level floor plans as much as they used to."

Me: "Oh, so it said nothing about 'the blacks' and their skin color's effect on housing values?"

Abby: (Silence.)

I think she was catching on to my disapproval of her comment at that point.

Although Abby's exact phrasing was terrible, if the appraisal had actually said anything about "changing demographics" I could see how people of a certain generation (Abby is about fifteen years older than me) could interpret that as "the blacks are lowering my housing value." (To be clear: I do not agree, but that interpretation wouldn't surprise me.) However, the report didn't say *anything* about the color of Abby's neighbors' skin, and instead only stated that potential buyers might simply not like her house because of an outdated design. People of color had nothing to do with the appraisal value and Abby wasn't basing her comment off of any other information except her own feelings. Well, Abby, those feelings are racist.

Although I didn't expect the conversation with Abby to end there, I had hoped that my clarifying questions might help to show Abby how her assessment of her home appraisal was erroneous. Instead she doubled down on "alternative" rhetoric to support her argument by citing other feelings and statistics that she believed to be true.

As I listened, it seemed that some of Abby's statistics may have been referring to "white flight," which is a term to describe what happens when minority populations increase in predominantly white neighborhoods (and white residents move away), which can appear to lower the values of the homes in that area. But is it really the color of the new neighbors' skin that makes housing values decrease, or is it economics—most notably supply and demand—that causes this? When racist white people decide to sell their homes and thus flood the market with product, which causes home values to decrease to accommodate consumer demand, it seems to me to be a function of economics. While it's an interesting argument that the melanin in a person's skin can directly decrease the value of drywall and hardwood floors, I simply don't buy it (no pun intended).

Abby is a wonderful person. She is kind, caring, and loving. She works hard to ensure a healthy positive lifestyle for herself. She has supported her children many times at the expense of her own personal lifestyle, and even defended them when she probably shouldn't have, because that's what a loving mother does. Many people have a relative, friend, or acquaintance who may be a wonderful person, but who has also made comments like "black people have extra muscles in their calves, that's why they can jump higher" or "I've seen photos of kids from that new school and I don't think it's a good school" or "the blacks have moved in so my housing value has gone down." Although these good people in our lives may not think the comments are racist, they *are* racist to someone else, most notably people of color—like the people who white folks once owned as property and who, at one time, were legally declared by our Constitution to be only three-fifths of a regular person. Until you or your ancestors have been owned by another person, I think requesting white people to have a little humility and to use caution when making comments about people of color is not too much to ask. We cannot know another person's experience until we've walked a mile in their shoes (or their ancestors' shoes).

For whatever reason, when she said it, Abby didn't believe that her comment was racist. And while I disagree, I knew I couldn't control her interpretation. I can only control my own words and continue to explore beyond my original Iowa bubble to clarify and understand the truth—even though others haven't always done the same. Whether their exploration merely takes them outside their neighborhood, or outside their state or country lines, I can't control that. But I can let them know some things are not okay to say around me. Not everyone in my hometown says potentially racist things, but those types of comments can be prominently heard within the community more often than most may want to admit.

In that moment on Christmas Eve of 2015, I decided that although I love my friends, I would not allow Abby (or anyone) to say things like that around me anymore. After further conversation, it was clear that if she had put more thought into her comments at the bar, she wouldn't have said what she did. I know Jayme and Abby are not bad people, they're actually great people. And although I know their hearts are in the right place, I simply won't stand idly by if racist comments are being said.

Hopefully, with time, we can foster a new generation of individuals who, when we see or think about people who appear different than us in appearance and culture, will realize those people are *not* actually all that different. They're human, just like us.

❆ ❆ ❆

For me, it was past experiences like these that spawned my return to the trail, and reflecting upon them crossed my mind almost daily while hiking. I can only describe a pretty tree or a beautiful view in so many ways. To truly understand what it's like to hike thousands of miles through the woods, it's imperative to have an idea of what someone actually thinks about when hiking through the woods, which, for me, often included reflective ruminations about life events from off the trail, as well as on it. I found myself mulling over experiences with family members, friends, loved ones, jobs, and everything in between. These relationships and interactions shape our thoughts, and those thoughts acted as hiking fuel with every step I took.

CHAPTER 28

Appalachian Trail 2016
158 Days, 2,074 Miles

We develop relationships at every switchback of our lives. We foster a rapport with colleagues at work, acquaintances at local meet-up groups, buddies at fantasy-football drafts, and even with inanimate objects like smart phones, cars, and clothes. The relationships we develop with these people or items absolutely shapes our lives—whether we like it or not—and it's up to us to manage their impacts accordingly.

For a thru-hiker, the impact of our backpack is not metaphorical. It can be an actual heavy weight on our shoulders and we develop relationships with the things inside of it. And, just like in our personal relationships, the outcome of those relationships with items inside of our pack may not be what we expect.

For example, I carry a micro-stove that I bought years ago from Amazon after I found an unused gift card in the middle of Cherry Creek Drive in Denver. Although I was skeptical of the cheaper off-brand model, it still works to this day. During one stretch of the AT, one thirteen-ounce cylinder of compressed isobutane lasted for twenty-seven days with this stove. (I normally only get about two weeks of use.) Having one canister of fuel last for almost a month while traversing through two and a half states was astounding! I have absolutely developed a positive relationship with this stove because of the reliability it has shown. My tent is another story.

When an airline lost my tent, I was forced to expedite the purchase of a new one before heading to Georgia to start the AT in 2014. I bought a box-store brand that was labeled as a single-person, light-weight backpacking tent. Its bivy-style design was intended to stay low to the ground and not hold much more than what is needed to lay down and fall asleep inside. It was similar in design to my previous tent, which I liked, and it appeared to meet my needs after a few test setups in the backyard. It turns out that setting up a tent in the backyard doesn't quite give you the full picture you may get after setting it up for your twenty-fifth, fiftieth, hundredth, or hundred-and-fiftieth time while hiking in the woods. Let me cut to the chase: I hate my tent.

Although the lower profile of the bivy-style design is meant to mitigate the effects of high winds, in actuality it's probably two or three inches lower in total height than my previous model, resulting in it being *just* low enough that when I needed to sit up and scratch the ground-hornet stings on my right leg, I got a face full of mesh netting before my dirty fingernails even came close to my leg. My new tent is also about two to three inches shorter in total length than my previous model, thus forcing my disgusting feet or my beautiful face to fight a battle to the death to decide which gets more wiggle room. My face usually wins those battles and my feet are then shoved into the end of the blue and grey netting.

The zipper situation is in a category of its own. First of all, there's only one. *One* zipper! As if the designers of this tent decided that all users shall be forced into one direction of entry and exit regardless of sun, wind, or general layout of the campsite. How am I supposed to allow the tent to air out during the day with only one zipper?!?! Do I dare even mention where this one zipper is located? Yes, I will. It's located where my feet are positioned—shoved down at the end of the mesh netting—which means when my internal bathroom clock wakes me up at three in the morning, I must lean forward, get a face full of mesh and a whiff of my smelly feet, *and* find a zipper in the dark while I'm trying not to piss all over myself!

Hopefully you grasp my point. My tent is terrible. I hate my tent.

On my 151st night of the hiking the Appalachian Trail, I set up my tent at a campsite next to Black Brook, a murky, slow-moving water source near South Arm Road just outside Andover, Maine. There were quite a few hikers at this site on that evening, the most memorable being a family group that included a mom, two sons, a daughter, and two dogs who collectively went by the trail name Moon Spread and the Valley Dogs. Although their exact itinerary was hard to discern as they had been doing sections of various trails (not just the AT) for the past two years, when I met them, they were about five days from finishing and heading back to Missouri where the mom had recently closed on a house.

As the sun began to set and the trees turned from barky totem poles to dark thin lines indiscernible from the next, a few cracks of lightning and thunder were heard in the not-too-far distance. The group of hikers at the campsite congregated near what was determined to be the center of camp, and we were sharing stories and passing around one Pabst Blue Ribbon, a small bottle of whiskey, and a few shots of butterscotch schnapps when the first few drops of rain began to fall.

Even though the leaves of the surrounding trees provided a nice canopy, this storm decided it was going to take more than a few leaves to stop its droplets of precipitation from reaching the top of my head. Within a few seconds, the rain picked up and, as usual, the happy group of hikers exchanged a few well wishes (knowing that most of us would likely never see each other again) and scattered to our various houses for the evening, some in tarp-covered hammocks, some in large four-person tents like Moon Spread and the Valley Dogs, and some, like me, into my bivy-style one-person tent.

The storm hit with a fury. The lightning seemed as if it were directly over the campsite and the ground shook with every thunderous strike. I could feel my tent vibrate from the heavy droplets of rain as they pounded the fabric from every side. Although there were a few spots where the fabric had worn thin over the last few years, the inside stayed dry and sprouted no leaks.

The wind continued to blow with increasing turbulence, bending the two rods that held my tent in place almost to their breaking point, but with the aid of the taught guy lines and

My bivy-style one-person tent set up next to Black Brook

all the available stakes pounded into the ground, my tent held strong. As with most storms in the woods, the trees and other foliage generated their own sounds as some branches swayed from left to right and some were on the brink of snapping off. Although the weather tried its best to disrupt this camping experience, when the storm subsided, my clothes, my sleeping bag, and my face remained dry and cozy for the entire evening.

Although I have endured an innumerable number of evenings where my disdain for my tent was elevated, on that evening, while camping in the middle of the wilderness in Maine, I *loved* my tent.

If I replaced the word "tent" in that story with the name of anyone with whom I have been in a personal relationship, there would be a similar love/hate feeling. This isn't to say that we should blindly accept someone's attributes regardless of how terrible they are, but if we *choose* to only see the negative, then that's all we'll see. Relationships of all kinds can be hard, and they absolutely require effort to succeed, but losing sight of the positives they provide only clouds our emotions. Hopefully, I will continue to see the positives in both my camping gear and my personal relationships while on (and off) the trail.

But I still want to buy a new tent. That thing is terrible.

❉ ❉ ❉

In April 2013, a sixty-six-year-old woman named Geraldine "Gerry" Largay began thru-hiking the AT. Sadly, she went missing when she was somewhere in Maine in July 2013 and her body wasn't found until October 2015 when a logging company came across her tent with her remains inside. I had heard of Gerry's story in various news circles, but never put further thought into it until 2016 when I returned to the AT. The Maine Warden Service had finally released its files regarding her disappearance and the subsequent investigation, thus reigniting the story among AT hikers.

With all AT stories, there is a bit of a rumor mill that aids in distorting the facts which, unfortunately, was one of the reasons why authorities supposedly had problems putting together a timeline regarding Gerry's whereabouts during the initial search. Although she had begun her hike in 2013, one false piece of information I heard was that she was hiking in 2014 (when I did my first section of the AT). What most peaked my curiosity about Gerry's story was when I discovered that Gerry's trail name was "Inchworm" (likely a humorous reference to her slower hiking pace). During 2014, there was a small section during which I had hiked with an older woman whose trail name was Inchworm! The story had become personal. However, after finally reaching a town with some decent Wi-Fi, I determined it was not the same woman I had previously hiked with. (Catchy trail names tend to get chosen by new people each hiking season.)

What makes this story even sadder is that so many things had to occur for this tragedy to unfold. I lightheartedly refer to the AT as being a "pampered trail," alluding to the many resources available to hikers like the thousands of white blazes, well-maintained trails, and multiple books and mobile apps with spreadsheets describing the locations of water sources and road crossings. This is why there are a lot of people who attempt to hike the trail every year who have never been camping, let alone backpacking for many months in the wilderness. I was shocked to learn that there are many people who either read a book about the AT or hear about it from a friend, and then decide to buy some gear and show up at Springer Mountain in Georgia with the intention to hike over two thousand miles with very little experience. The inspiring part is that some of these people actually finish! This is possible because the AT community has built up numerous resources to help hikers succeed, but a lot of these resources are only *on* the trail. Inchworm, unfortunately, had wandered off the trail, so she couldn't take advantage of the traditional resources.

I have an app on my phone with USGS topo maps and waypoints along the entire AT. It's called Guthook, which refers to the trail name of the guy who developed it. Although it was in its early developmental stages in 2013, it was available then, along with a few other GPS-locating devices that could be used in emergency situations. However, back then, not everyone wanted to bring a smart phone on the trail, and the other devices were pricey, and, in some hikers' opinions, "too heavy to carry." It blows my mind that, of all the gear that gets put to the wayside when planning a two-thousand-mile hike, a map would be on that list. I heard my fellow hikers expressing a general opinion that was fairly "anti-map" because of the additional weight it would add to a pack.

Fast forward to 2016, a time when almost everyone had a smart phone. In fact, I was hard pressed to not see at least one person on the top of every mountain making a phone call or "gramming" a selfie. At an earlier point in my life this might have annoyed me, but if it's done in moderation, I don't feel that calling a loved one from the woods is a terrible thing. Purely from a safety standpoint, it's not a bad idea to let someone know where you're located from time to time. In addition to better cellular services, 2016 also brought access to more, and cheaper, lightweight devices that could be loaded with maps.

Despite all the debate around what gear to buy, I still believe that the traditional essentials are the most important. The only roadblock to everyone having some sort of GPS device is, unfortunately, the cost. However, I think if you can justify a $9 mixed drink at a bar (which many hikers do while visiting towns on the trail), an app that costs $8.99 and could tell you where you are and potentially save you in an emergency should definitely be excused. To be clear, I am absolutely *not* implying that Inchworm did anything wrong with her backpacking preparations or intentions, or that she was not a skilled hiker at that point in her journey, but I do believe that her story highlights how, even with all the current resources available, accidents can and do happen along the AT.

When I stopped at the Poplar Ridge Shelter—the last location where Inchworm was seen before her disappearance—just after Saddleback Mountain and before entering the town of Stratton, Maine, it was clear that if someone became turned around in this area, the thick tree coverage that begins almost immediately once you step off the trail could easily obscure the way back. I wish Inchworm's family, and the families of all who have experienced hardships while trying to enjoy the beauty of the AT, all my condolences. I just hope her story can help future hikers be prepared and stay safe while exploring and enjoying the wilderness.

❦ ❦ ❦

Around 1876, in the town of Lowell, Massachusetts, Dr. Augustin Thompson patented a medicine called "Moxie Nerve Food." He claimed it contained a rare unnamed South American plant and that this magical elixir helped eliminate "paralysis, softening of the brain, nervousness, and insomnia."

Sign me up.

The ingredients, brand, and overall understanding of this product transferred hands several times over the years, and are currently the property of Kirin Holdings Company, which is a member of the Japanese Mitsubishi Group. The beverage was eventually filled with sugar and marketed to children as a healthy soft drink that was simply called "Moxie." So, it only makes sense that on May 10, 2005, a nineteenth-century magical elixir that was originally made in Massachusetts and is now a soda owned by a Japanese car company, became the official soft drink of the state of Maine (sarcasm intended).

I'm going to anger a lot of people with this next comment: I hate Moxie. The second ingredient listed on each can is "high fructose corn syrup and/or sugar." And/or? This liquid is so mysterious that the manufacturers don't even *know* which glucose-based product made it into that particular can of soda?! Imagine a bitter cough syrup (that doesn't cure a cough) was mixed with soda water and other "added flavors" (an actually listed ingredient), compressed into an aluminum can, and then marketed to the people of Maine. That's what I think Moxie is. I take back what I said earlier: please do not sign me up.

The advertising behind this product would lead us to believe that even with its mysterious ingredients we should still desire this drink. It is available in every vending machine, gas station, and supermarket in Maine. It even replaced Coca-Cola as the main soda available in many trail angels' coolers when I was fortunate enough to cross one.

The entire population of Maine seems to have come down with Moxie "fever." (Ironically, Moxie does not treat Moxie fever.) Natural and human-made landmarks include references to the drink—like Moxie Bald, which is a 2,600-foot rock face that AT hikers scramble up as the last climb before reaching the town of Monson, Maine. I admit it's possible that these landmarks' names were derived from an Abenaki Native American word meaning "dark water." Regardless, that definition still supports my opinion of the soda.

Atop North Crocker Mountain before heading into Stratton, Maine

After leaving Stratton and climbing to the top of Moxie Bald, I passed a father and daughter, the latter of whom was visibly winded and resting on a rock when she reached into her bag for what I assumed would be a bottle of water. Nope. As she pulled out a two-liter bottle of Moxie, I had to force down the little bit of vomit that entered my mouth. I'm sure Dr. Augustin Thompson is laughing in his grave knowing that his magical elixir is now being used to hydrate humans while climbing mountains.

Moxie: it's what Mainers crave.

Thirteen states and 2,074 miles down. One state and 115 miles to go.

CHAPTER 29

Iowa 2016

In the early months of 2016, as I managed my frustration with the racial divide across our country—and specifically in my hometown—I also continued my efforts to grow the reach of the brewery by increasing our distribution. I hit my networking stride and expanded my active draught list to nearly seventy bars and restaurants. Although I couldn't compete with the level of coverage that a large distribution company could offer, I also knew that I was close to reaching my max capacity with the resources I was provided, which consisted of a white van and my personal cell phone. The marketing emails, sales meetings, tasting events, draught-line maintenance, and carrying of 160-pound kegs in and out of basement coolers—all tasks that fell under my job description—would be done by a team of people if the brewery had signed with a large distributor. But ever since my first day on the job, it had been made clear that was not part of the business plan and that we wanted to keep everything in house.

My competition was Anheuser-Busch InBev (also known as AB InBev, which is the company that owns Budweiser) and MillerCoors—two of the largest beer companies in the world.

These companies' beer selections, and their respective subsidiaries, are distributed by regional distribution companies.

Next time you see a sign advertising a beer event or a new product at your neighborhood grocery store or bar, if you look closely, you'll likely see a small logo that tells which distribution company paid for the advertisement. Little perks like paying for signage aren't illegal in any way, and I applaud the effort to relieve some of the financial burden incurred by small businesses; signs are decorations, and customers expect their pubs and restaurants to look nice. However, those types of perks fell outside the scope of what I was able to provide from our little brewery.

But it doesn't stop at event marketing or new-product rollouts; almost all beer-related signs in an establishment are paid for by the distribution companies. So if a bar owner wants to take Budweiser off the main tap line (possibly because he wants to support a new local beer), the bar's Budweiser sales representative could choose to remove from that bar every advertisement, tap handle, and neon sign that supports any product from Budweiser. Even just the possibility of losing all those decorations is enough incentive to local bar owners to keep the major brands on tap.

These advertising perks can add up to thousands of dollars each year, which is a lot of money to a small-business owner. It might even limit a bar's draught-beer selection to whatever taps are left open after filling the others with beer produced and distributed by the larger companies. If you consider all the brands that those companies own, this game of tap-handle roulette frequently only leaves one or two (or possibly zero) beer lines open for, say, a small self-distributed brewery like the one I was schlepping kegs for. This isn't to say there aren't plenty of beer drinkers who prefer Budweiser to other beverages, but it's no secret that marketing dollars can potentially influence the sales and availability of any product. Upon learning these nuances of the beer-distribution game, my only thought was *challenge accepted*.

Naturally, I had to find whatever advantages I could to gain an edge without any additional financial or marketing support. I built my sales pitch on a foundation of why we "have not signed, are not signing, and will not ever sign" with a large distribution company. After surmounting the initial learning curve necessary for the direct-sales position, I expanded my elevator speech to show why our company's shortcomings were actually assets and why our competitors' perks weren't as great as they might seem. I rarely said negative things about my competition outside of what could be considered acceptable sales tactics because, at the end of the day, we were still just selling beer.

So, when I sat down for my weekly meeting with the owners of the brewery on the morning of March 1, 2016, right after closing the largest distribution sales month since the company's inception, I was surprised that instead of discussing the logistics needed to hire a part-time worker to allow me more time for marketing and sales meetings (which was something we had discussed just a few months before), they started the meeting by saying, "Big news, we're signing with a distributor!"

Well, shit.

Later that afternoon, Potter sent me a Facebook message to ask if I would be available to dog-sit in Santa Barbara for a few months after that year's Memorial Weekend Death March, as he'd be taking his wife and children to Europe for the summer. Although signing with a distributor was the best business and financial decision for the brewery (and there are absolutely no hard feelings), it was definitely not part of a plan I was expecting, and there was no guarantee that I would still have a job. After contemplating what I would do about Potter's request, when I responded to him at the end of the week, my answer was a resounding "yes."

And after what happened with my friend Dale and his wife Maureen five weeks later, I'm sure grateful I had a cozy spot waiting for me near the Pacific so I could clear my thoughts.

❉ ❉ ❉

I met Dale shortly after beginning the job at the brewery. He was a regular at one of my accounts and since my job was all about building connections with bar owners and patrons, it was only natural that he and I became friends. Besides, he was a Cubs fan, so that sealed the deal on our friendship. Dale has a couple of adult children and works at the Quaker Oats factory in Cedar Rapids. He also has played the lottery for, in his own words, "as long as I can remember." One time, a group of Quaker Oats employees won the top Powerball jackpot that was valued at $241 million. I had asked Dale if he was a part of that group.

He wasn't.

A few months after that jackpot, another group of fifty Quaker Oats employees had won a Powerball prize valued at over $10,000. Again, I thought for sure Dale had been a part of that group.

He wasn't.

Despite missing out on those previous jackpots, Dale continued to play the Powerball and even started his own pool with twenty members at a local bar, an establishment that's only about a ten-minute walk from the Quaker Oats factory. They pooled money twice a week from the twenty members to purchase tickets.

By the beginning of 2016, hearing Dale talk about his lottery pools had become white noise to me. This is why in May of that year, shortly after the brewery decided to sign with the distribution company, when I heard from Dale's daughter that "Dad won the Powerball," I really didn't have any elevated emotions. Dale's lottery pool had purchased a ticket that matched four white balls and the Powerball, and collectively they won $150,000. They missed the top multimillion-dollar jackpot by *one white ball*. After taxes and splitting the winnings among the members, each person was awarded just over $5,000—not a life-changing sum of money for most of them, but still a nice chunk of change. With $5,000 a person could go on a vacation, pay off a car loan, complete some home projects, contribute to a Roth IRA, or simply save most of it and go to a nice restaurant a few times.

Which one of those options did Dale and Maureen choose? *None of the above.* Instead, they decided to take two days off from work and get stupid drunk for four straight days. I suppose that's an option, too. By the end of the four days, once we factor in the bar tabs, clothing and carpet replacements, new paint that was required, and the emergency room visit, I imagine most of the $5,000 was gone. Although Dale might not remember it the same way I do (for obvious reasons), below is an account of what one sober person experienced on May 8, 2016, four days after Dale (and his nineteen buddies) won the Powerball.

Dale's daughter was in Oregon visiting her brother. I was watching her dogs in Cedar Rapids when she called and asked, "Can you go over to Dad's place?" Her concern stemmed from a phone call she had received from her father regarding their mom. Maureen had supposedly fallen in the bathroom and was possibly in need of some help. This didn't seem like too big of a problem to me, because I figured that Dale—a man in his sixties—would know to call 911 if his wife was in real trouble. However, in his state of inebriation he couldn't even process that his daughter was two thousand miles away and therefore unable to help, and he had not contacted any of his family or friends who were in the same city as him. So, it turns out that expecting he would know to call 911 if something serious had happened *was* a lot to assume.

It was after ten at night when I called Dale only to hear a jumbled mash of information regarding winning the lottery and how he couldn't find his can of chewing tobacco. Due to the late hour and this not being the first drunk conversation I ever had with Dale, I wasn't really paying attention. But then I heard him say "we can't stop the bleeding."

I hung up the phone, dialed 911, and gave them Dale's address.

When I arrived, the paramedics had already beat me there. I'm grateful they did because when I arrived, I saw Maureen sitting on the porch of their trailer, head bandaged, while the rest of her body was visibly covered head to toe in blood. If I hadn't called 911 when I did there is no doubt in my mind that Maureen would have died that evening—on Mother's Day. Thankfully, Dale's daughter had the foresight to call me when she did.

While the paramedics were attending to Maureen on the front porch, one of them gave me a report of the situation and said, "We located the woman just inside the front door. We're trying to stop the bleeding and another male is still inside the residence."

Confused, I responded, "Another male? That's Dale, her husband."

The paramedic responded with a very surprised "Oh," and went about helping his fellow coworkers in caring for Maureen. Dale had apparently refused to give them any information as to who he was or why his wife was covered in blood with a massive head injury.

When I walked inside the trailer, it looked like a murder scene from an episode of a television drama. There was blood splattered on almost every wall, all over the kitchen counter, on the shelves that housed family photos, on the entire bed and comforter, and there were pools, literal *pools* of dark red blood all over the living room and bedroom carpeting.

Over the next few hours, I learned why Dale had refused to call 911: His vodka-soaked brain was concerned that he was the only witness to a woman dying in his house. He finally slurred, "I didn't want them to think I did anything."

Of course, Dale did not harm Maureen in any way, but the alcohol made his brain think that's what others might have assumed. She had fallen in the bathroom and landed on a metal edge that split a two-inch wound on her head. Blood from a head injury does not clot as quickly as it does in other areas of the body. Also, alcohol (which they had been consuming for four days) and the pain medicine she was taking for a previous ailment both thinned her blood and further decreased her body's ability to clot the wound. As Maureen continued to bleed from her head, she wandered around trying to find a towel to stop the wound from spewing blood in quantities that I didn't think were in the human body, which explained why everything was covered in blood when I entered the home.

As the paramedics and I continued to question Dale, he countered all of our questions with his retelling of the events from the previous four days. With every attempt to find out where and how Maureen fell, so as to piece together an explanation of what occurred for medical reasons, Dale proceeded to retell the story of how they won the lottery. As with many drunk stories, he would inevitably get to a certain part, forget what he was saying, and then start over from the beginning.

I had to put a bottle of Black Velvet back into the cupboard *twice* while he was attempting to pour another drink. (They had finished all the vodka.) While I was assessing the damage around the home, he succeeded in pouring a full glass of whiskey for himself. I promptly poured the amber liquid down the sink when I returned to the kitchen, which only angered Dale—seemingly more so than the fact that his wife was bleeding to death on the front porch. Although arguing with an intoxicated person is never a promising idea, I felt it was prudent to remind Dale that his wife was dying outside, to which he ultimately replied, "If she dies, she dies. Fuck it. It's what we do. We drink." No matter how many good memories I have with Dale, whether it was going to a Cedar Rapids Kernels baseball game or fishing at Lake McBride in eastern Iowa, I will never forget the time when he said those words to me.

Due to the lack of information we were able to glean from a very intoxicated Dale, the paramedics made the decision to transport Maureen to the University of Iowa Hospital in Iowa City. After they left with her in the ambulance, I made a few more feeble attempts to convey the seriousness of the situation to Dale; however, as expected, this did nothing to change his attitude at the time. I pulled the blood-soaked sheets off his bed, being careful to trap the pooled blood inside the sheets and set them in the bathroom. I ensured the bottles of liquor were put away, and then I walked Dale into the bedroom where I removed his shoes and laid him in bed.

It was well past midnight by the time I left their home and drove to Iowa City. I found Maureen in the emergency room where I discovered that the blood had not been cleaned off her body. So, after midnight on Mother's Day in 2016, using a box of wet napkins that were available in the room, I thoroughly cleaned dried blood off Maureen—head to toe. It took almost an hour before she looked like a human again and not like an extra on the set of a zombie movie. She was still visibly out of it because of both the blood loss and the alcohol that remained in her system. I knew she would be staying that evening in the hospital, so I tucked her into bed and drove home.

When I arrived back at Dale's home the next morning, to my surprise, he was missing. *He was back at the fucking bar.* Another thing that was missing, not to my surprise, was the entire bottle of Black Velvet. He woke up at some point and drank the rest of the bottle. Although he wasn't drinking at the bar and was just having breakfast the next morning, it was difficult to swallow that the first choice Dale made—after waking up in a home that was covered in pools of blood with his wife missing—was to go back to the bar.

When I arrived at the hospital that day, Maureen was in surprisingly good spirits. I took her back home where I helped her into bed and made sure she was comfortable. Dale was also back home by that time. We didn't speak. I left, and that was the end of it. To this day, I still wonder what would have happened if they had matched the fifth white ball.

❖ ❖ ❖

Dale is a good man. He is a kind man. He would offer the shirt off his back to a person in need. He has always offered me help, whether it's to lend me his truck or just to pay for a few drinks at the bar. He has told me stories about his children that lead me to believe that he is a good father. He was their basketball coach and was likely around for more extracurricular activities than the other kids' fathers. However, watching the aforementioned events unfold and hearing the words Dale said to me that evening are things I wouldn't wish upon any human. I can only imagine what his children would have thought had they witnessed such a disgusting example of Dale's alcoholism.

❧ ❧ ❧

The events that took place on Mother's Day in 2016 engulfed my thoughts many times while I was on the AT later that year. With almost every step up a mountain, every pump of my water filter, and every bite of a camp dinner, I'd find myself thinking of that night and how I could use the memories of that experience to make *me* a better person. I love all my family and friends who struggle with alcohol abuse, but I can't do anything else to help Dale beyond support his positive traits. Only Dale can make the decisions best for him.

I had been home allowing my heart to recover for almost two years on the evening that I discovered Maureen bleeding from a head wound. After the experiences with my friends, the way my job ended, and my failed relationship with Erica, it became clear that it was time to make a change. Although my heart condition had improved, I knew that it had probably taken some years off my life. I could sit around and let that bother me, or I could take control of my future. It was time for me to get back on the right path. Besides, I had just finished rebuilding the motorcycle. It seemed the perfect time to test it out on a longer road trip.

CHAPTER 30

Appalachian Trail 2016
159 Days; 2,074 Miles

After descending Moxie Bald I spent a few days in the town of Monson, Maine, where I resupplied before beginning the final stretch of trail that would take me to the base of Mount Katahdin, the summit of which is the northern apex of the Appalachian Trail. Although finishing the trail was not my only goal when I had started hiking it in 2014, after overcoming the worst of my heart condition you can bet your ass there was a feeling of redemption the second time around, and the top of Katahdin was exactly where I needed to be. *Nothing was* going to stop me.

Mount Katahdin is in Baxter State Park, which is not a traditional state park, but a large piece of land deeded to the state from former Maine Governor Percival P. Baxter. According to an informational flyer available at the park, young Percival enjoyed fishing trips in the woods of Maine. His passion for the outdoors inspired his efforts to turn the area surrounding Mount Katahdin into a park. When those attempts failed, he began personally purchasing the land and formally donated the parcel to Maine in 1931, with the condition that it be kept in its natural state. That wish is evident still today. If you ask the park ranger on duty to use the office phone—there isn't one.

Through legislative precedents and separate deeds for each donation, Baxter ensured that his park could never be broken apart. Although his first donation was around 6,000 acres, the park currently encompasses 209,501 acres of land. He also left a trust of nearly seven million dollars to ensure that his park would never be a burden on the taxpayers of Maine, and the park is still self-funded to this day (though, of course, additional outside funds are appreciated). The core of the park is managed as a wildlife sanctuary and another section is managed as a Scientific Forest Management Area—a showplace for sound forestry, hunting, and trapping practices.

Baxter State Park is one of Maine's, if not the entire country's, most admirable examples of a pristine wilderness. Before he passed, Baxter shared these words for future generations: "Man is born to die. His works are short lived. Buildings crumble, monuments decay, wealth vanishes. But Katahdin, in all its glory, forever shall remain the mountain of the people of Maine."

What a cool dude.

❖ ❖ ❖

The final one-hundred-mile section of wilderness that an AT hiker passes through before reaching Baxter State Park is called the "100 Mile Wilderness." Depending on the measurement tool or the specific map that is referenced, I'm sure some purist hikers might argue that this section isn't *exactly* one hundred miles. But whether the trail was already one hundred miles long and they named the wilderness after the length, or whether they named the wilderness and *then* had to build a trail that was one hundred miles long, quite frankly, didn't matter to me. It could have been 120 miles, 140 miles, or 250 miles for all I cared. I just knew I was going to finish the damn thing!

Some hikers decide to complete this section of the trail in the middle of their journey, which makes them "flip-floppers." This term refers to hikers that decide to not hike the entire two thousand miles of the trail all in the same direction. Instead, these hikers are shuttled to various trailheads and hike sections of the trail however they please, and some of them end up piecing together and finishing the entire trail in the process. Because of the logistics involved in hiking the 100 Mile Wilderness, some flip-floppers decide to hike southward through the wilderness and meet back up with a section of trail on which they had previously been hiking north. However, for traditional north-bounders (NOBOs) like me, who started in Georgia and hiked every step of the AT in a northerly direction, reaching the 100 Mile Wilderness represents the beginning of the end, the home stretch, the point of no return, or any other cliché meant to imply that the end is near. No matter how you look at it, reaching the start of the 100 Mile Wilderness is a big deal.

For most NOBO thru-hikers, if you've made it that far it would take a huge obstacle or life event to keep you from finishing, and that was definitely how I felt when I reached the town of Monson. What separates the 100 Mile Wilderness from other hundred-mile sections on the trail is that it's almost entirely cut off from the outside world—there are no main roads to a town; no regular restaurants, grocery stores, or gas stations nearby; and no easy access to emergency services if any were needed. At least, that's what I was scared into believing and, to some extent, it's very true.

❈ ❈ ❈

The population of Monson is approximately six to seven hundred, and it offers a small community center, a historical society, a gas station, and the Lakeshore House Lodge and Pub. It's also home to Shaw's Hiker Hostel, which is a family-owned property that offers beds, community meals, provisions, and even a fully stocked garage with both brand-new and used hiking gear.

I took a zero-day at Shaw's and used the time off to plan my attack on the 100 Mile Wilderness. My legs were healthy and felt strong, and my mind was in the right place with the right attitude. I hadn't even thought about my heart in a few days. Everything seemed to be operating normally and I wasn't about to let any anxiety keep me from reaching Mount Katahdin. I stocked up on food and supplies. My goal was to complete twenty miles per day and either get through, or pretty darn close to through, the entire wilderness in five days.

While at Shaw's, I also began to think about some logistics that would need to be attended to after I finished with the trail. I had been applying for jobs for the last two weeks while I was in Maine, taking advantage of Wi-Fi whenever it was available in towns that I went into to resupply. I even formatted my resume and wrote a few cover letters entirely on my phone while staying in shelters along the trail. While this was counter to "enjoying nature" being my only goal, after meeting new friends at campsites and staring at the stars before retreating to my tent in the evenings, I didn't see any harm in spending a few hours planning for my post-trail life. Besides, I had some cool "offices" to work from during that time and I felt pretty darn happy after I hit "send" and applied for a job while in the middle of the woods (even though I didn't get the position).

After packing up my bag one last time at Shaw's, I caught a shuttle up the small Highway 6 toward the trailhead and began wandering into the wilderness for one hundred miles of untouched natural serenity. I wasn't scared one bit.

Thirteen states and 2,074 miles down. One state and 115 miles to go.

CHAPTER 31

California 2016

I walked into a room, removed my shirt, and let a very friendly woman rub a cold gel all over my chest. The room belonged to my cardiologist, the friendly woman was an ultrasound technician, and the cold gel was so the sound waves emitted from the transducer could more effectively reach my heart. This echocardiogram was one of many that I had received since being diagnosed with Lyme disease and total heart block.

For two years, I had follow-up appointments with family doctors, infectious-disease doctors, and my cardiologist. After some time, my heart began to heal itself, and although I was still able to perform everyday tasks, even strenuous activities such as running and playing in city league softball games, a constant feeling of uneasiness and anxiety continued. Whether it was after a workout, a second cup of coffee, or even doing completely inert activities like reading and catching up on Netflix, I still sporadically experienced an acute awareness of the activity in my chest.

After much back and forth with my cardiologist, we determined these feelings were mostly nerves or anxiety, as nothing was consistently measurable while I was hooked up to Holter monitors or EKG machines, or while receiving lubed-up heart sonograms. Isolated readings would still exhibit signs of carditis, but we could never determine when or why it was happening.

When various results determined that my heart rhythm and telemetry was normal, albeit on the lower end of the spectrum (whatever that means), I was presented with two choices: avoid all activities that might scare me when episodic attacks happened or drink a second cup of coffee and move on with my life. I decided to drink a second cup of coffee *and* ride a thirty-seven-year-old motorcycle from Iowa to California.

❦ ❦ ❦

After I learned my job at the brewery would not continue in the way I had hoped, and after witnessing the aftermath of Dale's Powerball celebration, I was grateful for the opportunity to dog-sit in California for Potter, who had become one of Santa Barbara's premier landscape artists. Staying in a house that has wall-to-wall paintings of beautiful views is a nice perk, lest I forgot to just walk outside to see the same.

To get to Southern California, I decided to ride my 1979 Honda CM400T motorcycle. Although I was literally rebuilding the carburetor up until the day before I left Iowa, I determined it was now or never to test the bike's ability to make a cross-country trip. *I had to get out of town.* After discovering the primary jet in the battery-side carburetor was clogged, which caused the bike to sputter and die before any power could be transferred from the crankcase to the rear tire, I cleaned it with a small wire needle and a full-immersion soak in a concentrated cleaning agent. After I tested the fix and determined the bike would at least get me out of Cedar Rapids, I immediately packed the saddlebags with camping gear and warm-weather clothes, handed my keys to my subletter, and took off across the freshly planted corn fields of Iowa on a very chilly day. Although it would have been prudent to bank more riding time before embarking on a two-thousand-mile journey—to ensure the bike was mechanically sound after completing a carburetor rebuild—after witnessing Maureen's brush with death only four days before, it was time for me to go.

Along with the carburetor problems, two weeks before leaving on the trip my tubeless rear tire went flat while on a ride near the Amana Colonies in Iowa. I was miles away from a town and only carrying a limited number of tools. After borrowing some scissors from a nearby gas station, I carefully cut pieces of plastic from the ends of a pair of sunglasses into two small gaskets. After placing the homemade gaskets on the inside and outside of the valve stem (the part that connects to an air hose when filling up your tires with air), I squeezed in some tire slime and filled the tire with air. The tire pressure held with no further leaks. However, when riding to California a few weeks later, by the time I crossed over the Grand Tetons in Wyoming and entered Idaho, I noticed the rear tire was going bald and decided it would be prudent to get a new tire as soon as possible.

At a motorcycle shop in Boise, the technician showed me exactly why the tire was going bald—it was *not* a tubeless tire.

When I got the flat tire back in Iowa, I had actually ripped the valve stem from the inner tube, but I hadn't seen the busted tube inside of the tire. Miraculously, the two homemade gaskets from the pair of sunglasses had created an airtight seal around the rim of the tire that held for over one thousand miles of riding. In fact, except for the tire balding due to the lack of a tube, the tire pressure had held. The mechanic was shocked (and frankly so was I) when we both saw the slime-covered tube that had been spinning around inside of the tire once we removed the old one from the rim. With the new tire (and tube this time) in place, I was ready to make the final push down the eastern California border past the Modoc, Lassen, and Plumas National Forests.

The ride was purely spiritual and the nine days and two thousand miles of riding through rain, wind, sleet, and snow was epic. Up to Mt. Rushmore, over the Tetons, and down the eastern Sierras is one of the best captions I could have thought of for such a journey, and I made it happen. I arrived in Escondido, California, with about fifteen minutes remaining in my nephew Monty's third birthday party.

❊ ❊ ❊

Almost two months passed, and my time spent dog-sitting on the West Coast provided the exact escape I was looking for when I left Iowa. It was filled with backpacking and camping trips, beach time, motorcycle rides up the coast, and singing on stage with Vanilla Ice at an "I Love the 90s" concert at the Santa Barbara Bowl. (Yeah, that happened.) Any one of these

Monty sporting a Batman shirt before I head
to Santa Barbara for the summer

things are good for the soul, but compile them together in two months with no real responsibilities and it can do wonders, albeit with a little strain on the bank account. I had to remind myself, though, that I don't need to have it all laid out in a spreadsheet. My bills were paid, my mind was filled with ideas, and my gas tank only cost six bucks to fill up. Life was good.

❦ ❦ ❦

Toward the end of my dog-sitting time, while I was at my favorite coffee shop in Santa Barbara, Handlebar Coffee Roasters, I was contemplating what my next move would be when Potter and his family returned from Europe. I sat down in my normal spot, which was a stool next to the outside window that faced Canon Perdido Street. It seemed like a normal day, which was why I hadn't noticed who was sitting in the booth just to my right. It was Kathy Ireland, and she was looking as good as ever.

I had always wondered what I would say to Kathy if we were to ever meet. Jokingly, I have always said that if she were to burst through the doors at my future wedding and proclaim her love, I absolutely would leave whomever I was about to marry and live happily ever after with Kathy. But, when it happened in real life, although I did pick up her handbag when it fell from her chair at one point, in the end, I said nothing. She was clearly having a meeting with a friend and I felt an awkward fanboy introduction from a thirty-two-year-old bearded man just wasn't appropriate. I'm pretty certain, though, that Kathy's friend noticed me looking at her throughout their entire meeting.

When Kathy left the coffee shop, I had a good laugh to myself. Although my inner twelve-year-old was crying about the missed opportunity to meet the woman on the cover of the best-selling *Sports Illustrated Swimsuit Edition* of all time, I took solace in knowing that my life would be okay.

I suppose it wouldn't have hurt if I had introduced myself to Kathy that day at the coffee shop, but I like that it left the door open for the mystery to continue. I'm sure she is a wonderful, normal person with whom I could have had a friendly conversation. However, part of me also enjoys keeping her as that childhood dream girl—traveling around the world on photoshoots and making cameo appearances in slapstick comedy movies. I hope she still feels that way sometimes, too.

CHAPTER 32

Appalachian Trail 2016
164 Days; 2,173 Miles

After scrambling down the rocky descent of Chairback Mountain, I finally reached Katahdin Iron Works Road where, to my surprise, a wonderful spread of trail magic was waiting for me. I was shocked that, after passing this spot a few days earlier on her way to summiting Mount Katahdin, a thru-hiker had then driven down one of the very few gravel access roads inside of the 100 Mile Wilderness and left a few snacks and a note wishing luck to her fellow hikers.

I sat for over an hour devouring a few of the treats, enjoying the little bit of shade that was provided by the trees along the edge of the road, and reflecting on how—after I finished the trail—I could move forward as a better person. After another six miles of hiking and climbing up one thousand feet of elevation, I reached the Carl A. Newhall Shelter. I was alone when I arrived but was later joined by a small group of high school students on a wilderness trip and a few other thru-hikers, one who was headed south named Firecracker. There was plenty of sunlight remaining but, seeing as I was in no rush to end my journey, I settled in for the night. I knew I would have a steep climb in the morning, one of the last big climbs before Katahdin, and this seemed like a suitable place to set up camp.

❦ ❦ ❦

As the pace and cadence of my legs reach full stride during a hike, my body's natural endorphins kick in and the hardcore thinking really begins. This is exactly what happened on the morning that I left the Carl A. Newhall Shelter in the 100 Mile Wilderness. On that day, my thoughts were focused on my family and friends, and on my relationships from the past two years since my initial time in the hospital. I found myself ruminating on the interactions that occurred between me and my friends during the months leading up to my departure from Iowa. I love my friends, but whether or not I agree with them about everything is an entirely different ball of wax.

As I began my ascent that day, I started doing the math and realized I had known Jayme and Abby for over fifteen years, and I have continuously sparred with them on pretty much any topic that could be imagined. Whether it be finances, politics, or whether Ross and Rachel were truly on a "break," we've found a way to be on opposite sides of many arguments. From an objective perspective, it's a good thing that we have different opinions. There are times that they have presented a topic in a way that resulted in a modification of how I think. This is good for me. As I discovered on the AT, meeting people who are different from me helps me to grow and mature as an individual, and this includes the people with whom I don't entirely agree.

I have no idea who that is, but this is the Carl A. Newhall Shelter.

I believe that bringing others with multiple views together to participate in a discussion only makes us better people.

However, some topics aren't just a matter of pushing buttons but are matters of humanity. When Abby said, "The blacks have moved in so my housing value has gone down," it drastically changed the way I communicate with her. I love Abby, but *some things you just can't unhear.* It was frustrating to hear her say those words, but it also changed the way I think about my own speech. It affirmed my resolve to consciously pay attention to what I say and who my words may affect. I've said a lot of stupid things in my life, and sometimes the person whom my words most affect is me.

As thoughts of my friend's comments swirled in my mind, and I formulated plans for how I could move beyond their comments and continue to love them for all of their good qualities, I began climbing Gulf Hagas Mountain. By that point—possibly because of gaining eight hundred feet in elevation in less than a mile or maybe because of the emotions that were attached to my thoughts—I was practically levitating when I crested the climb and hiked past Sidney Tappan Campsite at full stride. I strangely remember seeing a ridiculously large fungus on a tree stump and some not-so-fresh moose droppings a bit later. The number of feelings permeating my being would have provided a healthy dose for reflection at any time, but it was barely eight in the morning and I was just getting started.

❖ ❖ ❖

Although I have spent a night in jail from a public intoxication charge in my early twenties, I have never received a DUI. (As I've mentioned, though, there were some close calls.) I've never been court ordered to seek out therapy for an alcohol addiction, nor endured anything else beyond the typical growing pains involved when a man in his twenties and early thirties is learning what is an acceptable amount of alcohol consumption. Even though some people would tell me I am not an alcoholic, mostly because I haven't been in substantial amounts of trouble with the law, I *absolutely* believe the possibility exists.

It's sad that for some people to take a problem seriously they need something terrible to happen. It's unfortunate that we don't have more programs for people to identify addictions before they ruin their lives with a DUI or, worse, before they ruin someone else's life—rock bottom shouldn't be the place where recovery begins. After the weekend that Dale won the lottery, as was the case with my experience with Jayme and Abby, it wasn't my feelings toward Dale that imprinted on me most—it was my feelings toward myself.

I've told many drunk stories in my life, but for some reason, telling a drunk story just doesn't have the same appeal when you see the negative side effects hit so close to home. After leaving Iowa on the motorcycle trip, I spoke with Dale's daughter multiple times about the evening Maureen went to the hospital. She loves her father. Her father is the person she wants to talk to about finances and politics; he's the person she wants to talk to about friends and relationships. But she can't actually talk to him about any of those things because of his addiction, and she can't change that. I can't change that. Only Dale can. I can only change myself.

After the evening of Mother's Day in 2016, when I witnessed the disturbing aftermath of Dale's alcoholism, I decided that I didn't want that as my future. I never wanted to allow my drinking habits to affect another person like that experience affected me, especially any future children I may have. *Some things you just can't unsee.* I see things a lot clearer now, and since I began writing this book about my AT experience, I have not consumed a single alcoholic beverage. I don't know how long I plan to keep this going, but the sobriety continues for now, and I love it.

❊ ❊ ❊

As I reached the top of Hay Mountain, the AT turned into a skinny path that was completely engulfed by trees and rocks. I was crushing a nearly 3 mph pace as the sign for the White

Brook Trail junction came into view. I stopped for a break to drink some water and eat a snack, but I couldn't sit for long. My mind was racing right in step with my feet, or perhaps my feet were racing right in step with my mind—I couldn't tell which was the inciting force. As thoughts of my friends further consumed my brain, I could sense that some closure was at my fingertips. I was crushing miles and, more importantly, crushing thoughts that were negative weights on my soul.

To reiterate, I love all of my family and friends, both their good and bad qualities and, as I have mentioned, I am far from a perfect person. However, the things we see and hear can and do affect ourselves and others. Words matter. Actions matter. Be careful what you do with them. *Some things you just can't unsay.*

After spending thousands of miles thinking and having out-loud conversations with myself regarding my friends back home, Megan, Erica, past jobs, my heart problems, and my own words and actions over the course of my life—and after trying to determine the best path forward upon finishing the 2,189-mile-long Appalachian Trail—I decided that I needed a platform for telling those stories and the lessons I learned from them. So, at the top of Hay Mountain I decided to write a book—*this* book.

As I continued along the AT and reached the top of White Cap Mountain, which is the last big climb of the 100 Mile Wilderness before it levels out into Baxter State Park at the base of Mount Katahdin, I knew that all these topics could have left my mind cluttered, confused, and angry. But that wasn't the

A profile view of Mount Katahdin, the northern terminus of the Appalachian Trail

case. Not even close. Even though it was overcast and windy that day, and the clouds rushed past my face as I sat behind a pile of rocks to shield myself from the weather, my mind was clearer than it had been in a long time. Thinking and attempting to make myself a better person is *what I do all day on the AT.* Then I eat Pop-Tarts and hike over mountains.

Thirteen states and 2,173 miles down. One state and 16 miles to go.

CHAPTER 33

California 2016

After completing another Memorial Weekend Death March with the Santa Barbara crew—my first major backpacking trip after going into complete heart block—I was confident that my physical capabilities had returned. Although I wasn't operating at quite 100 percent, completing that year's Death March was the final test I needed to pass to assure myself that if I ever wanted to go back and finish the AT, I would be physically able to. But my mental desire to do so just wasn't clear.

For starters, the logistics that would need to be coordinated to make it happen were daunting. The date of the wedding that I had agreed to officiate meant I was up against a very tight deadline to complete the remaining six hundred miles of trail. There was also the issue of money. Even though the Potters graciously paid me for watching their dogs for a few months, and I held a few part-time jobs while living in California (one of which was shuttling cloth baby diapers for a company called Tinkle Bell Delivery Service), it was not enough to purchase a cross-country flight, afford six weeks of provisions and lodging on the East Coast, *and* keep paying rent on my apartment back in Iowa (since my subletter didn't work out). Although I had money set aside in a few retirement accounts, I wasn't actually retiring and wasn't even sure if I should attempt a return to the trail. I just couldn't decide and considered that perhaps I needed to save more money and try again in a few years.

As is often the case when I'm making big decisions that don't seem to make great logistical sense, my ultimate push to return to the AT came down to recalling one particular past experience in my life, from when I had traveled to Italy in college for a Roman archaeology course. Upon arriving on the Isla de Capri, a small mountainous island off the Mediterranean coast of Italy, our group was about to hike up the mountain to the town center when we came upon an elderly couple sitting on a bench at the base of the mountain. They spoke English, and after a few introductions and travel banter, I asked them why they were sitting on the bench. The elderly gentleman looked me right in the eye and said, "Do as much as you can while you're young. We waited our whole lives to visit this island, and now we don't have the energy to climb up it. Hell, we don't have the energy to wait in line for the train ride to the top!"

Since this chance meeting at the base of a mountain in the middle of the Mediterranean, I've had many other interactions with members of older generations and received life advice with the same theme: "Do it." I believe that the hundreds of years of collective life experience from all of these sage individuals, many of whom I've met while traveling, all boils down to something that isn't that much of a secret: We just don't know what's going to happen. We can't predict the future, not even a few weeks, months, or years. We don't know if we're about to get sick or get a new job or meet someone who makes us want to change our life path. I'm not saying there isn't value in devoting prolonged time or energy to something, but we don't know what the future holds. We only know what resources and opportunities are available *now*, and sometimes we just have to take that leap of faith and go for it.

Ten years after visiting Capri, as I was dog-sitting in Santa Barbara and toying with the idea of going back to the East Coast to finish the AT, the elderly gentleman's words were resonating very clearly. I had been given a second chance at health and, after two years of recovering from Lyme disease, had regained the physical ability to at least attempt finishing the AT, and I didn't want to take that for granted. I knew that piling up credit card debt and taking money out of tax-deferred retirement accounts were terrible long-term financial decisions, but I was also certain that waiting even just a few years—during which my heart condition could worsen and physically prohibit me from trying to finish the trail—would be more disastrous for my life than a credit score that is a hundred points lower. Besides, I wasn't planning on buying a house any time soon and there was no one else in my life for whom I needed to plan a future. It was just me, a healthy heart, and a second chance.

Before seeing Kathy Ireland in the coffee shop that day, I had already discussed my options with family and friends, and I was leaning toward heading back to the AT. Perhaps, though, I also needed a timely reminder from my childhood that I shouldn't always take life so seriously. My heart was better. I had no prior commitments. If I was ever going to do it, the time was now. Over the next few weeks I prepared to fly from one coast of America to the other. I sent items back home that I wouldn't need for the hike, and I even found a friend in California to purchase my motorcycle. Everything was coming together. I was going back to finish the Appalachian Trail.

CHAPTER 34

Appalachian Trail 2016
166 Days; 2,189 Miles

On my 164th night on the Appalachian Trail, I stayed a mere few miles from the base of Mount Katahdin. I had just exited the northern terminus of the 100 Mile Wilderness, the final fifty miles of which included numerous large ponds, gigantic boulders, and a seemingly endless supply of frogs. (Seriously, there were frogs *everywhere*.) I crossed over Abol Bridge and set up at the campground with a few other hikers. This campground was used by AT hikers and car campers alike and my neighboring campsite that night was occupied by two amazing individuals, Darek and Aleksandra, who were from Poland.

It was Aleksandra's birthday. They were already celebrating and quickly invited me over to join in the festivities. Darek was wearing a *Game of Thrones* shirt and Aleksandra had on a Slipknot one, and they were both self-described metal heads. When I told them I was from Iowa, Aleksandra shrieked in excitement because Slipknot is from Des Moines. The evening proceeded as expected, with a case of beer, a bottle of whiskey, and a delicious dish that I can only describe as a kielbasa jambalaya that Aleksandra whipped up toward the end of the night.

We drank and talked until the combination of hiking twenty-three miles and drinking alcohol finally became a bit too much for my body to handle in a twenty-four-hour period, and it was time for bed. It was the perfect way to celebrate reaching my goal of hiking the entire 100 Mile Wilderness in five days.

❋ ❋ ❋

On the morning that I planned to summit Katahdin, it was bit chilly and the forecast called for strong winds. However, it was going to take a lot more than a little harsh weather to prevent me from hiking up that mountain.

My ascent began like any other climb. The first mile or so included a canopy of trees hanging over the top of the small single-track path. That was followed by a steeper section with a few boulders over which I had to climb. The rocks grew larger with every step I took up the trail. As the elevation increased the trees began to shorten in height, as expected. Although I could hear the wind howling above the tree line, adrenaline kept my body moving forward and upward without giving it a second thought. As I climbed up and over rocks, hopping over small remnants of streams from a previous day's rain, my mind began to wonder, *Is this it?* And, just as the AT had done time and time again, just as I thought I had it all figured out, it showed me the truth like a game-show host pulling back the mystery curtain to reveal what's behind it.

Somewhere around the third mile of the day I encountered a boulder field known as "The Gateway," which required a lot more concentration than I anticipated. This, combined with the howling winds and the trees vanishing, meant I was completely engulfed in the elements. All of a sudden, my internal emotions quickly went from excited to (dare I say it) scared! That feeling intensified when an older couple who began their ascent before me came back down the mountain, saying, "We don't need to risk this." *I do*, I thought to myself.

While staring up at a ridiculously steep pile of large boulders, and drop-offs on either side that were equally as treacherous, I mistakenly thought the small wooden post at the top was the Katahdin summit sign—wishful thinking, I suppose. I continued scrambling up the Gateway and was knocked off my feet multiple times by perpendicular winds; I was even forced to drop to my stomach a couple of times out of fear of losing my footing. Being blown off a mountain onto a pile of sharp rocks was a situation I wanted to avoid.

At the top of the first climb there was a long traverse across what appeared to be the ridgeline. As it was early in the morning, the clouds were still thick, but a bully of a wind was showing just how fast it could push its way through. Every so often there was a gap in the clouds and I would see it—the famous wooden summit sign. Although still at least a mile away, that wooden sign with its white lettering gave me all the energy I needed to know that nothing could stop me now.

After passing Thoreau Spring, the wind and clouds continued to do their best to force me to turn around, but I continued along the ridgeline, up more rocks, across more ridgeline, up more rocks—it didn't matter how many times I had to climb up, I was determined to finish this thing. Then, after hiking for just over five miles and gaining almost four thousand feet of elevation since I started hiking that morning, I saw it. Not just between openings in the clouds or on a magazine cover or on a postcard sent to me by someone else who had just finished the trail, but I actually saw it with my own eyes. The famous wooden summit sign on top of Mount Katahdin was in clear view just a few feet away.

❖ ❖ ❖

While I can't describe the exact thoughts going through every hiker's mind when they reach the wooden sign after thousands of miles of hiking, I *can* tell you what I was thinking on that early morning of September 12, 2016: nothing.

My mind was empty.

I can tell you what I did, too: nothing.

I didn't immediately touch the sign when I arrived, like most do, because I didn't want to disrupt the special moment being shared by the other hikers who were already touching, kissing, and taking photos with the weathered slab of wood. After all the time and effort that I spent striving to arrive at this place and complete this goal that seemed impossible, I still had the patience to pause and consider how I could ensure that my fellow hikers got to fully enjoy their moment of elation. I can't say I would have done this if it hadn't been for one of the main tenants of trail life—to look out for each other—and in this moment of exhilaration and sensory overload, watching respectfully as another person celebrated was wholly fulfilling.

Besides, the mountain wasn't going anywhere anytime soon, and I was at somewhat of a loss as to how I should let my emotions spill out. Thankfully, the hiker who was posing for his long-awaited summit photo with the Katahdin sign recognized the importance of the moment and yelled at me, "Get over here and touch this thing!" I happily obliged.

What proceeded to take place next can only be described as a redneck photo shoot. The inclement weather that morning had stymied a few hikers earlier in the day, so there weren't many people at the top of the mountain. But the few of us who did fight through the heavy winds and cold temperatures took full advantage of the extra time we had with the wooden sign. We captured every shot and angle we could possibly want for our social media sites. Hell, I even did three outfit changes. I also took a few photos of just my pack because I felt my fourteen-year-old, faded green, external-frame backpack carried me just as much as I carried it some days, and it deserved its own photo roll.

The clouds began to clear away from the summit area as condensed droplets of moisture hurtled past my face. The temperature began to rise just enough to make me feel confident that I wouldn't suffer the effects of hypothermia, so I decided to stay at the top of the mountain for as long as possible. I even brought out my mini coffee grinder, my isobutane micro-stove, and some whole coffee beans so I could brew a cup to enjoy while I observed more hikers find their way to the wooden sign and soak in all the glory that Mount Katahdin had to offer.

34: Appalachian Trail 2016

This is what achieving your goal looks like.

It's an interesting spectacle at the wooden sign. According to pamphlets available at the ranger station, over sixty thousand people visit Baxter State Park in northern Maine each year, and many of them witness the same sign I was staring at in the moment I just described. But not all of those folks have just completed a 2,189-mile journey through the woods—the total length of the Appalachian Trail in 2016 (a feat that took me, in total from before and after the heart condition, 166 days). In fact, most people are there to enjoy the park for just a single day, so it's a bit humorous to see a small oligarchy form among those taking photos next to the wooden sign. The day hikers are very cautious to not keep a thru-hiker waiting too long, even though, as I mentioned, most of us realized that after a few thousand miles we could wait a few more minutes because the mountain wasn't going anywhere.

Even though my mind was empty when I arrived at the sign, if there was one place where I knew I would need time to reflect on my life, it was at the top of Mount Katahdin. My journey had been a far cry from a traditional Appalachian Trail thru-hike and was complete with plenty of side trips into neighboring cities, attendance at multiple weddings, a cross-country motorcycle road trip, two other backpacking trips, and a life-threatening heart condition. Not exactly by the book, and absolutely not what I expected for the previous two years, but that's how this journey unfolded.

I had spent thousands of miles reflecting on past life events, all while enjoying the natural beauty of my country. It was fulfilling, gratifying, challenging, sad, happy, and every other emotion the body can experience. It was at the top of Mount Katahdin that I realized how truly privileged and blessed I am to have had the opportunity to complete this adventure, and to be surrounded by so many amazing individuals on (and off) the trail while doing so.

❖ ❖ ❖

After a few hours at the top of Mount Katahdin that included a lot of thinking, celebrating, taking group photos, and watching anyone with a decent cell phone service enjoy the ability to post and stream real-time videos, it felt like it was time to go home and start the process of moving on from the trail.

A few hikers had arranged a shuttle to bring us to the nearest town. Once we arrived in Millinocket, a town known almost entirely for being the closest town to Mount Katahdin, a scattering occurred among the hikers. Everyone seemed to have a different itinerary for their post-summit activities, from staying at the local hostel to meeting friends or family who had come to meet them for their final day.

I kept it simple with steak and lobster. I was in Maine, I had just finished hiking the entire Appalachian Trail, and I wanted steak and lobster. Nothing is more of a metaphorical middle finger after overcoming a physical obstacle than consuming two of the most sinful items a person can eat in this world. All I needed was a side of pork chops and I would have equally offended most of the planet's religious conservatives. I think even

My external-frame backpack deserved it's own photo with the sign.

Leviticus himself would have been impressed with the amount of sinful shellfish I devoured that evening. The next few days were a tempest of travel logistics. A shuttle, a bus, a short walk, an Uber, a hotel stay, a taxi, and two layovers filled my life before my final flight landed at the Eastern Iowa Airport. And, just like that, my Appalachian adventure was over, and I was back in the real world.

Fourteen states and 2,189 miles completed.

A journey of a lifetime. Now on to the next one.

EPILOGUE

Colorado 2018

As I sat at the end of the bar inside the Novo Coffee near Cheesman Park in Denver, my mind was inundated with possible topics we might discuss when she arrived. It was Valentine's Day in 2018 and I was meeting a girl who, in spite of having very little time available, found a few minutes for me. She was always so busy. So much so, in fact, that she rarely included me in her plans, which was why we had broken up a month earlier. I was meeting my ex-girlfriend, Melanie.

❖ ❖ ❖

After finishing the AT in September of 2016, my feeling of accomplishment was indescribable. I had overcome a life-threatening heart condition to complete one of our nation's most beloved and cherished long-distance hiking trails. I used my time on the AT to reflect on past events in hopes of moving forward more positively in my life. When I arrived back in Iowa to move out of my apartment, I was enormously confident that my life would be very different. I was excited to just be happier, and for the most part, I actually was.

In the time that passed since I was standing on top of Mount Katahdin, I officiated a wedding, went dog-sledding in Mongolia, spent time with local Cherokee tribe members in North Carolina, hiked to the craters of active volcanoes in Central America, and once again hopped on a vintage motorcycle to embark on an American road trip. That last adventure ended in Colorado, just outside of Rocky Mountain National Park, for the wedding of a college friend.

❊ ❊ ❊

I've had a few follow-up appointments with cardiologists since finishing the trail, and every visit gives me reassuring information: my heart is strong, it just has some faulty wiring. I can hike up mountains, I can run for miles, and I can drink two cups of coffee and feel fine. I don't have Lyme disease anymore (thanks to antibiotics destroying the bacteria), but my heart does continue to have an electrical problem and, every now and then, probably once or twice a month, I feel a small *putter* on the left side of my body. Sometimes it's actually irregular beats in my heart, sometimes it's just anxiety, and sometimes I simply just need to eat a banana—there's no way to tell for sure in the moment. But I'm not going to call a doctor every time it happens, and I'm not going to let it stop me from doing the things I love.

While on the motorcycle road trip, I contemplated where I wanted to live. Although this feeling of having a blank slate and the freedom to choose any city to be home was pretty great, it also was quite daunting. I was living off of what could fit on

Epilogue: Colorado 2018

the back of a 1982 Yamaha Maxim XJ650, and with my financial resources exhausted and a massive credit card bill looming, I needed to find a consistent roof over my head and a steady paycheck—for the first time in eighteen months.

❖   ❖   ❖

The wedding was beautiful; it was held at a private location with a Rocky Mountain backdrop, and the wedding photographer had the keen ability to capture such a beautiful place and make it even more spectacular in the photos. She was a person who could see something ordinary and make it extraordinary, which is maybe why she agreed to start dating me a few weeks later.

Because of the new relationship, I decided to move back to Denver and, at first, Melanie and I exuded all the excitement one might expect from a new couple reuniting after a few months apart (I had returned to Iowa for a few months while she finished her wedding season). I started looking for an apartment and began working as an instructor at an interactive gym facility called Great Play, where we focus on developmental and athletic skills for toddlers and young children. After a few months, though, it was clear something was missing for Melanie. On the day I moved into a little studio in the Capitol Hill neighborhood, she told me she no longer wanted to pursue the relationship.

Much like my story of hiking the Appalachian Trail describes, although we can't control many things in this life, we also can't let that distract us. We must constantly strive to see the positive effects of placing one foot in front of the other, and learn that moving forward on (and off) the trail is the answer to a lot of obstacles that we face. Moving forward was integral in my overcoming the physical and mental struggles of my heart condition, and I now feel confident that I can take on anything. Moving forward was paramount in my acknowledgment that I don't need alcohol in my life to be entertained, and I haven't had a drink in fourteen months. Moving forward was essential to my continued growth as a man, a friend, and a human being. Moving forward allowed me the time and energy to write this book.

I could never have imagined that my post–Appalachian Trail life would include traveling around the world for a year and a half, much like I could have never imagined I would be meeting my ex-girlfriend on Valentine's Day. Although my relationship with Melanie didn't last, I'm a better person than who I was before I started the trail. Dammit—I'm a great person and someday I'll find a woman who wants to spend the rest of her life with me. That day just hasn't arrived yet.

Melanie and I chatted for a bit. She ordered a beer and I had a refill of my Ethiopian-origin coffee. The conversation was civil and after an hour she had to go meet some friends, which was fine as I had plans as well. I was meeting my friend Krista to attend the Avalanche hockey game that evening. It was a first date.

ACKNOWLEDGMENTS

The list of people I have to thank for making this adventure possible is innumerable. Thank you to the hostel owners, local restaurants, other hikers, and all the members of my various trail families that I met through the course of this crazy journey; you helped make the difference and I hope we can keep in touch in whatever ways we can. Thank you to my family and friends back home and abroad supporting me: it truly is humbling to chat with people who have followed me through this journey over the past four years, from reading my original blog posts to my journey of traveling and writing this book. I am grateful for the care packages (thanks Amy, Marie, and Morgan) and kind words, for rides into towns and places to stay. I would never have had as great of an experience if it hadn't been for the people that were there along the way. It is only proper I mention all the doctors who provided care for me during my initial infection. At the 510 Clinic I owe a debt of gratitude to the physician assistants, Jaimie and Bruce; their PA student, Ashley; and Dr. Fribush, for recognizing the greater concern of the situation. Thanks to all the doctors at Berkshire Medical Center: my cardiologist, Dr. Leppo; the hospitalist, Dr. Ramalingam; my resident, Dr. Walker; my infectious disease specialist, Dr. Aucoin; and a number of other interns and residents. Thanks to all the nurses who put up with my attempts at humor: Lisa, Kristen, Dawn, Jo, and Fredina, and the many others who came in and out for various reasons. A great deal of thanks to my mother, Jeannie, and my sister, Dawn, who made the trip out to Massachusetts to be by my side. Thanks to my father and step-mom, Dan and Connie, for constant reassurance that things will work out okay. Taryn, thank you. Thank you for the texts, phone calls, and Facebook messages and reactions, they truly did mean a lot and were overwhelmingly positive daily occurrences during all the time I was in the hospital and afterward. Thank you to everyone who helped during the writing process from beginning to end: Elyse, Andy, Evan, Dave, and Matt, who read over initial manuscript excerpts; and my team toward the end, Timm, Meredith, Annie, Afton, Daniela, Matthew, the staff on the fourth floor of the Denver Public Library, the Denver Metro Small Business Development Center, Legal Shield, and the attorneys at Riggs & Abney Law Firm. Special thanks to my editor, Brooke: you were a spark that really helped ignite this project. Finally, to anyone who took the chance and bought this book, from the bottom of my physically and emotionally healing heart, I thank you.

In Memoriam

To those who were a part of my journey both on (and off) the Appalachian Trail and left this world before I had a chance to thank them properly:

Baltimore Jack, Geraldine "Inchworm" Largay, Jessa, and Courtney

In Support

Dave "Penguin Man" Transue, who shortly after battling the cold temperatures with me in North Carolina, learned his next uphill battle would be with cancer. My thoughts are with him as he climbs a different kind of mountain.

Original Photo by Jean Baker

Dustin Waite is an exploration geologist for Crystal Geyser, working remotely in Denver, Colorado. Although his BA from Cornell College is in Geology and Marine Sciences, his career has included an eclectic mix of professional experience: geological consultant in Santa Barbara; Colorado Certified Environmental Educator with the Greenway Foundation in Denver; Assistant Curator of the Lahaina Heritage Museum in Maui; Head of Sales and Distribution for a local brewery in Iowa; and instructor of developmental education for toddlers at a gym facility in Denver.

Dustin's travels have included riding his motorcycle across the United States multiple times and extended trips in New Zealand, Australia, Italy, Peru, India, Mongolia, and Central America in addition to hiking the entire Appalachian Trail, the inspiration for *External*.